AF553814

EFFECTIVENESS OF ADVERTISEMENT

EFFECTIVENESS OF ADVERTISEMENT

By

Dr. C.Mahimai Arul Ignatius

M.com., M.Phil., M.B.A., Ph.D.
Assistant Professor
Dept. of Commerce
St. Joseph's College
Tiruchirappalli (Tamil Nadu)
(India)

&

I.Francis Ganasekar

M.com., B.Ed., M.Phil., M.B.A., Ph.D.
Associate Professor & Head
Dept. of Commerce
St.Joseph's College
Tiruchirappalli (Tamil Nadu)
(India)

DISCOVERY PUBLISHING HOUSE PVT. LTD.
NEW DELHI-110 002

Published by:
Tilak Wasan

DISCOVERY PUBLISHING HOUSE PVT. LTD.
4383/4B, Ansari Road, Darya Ganj
New Delhi-110 002 (India)
Phone : +91-11-23279245, 43596064-65
Fax : +91-11-23253475
E-mail : discoverypublishinghouse@gmail.com
sales@discoverypublishinggroup.com
parul.wasan@gmail.com
web : www.discoverypublishinggroup.com

***First Edition:* 2013**

ISBN: 978-93-5056-257-4

Effectiveness of Advertisement

Printed at:
Aditi Fine Art Press
Delhi

Preface

Advertisement plays a vital role in promoting the products. Advertising is a form of communication used to influence or to convince an audience to take some action with respect to products, ideas, or services. Advertising messages are viewed via various traditional media; including mass media such as newspaper, magazines, television commercial, radio advertisement, outdoor advertising or direct mail; or new media such as websites and text message. Out of these Television advertisements are very prevalent even among the general public. The result of the advertisement lies in the effectiveness in factors.

This book deals with the effectiveness of advertisement in the ethical outlook among youth particularly youth in Trichy corporation limit. This book documents the views of the opinion leaders and the student respondents about the ethical and unethical practices in advertisements. It also bears the record of opinion and attitude of the opinion leaders on role advertisement, celebrity in the advertisement and features of advertisement.

There are ten advertisements namely VVD Gold Coconut oil, Horlicks, Nescafe Sunrise, Medimix, Sandal Soup, Docomo, Yuva A810, Colgate Max Fresh, Spinz Deo, Bingo Chips and KFC chicken taken for research. The author has accentuates views expressed by the different professionals like Doctors, Engineers, Lawyers, Professors and auditors on the ethical connotation of these advertisements. The author also is keen in highlighting the outlooks of the opinion leaders like Actors, Directors, Cinematographers, Singers, Creative Heads and Music Directors. The ideas of the marketing executives and Editors of the dailies and also the Directors of different radio stations are documented in the book. The author has mainly emphasized the views expressed by the youngsters on the effectiveness of these advertisements. The effectiveness measures of the advertisements are the various factors like Values, Culture, unethical Practices and social impacts. The varieties of creative ideas expressed by the different youth groups based on age, colleges and locations have been appreciated in the book.

The research work has been recorded in the book. The various techniques like pre-test and post-test for measuring the effectiveness of advertisement are discussed in detail. The questionnaire used for the research is also attached which will enable the young research scholars to have an idea about their own research. The book files the evidences of the research study to check the effectiveness of the advertisement. The book furnishes the relevant statistical data collected and also the analyzed data. The pictorial representation of the research work adds embellishment to this book. The readers are enabled to understand the research study very easily by following the different tabulated data. The findings of the effectiveness of the advertisement are highlighted by the author.

This book caters the necessary information to the researchers who carry out their research in advertisements. This book makes the study of advertising more important today than ever before, not only for students of business or journalism who may be contemplating a career in the field but also for students of sociology, psychology, political science, economics, history, language, science, or the arts. Many of these people will become users of advertising; all will be lifetime consumers of it.

By studying this book the readers will learn to:

- Discern the real social, and cultural role of advertising and, conversely, the impact of a society's values on advertising.
- Understand how advertisements have its impacts on individuals life
- Appreciate the important effectiveness advertising on business, industry, and national economies.
- Comprehend the strategic function of advertising within the broader context of ethical practices of society.
- Evaluate and appreciate the impressive artistic creativity and technical expertise within boundary of the value system of the society required in advertising.

Dr. C. Mahimai Arul Ignatius

Acknowledgement

I praise and thank the *Almighty God* from the depth of my heart who has showered His manifold blessings on me throughout my study.

At the very outset I thank my guide *Dr. I Francis Gnanasekar, M. Com., M.B.A., B.Ed., M.Phil., Ph.D.,* Associate Professor and Head, PG and Research Department of Commerce. St. Joseph's College, Tiruchirappalli, who guided me by his scholarly approach, constant encouragement and committed help during my dissertation work.

I thank the *Management* of St. Joseph's College and the Principal, *Rev. Dr. R. Rajarathinam, SJ,* for allowing me to do the thesis work.

I place a record of my profound gratitude to *Dr. L.J. Chaarlas,* Associate Professor, Department of Commerce, St. Joseph's College, Tiruchirappalli and *Dr. Gnanasekaran,* Associate Professor and Head, Department of Economics, St. Joseph's College (Autonomous), Tiruchirappalli for their academic help, suggestions and systematic approach which gave a lot of clarity to the layout of this thesis.

I extend my sincere thanks to *Dr. Stephen Vincent Raj,* Associate Professor, Department of Statistics, St. Joseph's College (Autonomous), Tiruchirappalli and *Prof. Suresh Kumar,* Department of Social Work, Bharathidasan University, Tiruchirappalli specially for helping me to use various statistical tools in the processing of the data and for carefully going through the interpretation.

I thank *Mr. Fernandez Garnet,* Dean of UGC Affairs, St. Joseph's College, Tiruchirappalli and *Mr. Thomas Romauld* who offered help in evaluating the language content of the dissertation.

It is also my earnest duty to thank *Mrs. Anuradha,* Assistant Librarian, Indian Institute of management, Bangalore and *Mr. Balasubramanian,* Assistant Librarian, Bharathidasan University, Tiruchirappalli for permitting to collect the materials for my research work.

I sincerely thank *Kiruhthika* and *Mr. Ravichandar* Media Supervgisors of *R.K. Swamy BBDO Pvt. Ltd.,* in Chennai for furnishign details on media presentation.

It is my hearty thanks to *Advertising Standards Council of India,* Mumbai and *Association of Advertising Agency of India* for their assistance given to me.

I will be failing in my duty if I don't remember *Mr. Ilakiyan,* Cine music director, in this context for getting the interviews from the famous cine professionals in Chennai.

My heartful and sincere thanks for all my family members *Dear Amma Mrs. A. Kulandai Therese, Dear Appa Mr. A. Christhu Rathinam, my dear spouse Mrs. A.V. Sona* and *my loving daughter M.S. Maryln Rowena* for their full cooperation, for accomplishing this great work.

Last, but not the least I owe my heartfelt thanks *to all* those who have helped in a special way for completing my research work.

C. Mahimai Arul Ignatius

Contents

Abbreviations

ACB	—	Aberrant Consumer Behaviour
		Advertising Result
AMA	—	American Marketing Association
ASCI	—	Advertising Standards Council of India
CCA	—	Concept Convergence Analysis
CSR	—	Corporate Social Responsibility
CTR	—	Click-Through Rates
DAGMAR	—	Defining Advertising Goals for Measured
DCV	—	Dynamic Capability View
DEA	—	Data Envelopment Analysis
DSA	—	Decision System Analysis
DTC	—	Direct-to-Customer
DWA	—	Discomfort with Ambiguity
FSI	—	Free Standing Inserts
LOV	—	List of Values
MAQ	—	Magazine Advertisement Questionnaire
NCAER	—	National Council of Applied Economic
NFS	—	Need for Sensation
PMS	—	Perceptual Meaning Studies
PPC	—	Paper per Click
PVR	—	Personal Video Recorders
RBV	—	Resource-Based View
		Research
TPB	—	Theory of Planned Behaviour
TSD	—	Theory of Signal Defection
UAI	—	Uncertainty Avoidance Index

1

Introduction

Human beings are interested in getting news about what is happening in and around them. People may be interested in getting the news about the marriages in the neighbourhood, child birth, school admissions, deaths, public appointments, accidents, incidents and so on. In day-to-day life, there is a possibility to encounter hundreds of such messages through myriads of media. The media help remove the hindrance on knowledge. In the commercial world advertisements are indispensable. When a new product is introduced in the market, advertisements are used to find a suitable place in the mind of the viewers and consumers. Thus, an advertisement removes the hindrance on knowledge. So, marketers highly depend on advertisements.

Market is a place where both the buyers and sellers meet. In economics a market is classified into perfect and imperfect market. In the present day market condition, monopolistic competition is prevailing under imperfect market. Product differentiation and selling cost are the two special features of monopolistic competition.

In the monopolistic competition, the manufacturer of a product can very well differentiate their brand or product with the help of advertisement. In this way advertisement is an unmixed blessing. On the other hand, it is said that advertisement could increase the selling cost. As a consequence, advertisements are brutal business promotion tools where mistakes can be costly if the perceptions created by the producer does not reach the customer.

According to Herbert Marcuse, "Advertising provides a culture of exaggerated self awareness, self righteousness and monetary pleasures of self assertions a kind of mass Narcissism – which destroys the bonds of basic human loyalties in the family, friend groups and in the community".

The language, slogan and image of advertising is marked by hyper bole, superlatives and stereo types of men, women and different ethnic groups. The men are usually macho, the women glamorous, the children cute and innocent. Moreover men with busty moustaches, women with sense of humor, management graduates with ponytail .... and the same. The year 2010 is facing lot of turning points in sports, games, business, trade, commerce and so on. These areas have more changes for the marketers to launch and advertise their brands. Indian Premier League 20:20 Cricket match, Cricket World Cup 20:20 in South Africa, Wimbledon, Austria, French, US Tennis Matches, Expo-2010 in Shanghai, China are some noteworthy areas where the marketers find a suitable place in the mind of the consumers. Adding additional feather to the cap, the first real digital world cup for football is expected to smash overall viewing records, thanks in part to the development of online TV and of smart phones such as Apple's iphone that will allow fans to watch on the more or discreetly at work. (The Hindu, 2010). Thus the scope of advertisement enlarges.

Table 1.1 : Advertisement Expenditure of the Media from 2000 to 2009

(Rs. in Million)

Years	Press	TV	Radio	Cinema	Out of Home	Internet	Total
2000	35500	19800	1300	900	5400	NA	62900
2001	38000	28500	1350	945	5800	NA	74595
2002	40200	31600	1500	1020	6300	NA	80620
2003	43620	37330	2550	1200	7700	300	92700
2004	49380	41350	2750	1450	8420	950	104300
2005	59800	48200	4100	1600	8900	1400	124000
2006	71000	60400	5600	1600	9800	2600	151000
2007	84600	70400	5800	1100	12000	3050	176950
2008	97200	81100	6750	1250	13300	3500	203100
2009 (Est.)	97600	85400	7800	1200	13700	4400	210100

Source: Agency estimate, Media direction

NA— Not Available

The word "advertising" is derived from a Latin word 'advertere' that means to turn attention towards a specific thing. The dictionary meaning of the word 'advertising' is to announce publicity or to give public notice. (Gupta, 2009).

AMA (American Marketing Association), defines advertising as "any paid form of non-personal presentation and promotion of ideas, goods and services by an identified sponsor". (Mathur U C 2002).

Advertising is as old as civilization itself. It has the longest history. Though there is no answer to the question as to the exact age of advertising, it can be said that advertising began the moment man discovered the art of communication. It is believed that advertising started in Egypt about one thousand years before Christ. The Greeks and Romans took it up later. The Greeks who took a prominent part in politics used advertising and publicity to the maximum extent in their election campaigns. The Greek states were organized as city-states and elections to these city republics were conducted in the same manner as elections to the modern legislative bodies. It was during this time that the Greeks made use of various methods of publicity. Similarly, there are evidences to suggest that Romans practiced advertising. Romans made use of advertising and publicity in conquering various countries. Publicity was made in the form of cries of vendors in the streets and announcement by drummers, though its scope was limited. With the fall of Roman Empire there was set back in the use of advertising and publicity.

The next stage in the evolution of advertising was the use of signs as a visual expression of the tradesman's function as well as the means of locating the source of goods.

The potentialities of advertising multiplied when the hand press was invented at the end of the 15th century. By Shakespeare's time posters had made their evidence and there is evidence to prove that advertising had assumed the function of fostering demand for existing products.

It was in the latter half of the 19th century that mass advertising came into being, mass production became a reality and channels and distribution had to be developed to cope with the physical movements of goods, creating a need for mass communication to inform the consumers, speedy development of advertising was accelerated on account of (*a*) industrial production, (*b*) means of transport, (*c*) increasing literacy, (*d*) advent and development of advertising agencies and (*e*) media. (Agarwal, 2005).

Advertisement is really a good master but, at the same time, a bad servant. It creates knowledge, awareness and loyalty. At the same time it degenerates Indian culture. It is puffing, exaggeration and create narcissism. Narcissus, in Greek Mythology was the son of the river God Cephissus distinguished for his beauty. His mother told him that he would have a long life, provided he never looked upon his own feature. Rejection of his lover Ameinias drew upon him vengeance of the Gods. Having fallen in love with his own reflection in the waters of a spring, he pined away (encyclopedia Britannica, 1960). Advertising creates a vast narcissism among youth, especially in developing countries. At this point the researcher wishes to do research on the effectiveness of advertisements in the ethical perspective among the college students by post-test method. (Gerard J. Tellis, 2004).

Statement of the Problem

In Monopolistic Competition the producer has to differentiate his own brand by way of product differentiation and selling cost. The best way to arrest the attention of the buyers is through advertisement. Advertisement creates knowledge utility. On the other hand, advertisement is a brutal business tool where mistakes can be very costly if the perception created by producer does not reach the end user. Moreover, the consequences of advertisement are negative. It creates cultural degradation, mass narcissism, monetary pleasures of self-assertion, unethical norms, unnecessary and unwanted technical jargons, disproved scientific jargons, creating ambiguities in the minds of the consumers, creating fear, criticizing the competitors, use of sex appeal in advertisement, subliminal message and irrelevant statistical data.

According to 2001 census 45 per cent of the Indian population was less than 19 yeas old. The fear of degenerating the youth is real and despite the powerful lobby of the makers of these products. They may make our youths as slaves by dictating terms to the concerned use of puffery, exaggeration regarding product function and benefit claims which must be shunned at all cost by the culture, viewers, marketers, users and society. At this point the researcher is willing to find out the effectiveness of advertisements among college students in Tiruchirappalli Corporation by trying to find the answers for the following questions: How far are these advertisements effective? Do these advertisements create mass narcissism on the college students? Are they unethical? Do these advertisements dictate terms? Is any advertisement prone to puffery and exaggeration? Does any advertisement degenerate our culture? At the same time what is the role of enlightened citizens such as the academicians, economic planners, political thinkers, political elites, technocrats, bureaucrats, social activists, media experts, development professionals and all other people who have enjoyed the fruits of democracy for ever regarding the above said problems. i.e., opinion-leaders view. What is the role of Advertising Standards Council of India in this aspect? How far can Advertising Agencies Association of India act?

Objectives of the Study

The overall objective of the study is to find out the effectiveness of advertisement, in the ethical perspective, among the youth in Tiruchirappalli Corporation limit. The following are the specific objectives:

(*i*) to ascertain the personal profile of the opinion-leaders and the student respondents of the study;

(*ii*) to study about the views of the opinion-leaders and the student respondents about ethical and unethical practices in advertisements;

(*iii*) to ascertain the opinion and attitude of the opinion-leaders on
- (*a*) role of advertisement,
- (*b*) celebrity in the advertisement,
- (*c*) features of the advertisement; and

(*iv*) to measure the select advertisements' effectiveness in terms of their recall, remember, acceptance and ethical value by post-test techniques of the student respondents.

Hypotheses of the Study

Based on the above objectives the following hypotheses are formulated.

(*i*) There is a significant variation among the student respondents on the content of the advertisement and on remembering the contents.

(*ii*) The effectiveness of advertisement on the student respondents differs on the basis of their age, religion, income and major discipline they pursue.

(*iii*) There is a perfect unanimity among the respondents – student and opinion-leaders on views about unethical dimensions of advertisements.

Methodology of the Study

Bearing in mind the above said objectives the following methodology is framed:

Pilot Study

The researcher had several rounds of discussions with the media people like adverting agencies, professionals like actors, directors, producers, cinematographers, singers, music directors and lyric writers in Chennai. Similarly, the researcher met the college principals, professors, lawyers, doctors and auditors in Tiruchirappalli. The objectives of the study was well explained to them. Moreover, marketing executives of daily news papers namely The Hindu, Times of India, Daily Thanthi and Dinamalar, Trichirappalli were also interviewed by the researcher. Similarly, Directors of television channels like Clock TV, Ten TV and S TV were also interviewed. Again, All India Radio Director, FM radio directors of Suriyan and Hello and their jockeys, Trichirappalli and chief editors of daily news papers namely Deccan Chronicle, Indian Express and Dinamani also contributed their views and ideas to this research.

A pilot study was made by the researcher in December 2009 in Trichirappalli to elicit the information on various aspects. A draft questionnaire was prepared for the purpose of pre-testing. The researcher selected at random 20 students for pilot study. After the collection of data, the researcher checked the reliability of the data through Cronbach's Alpha and the results confirmed that the effectiveness is achieved by a high internal consistency of 92 per cent.

The following were the chief indications of the pilot study which were considered in the main study.

1. Ten advertisements were selected for this study. They are eight durable goods and two non-durable goods. The selected advertisements are as follows. (1) VVD Gold Coconut Oil, (2) Horlicks, (3) Nescafe Sunrise, (4) Medimix Sandal Soap, (5) Docomo, (6) Motoyuva Y810, (7) Colgate Max Fresh and (8) Spinz Deo, and (1) Binco Chips and (2) KFC Chicken.
2. Among various methods of pre-test and post-test for measuring the effectiveness of advertisements that are available in the literature Post-Test Recall Memory was selected for this study.
3. It was decided to collect data from the arts and science college post graduates and Master of Philosophy students only. Moreover, data also collected from the college Principals, professors, media people, lawyers, auditors as they are the opinion-leaders. (NCAER, New Delhi).
4. Select 10 advertisements were recorded in the lap top and they were all played in front of the select student respondents to test their recall memory in the college premises.

Table 1.2 : Number of Colleges and their students strength
(During the academic year 2009-2010)

Status	Name of the College	PG		M.Phil		Total
		Arts	Science	Arts	Science	
Government College	Periyar EVR (Co-Ed.)	186	369	33	42	630
Aided Colleges	SJC (M)(Co-Ed.)	261	393	81	115	850
(Autonomous)	HCC (W)	62	86	32	22	202
	SRC(W)	101	179	13	24	317
	JMC (M)	291	490	12	10	803
	BHC (M)(Co-Ed.)	148	164	39	17	368
Aided Colleges (Non-Autonomous)	National College(M)	172	207	50	30	459
Self-financing	Cauvery College(W)	112	391	31	45	579
Colleges	Shrimadi Indira Gandhi College W)	174	641	-	-	815
	Kurunji College (Co-Ed)	15	155	-	-	170
	Srimad Andavan College (Co-Ed.)	87	241	16	26	370
Total						**5563**

Source: Director of Collegiate Education, Tiruchirappalli.

(W) → Women; (M) → Men; (Co-Ed.) → Co-Education EVR → Periyar E.V. Ramaswamy College; SJC → St. Joseph's College; HCC → Holy Cross College; SRC → Seethalakshmi Ramaswamy College; JMC → Jamal Mohamed College, BHC → Bishop Heber College.

A different questionnaire was framed and structured for opinion-leaders and their views regarding the advertisements were collected.

The study area selected are students of Arts and Science colleges in the Corporation limits of Tiruchirappalli. With the help of the Director of Collegiate education, the total number of Arts and Science colleges are identified. There are 11 Arts and Science colleges in and around Trichirappalli corporation. The students strength in Arts and Science are as follows.

In the above table 1.2 colleges are classified into Government Colleges, Aided Colleges with autonomous and without autonomous and self-financing colleges, i.e., one government college with autonomous status, five aided colleges with autonomous, one non-autonomous college and four self-financing colleges. The total strength is 5563. Again, for sampling purpose it was decided to take one government college, one men autonomous aided college, one women autonomous aided college and two self-financing colleges (one is co-education and another is women college). They are as follows:

Table 1.3 : The students' strength of the select sample colleges (During the academic year 2009-2010)

Status	Name of the College	PG		M.Phil		Total
		Arts	Science	Arts	Science	
Govt. College	Periyar EVR College	186	369	33	42	630
Aided Colleges	St. Joseph's College	261	393	81	115	850
(Autonomous)	Holy Cross College	62	86	32	22	202
Self-financing	Cauvery College	112	391	31	45	579
College	Srimad Andavan College	87	241	16	26	370
	Total					**2631**

Source: Director of Collegiate Education, Tiruchirappalli.

From the selected sample colleges strength it was decided to select 10 per cent students for this study. Therefore, the sample size is as follows.

Table 1.4 : Sample size of the study

Status	Name of the College	PG		M.Phil		Total
		Arts	Science	Arts	Science	
Govt	EVR	18	37	3	4	62
Aided (Auto)	SJC	26	39	8	12	85
Aided (Auto)	HSC	06	09	03	02	20
Self-finance	Cauvery	11	39	03	05	58
Self-finance	Srimad Andavan	09	24	02	03	38
Total						**263**

Thus, the sample size for this study is 263 students. The researcher with the help of the college office assistants prepared the name lists of the student respondents by giving running numbers. With the help of TIPPET Random Sampling Numbers List from the Statistical table book 263 sample students' respondents were selected. Thus, multi-stage random sampling technique is used for selecting the sample size.

At the same time, opinion-leaders are selected by the researcher at random. They are as follows:

Table 1.5 : Category of opinion-leaders

Category	Number of respondents
I. PROFESSIONALS	
i. College principals	05
ii. Auditors	05
iii. Doctors	05
iv. Lawyers	05
v. Engineers	05
II. ADVERTISING AGENCY	
i. Mudra	01
ii. Lintas	01
iii. JWT	01
iv. Leevi	01
v. Archana	01
vi. Ray	01
III. MARKETING EXECUTIVES	
i. The Hindu	02
ii. Dailythanthi	01
iii. Dinamalar	01
iv. Times of India	01
v. Dinamani	02
vi. Clock TV	01
vii. Ten TV	01
viii. Suriyan FM	04
IV. MANAGER/DIRECTOR	
i. Clock TV	01
ii. Ten TV	01
iii. S.T.V	01
V. RADIO STATION DIRECTORS	
i. All India Radio	01
ii. Suriyan FM	01

Category	Number of respondents
VI. CHIEF EDITOR	
i. Decon Chronicle	01
ii. Dinamani	01
iii. Indian Express	01
VII. RADIO JOCKEY	
i. Suriyan FM and Hello FM, Tiruchirappalli	02
VIII. TIRUCHIRAPPALLI EMPLOYMENT OFFICE	
i. Regional Deputy Director	01
IX. INSTITUTE OF ENTREPRENEURSHIP AND CAREER DEVELOPMENT	
i. Director	01
X. ADVERTISING PROFESSIONALS	
i. Cine Actors	04
ii. Cine Directors	03
iii. Cine Producer	01
iv. Music Directors	02
v. Cinematographer	01
vi. Cine Singers	05
vii. Lyric writers	03
Total	**75**

Source: Primary data

A separate structured two different set of questionnaires were prepared and given to the opinion-leaders and student respondents. The data were collected during December and January from the opinion-leaders and data from the students were collected during the month of January 2010. The collected data were coded and they were tested by the SPSS. Tools used in this study are ANOVA, Chi-square test and 't' test. The collected data were analysed and interpretation were made.

Scope of the Study

This study covers the students of Arts and Science colleges functioning within the limits of Tiruchirappalli corporation.

The period of the study is the academic year from December 2008 to January 2010.

This study has been designed to ascertain and to analyze the data on the effectiveness of advertisements on college students measured in terms recall value and remembering the contents.

The outcome of this study will help the media people, advertisers, advertising agencies to have control over willful advertisements. The findings and suggestions made by the researcher will help to avoid mass Narcissism and its consequences.

The role of Advertising Standard Council of India is brought to the students community. In future, the students forum can file a complaint about any misleading advertisement. The Advertising Standard Council of India can stand as a moral pillar to the students community. The Association of Advertising Agencies of India, who is a spoke person for advertising agency can also have a link with the students forum.

The media, agency, will know the factors which are responsible for the recall memory of the advertisements and their effectiveness.

The role of opinion-leaders should be very much linked with the students. In future, this will lead to a collective bargaining power to any evil that affects our society. The ideas posed by the enlightened citizens, such as the academicians, economic planners, political thinkers, political elites, technocrats, bureaucrats, social activists, media experts, development professionals and all other people who have enjoyed the fruits of democracy for ever is an unmixed blessings for the society and in turn the standard of living of the people will be in accordance to the standards maintained in terms of their own culture.

Limitations of the Study

1. The researcher felt and realized the generation gap between the young respondents and the opinion-leaders with regard to spending their leisure time. However, the views of opinion-leaders are very much useful to avoid unethical, unfair advertisements as they are from the senior citizens of democratic India.

2. With the help of the pilot study it was decided to collect data only from post graduate and M.Phil research scholars due to their mental maturity, education and environment. Hence, this study did not focus its attention on the under graduate students.

3. The recall test made by the researcher and administered to the students has its own limitations. The views of the respondents will vary from time to time, place to place and person to person. The students have individual opinions but they are not ready to share the same when they are in their groups.

Inspite of the above limitations the researcher spent his time, and energy with a lot of sacrifice, to achieve the objectives of this study.

Chapter Scheme

Chapter-I	deals with the introduction
Chapter –II	gives review of literature
Chapter –III	provides profile of the study area.
Chapter –IV	provides analysis and interpretation of collected data from the opinion-leaders.

Chapter –V speaks on analysis and interpretation of the collected data from the students respondents.

Chapter –VI deals with findings, suggestions and conclusion.

REFERENCES

1. The Hindu, 10th June, 2010.
2. Gupta, C.B., (2009), Advertising and Personal Selling, Sultan Chand & Sons, New Delhi, p.19.
3. Mathur U C (2002), Advertising Management, New Age International (P) Ltd., New Delhi, p. 3.
4. Agarwal (2005), Advertising and Salesmenship, Pragati Prakashar, Meerut, p. 3.
5. Encyclopedia Britannia, Vol. 16, 1960, p. 17.
6. Gerad J. Tellis (2004), Effective Advertising, Response Book A division of Sage Publications India (P) Ltd., New Delhi, p. 43.
7. Rao. S.L., (1992), Socio-Economic Effects of Advertising in India, National Council of Applied Economic Research, New Delhi, p. 59.

2

Review of Literature

In this chapter, the researcher is going to discusses the review of literature on the following headings namely, effectiveness of advertisement, measurement of effectiveness of advertisement, pre-test measurement of effectiveness, post-test measurement of effectiveness of advertisement, celebrities/models/endorser of advertisement and ethical values in advertisements.

Effectiveness of Advertisements

Schleifer and *et al.*, (1968), their study tests in a controlled laboratory environment some basic factors that may influence the successful or unsuccessful transfer of advertising campaigns from one country to another.

David Corkindale (1976), investigated the use of advertising in marketing and its effectiveness. They suggests the establishment of objectives by setting a market share goal, determining the percentage of the market to be reached and agreeing the necessary budget. Looks into the difficulties of implementing this practice. They present a list of advantages, main considerations and general areas of objectives and evaluations for this practice. This study concludes that the advertising objective can be evaluated for its degree of achievement.

Kanti Prasad. V. (1976), recent debate on comparative advertising has focused on its ethical rather than its effectiveness dimension. A laboratory experiment was performed to assess the communication-effectiveness of a comparative advertisement in relation to its "brand X" counterpart. Results indicate that though a comparative advertising format can enhance message recall to some extent, it also can result in some loss of effectiveness from consumer perceptions of low credibility of its claims.

Stephens and *et al.*, (1982), time-compressed television advertisements have produced superior recall in college students. The current study indicates that young adults do recall more from time-compressed advertisements, but that elderly adults recall less and middle-aged adults are somewhere in between. These results hold for normal television advertisements as well.

Alpert and *et al.*, (1983), substantial interest has recently arisen in the study of advertisement miscomprehension and the role of repetitions in that inquiry. This study extends previous work in this area by specifically varying the number of exposures to advertisement messages for four products and measuring the impact on miscomprehension and other measures of advertisement effectiveness variables. Their findings suggest that repetition may not improve comprehension, and there is some evidence of a wearout effect. Problems and opportunities for further research are also addressed.

Lana Hall and *et al.*, (1983), the effectiveness of generic versus brand advertisement for yogurt is evaluated, using a polynomial distributed lag mod-el. Brand advertisement is found to be more than twice as effective as generic in increasing per capita consumption of yogurt. These results are then compared to the effectiveness of generic advertisement of fluid milk and used as a basis for recommending to dairy producers the best allocation of promotion funds. Generic advertisement of fluid milk is now common at state levels and has been shown to be effective in increasing per capita consumption of milk. Despite such advertising, fluid milk consumption has been declining steadily since the mid-1950s, leading dairy farmers to question whether promotion funds might better be spent on manufactured milk products such as cheese and yogurt, the consumption of which has been increasing. Some, such as yogurt, have shown especially impressive gains in sales in recent years. Yogurt sales, regulated under Federal Milk Marketing Orders, have increased by over 200 percent from 1970 to 1980. Given the structure of the milk pricing system, the benefits which might accrue to milk producers from the diversion of promotion funds are not obvious. Under Federal Milk Orders, Grade 'A' milk used for manufactured milk products is Class II or III; fluid milk is Class I. Milk producers do not receive higher prices as a result of an increased utilization of Class II or III milk, ceteris paribus. There may, of course, be some benefits to producers resulting from increased Class II or III utilization. In the present situation of milk surplus, increasing the consumption of manufactured milk products with advertising might reduce the quantity of surplus milk and the losses associated with it.

Kilbourne and et.al (1985), they presented the results of two empirical studies designed to assess the effectiveness of sexual embedding in advertising. In Study 1, a sample of 424 viewed and evaluated two advertisements with embeds or two matched advertisements without embeds. The results indicated that embedding was effective in raising attitudinal evaluations of a liquor advertisement but not a cigarette advertisement In Study 2, GSR *measurements* were taken on a sample of 36 subjects while they viewed both versions (with and without embeds) of two advertisements. The results of Study 2 indicated that embedding was effective in increasing GSR *measurements* for the versions of the advertisements with embeds.

Bruce A. Austin (1986), argued in favor of using motion picture screens as a medium for the presentation of advertising messages. The concept and history of cinema screen advertising is examined, previous and contemporary audience research on cinema advertisements is presented, and an argument favoring the adoption of cinema screen advertising is offered. Virtually all of the American mass media are characterized as commercial in the sense of being largely advertising supported. The most common place and pervasive media-newspapers, television, radio, and magazines—all share this characteristic. Cinema, however, is and has been supported almost entirely by patrons. Moreover, today there is much discussion as well as research on how new communication technologies might be employed to meet advertising and marketing needs. This article examines a mass communication technology which has been present for a century but has been virtually untapped as an advertising and marketing medium for reaching American consumers. Few individuals think of theatrically exhibited motion pictures as a likely medium to be supported by advertising. Introductory mass communication, advertising, and marketing texts regularly omit mention of this notion. This article argues that in an age of new communication technologies, use of this older technology for advertising and marketing carries many of the same advantages as does use of the emerging ones. This article explores the concept of cinema advertising, presents previous and contemporary audience research on cinema advertisements, and argues that today, especially, this long-neglected medium should be adopted for the dissemination of information by the consumer marketing and advertising industries.

Burton and *et al.*, (1988), have examined the effect of one content and two contextual advertising manipulations on several measures of attitude toward the advertisement. Results indicate that such antecedent variables, each of which requires some degree of cognitive processing of information, can impact in excess of their effects on perceptions of the value of the deal. Results also show that A_{ad} is a significant predictor of attitude toward the deal after co-varying out the experimental manipulations and perceptions of the value of the deal. Findings suggest that separate measures of cognitive and affective dimensions of A_{ad} may be more appropriate than the single composite measures which have typically been employed by researchers.

Loken, and *et al.*, (1988), have investigated three factors that could influence subjects' reactions to print advertisements for cigarettes. A total of 115 college women were shown cigarette advertisements that varied on two dimensions: whether an attractive model was shown and whether a general or specific warning label was shown. One half of the women were pre-tested on their beliefs about the hazards of smoking prior to seeing the advertisements; all of the women completed a post-test beliefs measure. Ratings of the attractiveness, persuasiveness, and credibility of the advertisements were collected, and the smoking status of subjects was assessed. Results indicated that specific warnings on advertisements can act as counterinfluence to an advertisements appeal by making it appear less attractive and less persuasive than if the advertisements contained only a general warning. This effect was especially true for smokers. Subjects also rated an advertisement as more attractive, more persuasive, and less credible when it showed an attractive model than when it did not. Being pre tested on their beliefs about the hazards of smoking resulted in high attractiveness and persuasion ratings and in smokers' recalling and recognizing more of the specific warnings that appeared on advertisements. Practical and theoretical implications for the results are discussed.

Mazursky and *et al.*, (1988), have examined the impact of encoding of product information on temporal changes in product attitudes following exposure to discounting appeals. The sleeper effect, which is manifested by increased message effectiveness over time, was observed in two replications when participants were induced to encode the message elaboratively. Under this condition, consumers were guided to imagine themselves consuming the advertised products while viewing the advertisements. The sleeper effect was not observed, however, when consumers were not induced to elaborate on and integrate message information (Experiment 1) or when the request to imagine themselves using the products was delivered after the discounting cue was conveyed (Experiment 2). These findings support a model that postulates that the magnitude of the sleeper effect is influenced by the relative availability of the product information and the discounting cue appeal. Additional mediating mechanisms are explored and discussed.

Okechuku and *et al.*, (1988), have investigated the consumer attitudes toward print advertisements made in China and available in the North American market. Cognitive evaluation of advertisements based on source and message credibility; extent to which respondents felt the advertisement was interesting, impressive, attractive and eye-catching; usefulness of balance theory representation in predicting the direction of audience reaction during copy testing were studied.

Pamela M. and *et al.*, (1990), have explained the interactive role of source expertise, time of source identification, and involvement was examined in an experiment on advertising effectiveness. In general, findings support an elaborative processing explanation. A three-way interaction among the manipulated variables emerged in the study, which utilized print advertisement stimuli. The findings also suggest that the source expertise information was processed more as a central persuasion cue than as peripheral information. Managerial implications are offered.

David W and *et al.*, (1991), have considered the long-standing debate over media effects on advertising performance, in particular the effects of television advertising material. Argues that the attentiveness towards involving programme material, rather than immediately dissipating with the onset of commercial breaks, remains activated to some extent, producing a positive effect on commercial performance. Provides a summary of the evidence and reports on research findings.

Stephen Ansolabehere and *et al.*, (1994), have used a realistic experimental design, this article tests two hypotheses concerning the relative effectiveness of campaign advertising. The first (issue-ownership) hypothesis predicts that candidates gain the most from advertising on issues over which they can claim "ownership." The second (riding-the-wave) hypothesis predicts that candidates are better off when they synchronize their advertising with news coverage. Their two studies yield support for the issue-ownership hypothesis, but no evidence of interactive effects is witnessed between advertising and news.

Yang and *et al.*, (1995), this article presents an abstract of the research paper "Screen-Based Interactive Advertisements and Their Effectiveness: An Exploratory Study of Cross-National Computer Users," by Chung-Chuan Kenneth Yang. The purpose of this study was to explore the potential of interactive computer on-line shopping services as a medium for international advertising and to determine the effectiveness of on-line advertisements in this new medium. Repeated measure design was used with message types, product involvement and subjects' nationality as independent variables to test the effectiveness of on-line interactive advertisements. Four dependent variables were used to measure advertising effectiveness: subjects' attitude toward the advertisements, attitude toward the advertised products, purchase intention of the advertised products, and total amount of time spent on watching the advertisements. Graduate students from Taiwan, China and the U.S. participated in the experiment. No support was found for the hypotheses that interactivity would induce a positive attitude among subjects toward the advertisements and advertised products. It did not lead to a higher purchase intention of the advertised products or cause viewers to spend more time on the advertisements.

France Leclerc and *et al.*, (1997), have stated that the packaged goods manufacturers distribute cents-off coupons in free-standing inserts (FSIs) in newspapers. Free-standing insert coupons are typically composed of two parts: the coupon per se and a print advertisement. Using two laboratory experiments and a separate analysis of coupon measurements from scanner panels, the authors investigate whether the content of the print advertisement influences the effective-ness of the coupon. Theoretical arguments suggest that the impact on consumer attitudes will depend on the executional cues of the copy, the brand loyalty of the consumers, and the consumer's involvement with the product category. The results support the theoretical framework and suggest that it is possible to make FSI coupons more effective by choosing appropriate executional cues for their advertising copy.

Young Zhang and *et al.*, (1997), investigates the effects of different advertising appeals used across cultures. Cultural differences along the individualism-collectivism dimension are hypothesized to affect people's reactions to certain advertising appeals. Results indicate that appeals which emphasize individualistic benefits are more effective in the USA than in China. When appeals emphasizing collectivistic benefits are employed, they are generally more effective in China. However, such effects can be moderated by product characteristics. Different product types may serve to influence the effectiveness of culturally-congruent advertising appeals. Discusses the implications of the findings.

Charles F Hofacker and *et al.*, (1998), explore one of the many exciting advertising research possibilities spawned by the Web, namely the efficacy of banner advertisements designed to lure the browser to an external Web page. Traditional advertising research usually relies on self-report or memory. With Web advertisement banners, on the other hand, they could track actual behavior. In their pilot study, they demonstrate conclusively that click-through rate, the percentage of visitors to a Web page clicking on an advertisement banner, can vary according to the advertisement copy. They also find that the imperative call for behavior, "Click here", has a positive effect. These findings, using a new research method with a new medium, open the door to further advertising and communication research on Web advertisement banners.

Quester, and *et al.*, (1998), presents information on a study that examined the attitudes of Malaysian and Australian adults towards smoking, before and after exposure to an anti-smoking message. Effects of anti-smoking advertisements on consumer attitudes; Assessment of the attitudinal changes generated by anti-smoking messages were the parameters researched.

Rae and *et al.*, (1998), looks at the effectiveness of using sound and animation when launching advertisements by means of the World Wide Web increase in Web advertising; details on banner advertising which is the most common form of Web advertising; advantages of using Web based surveys are the aspects studied.

Deborah Roedder John (1999), twenty five years of consumer socialization research have yielded an impressive set of findings. The purpose of their article is to review these findings and assess what they know about children's development as consumers. Their focus is on the developmental sequence characterizing the growth of consumer knowledge, skills, and values as children mature throughout childhood and adolescence. In doing so, they present a conceptual framework for understanding consumer socialization as a series of stages, with transitions between stages occurring as children grow older and mature in cognitive and social terms. They then review empirical findings illustrating these stages, including children's knowledge of products, brands, advertising, shopping, pricing, decision making strategies, parental influence strategies, and consumption motives and values. Based on the evidence reviewed, implications are drawn for future theoretical and empirical development in the field of consumer socialization.

Mark Ritson and *et al.,* (1999), advertising research has focused exclusively on the solitary subject at the expense of understanding the role that advertising plays within the social contexts of group interaction. They develop a number of explanation for the omission before describing the results of an ethnographic study of advertising's contribution to the everyday interaction of adolescent informants at a number of English high schools. The study reveals a series of new, socially related advertising audience behaviors. Specifically, advertising meanings are shown to possess social uses relating to textual experience, interpretation, evaluation, ritual use, and metaphor. The theoretical and managerial implications of these social uses are then discussed.

Chanthika Pornpitakpan and *et al.,* (2000), an experiment involving 140 Singaporean students with four advertisements classified as either high or moderate in degrees of incongruity is used to investigate the influence of incongruity on the effectiveness of humorous advertisements. As predicted, participants' perceived humor, attitudes toward the advertisement and the brand, and purchase intention are higher for humorous advertisements containing moderate incongruity than for those containing extreme incongruity.

Elizabeth S. Moore and *et al.,* (2000), although the pre purchase effects of advertising on children are well documented, little is known about advertising's impact in conjunction with children's product usage experiences. Two studies, one using experimentation and the other using depth interviews, were undertaken to examine this issue. In addition to informational effects, special emphasis was placed on the role affective constructs play in shaping children's impressions. Experimental results indicated that both product trial and advertising have influences, but also that the interplay of these influences differ between older children

(10–11 year olds) and younger children (seven to eight year olds). Depth interviews offer further insights into these age differences such that their overall understanding of how older and younger children relate to advertisements and product consumption has been advanced.

Kumar, Anand (2000), the effectiveness of advertisements has been an issue of great concern to marketers, especially with the rapid increase in the number of marketing communications that the average consumer receives every day. Prior research has examined the impact of verbal interference on consumers' memory for different elements of the advertisement—that is, interference caused by similar verbal elements in advertisements for brands in the same product category. This study examined the impact of similar contextual or background stimuli on consumers' memory for different elements of the advertisement. Consumers were exposed to print advertisements for products in different product categories. The similarity of contextual cues-that is, background scenes-was manipulated (similar vs. dissimilar). Using a 2 (contextual cues interference: low and high) × 2 (processing goal: advertisement and brand) × 3 (cues: brand name, advertisement photo, product class) between-subjects design, it was found that exposure to advertisements with similar contextual elements reduced individuals' ability to recall not only contextual or background elements but also brand name from a target advertisement.

Katherine Gallagher and *et al.*, (2001), have replicated, using adult web users, a study comparing advertising effectiveness and content evaluation in print and on the web (Gallagher, Foster, and Parsons, 2000). As in the original study involving students, the replication found that advertising was equally effective in the two media. However, while the original study found that evaluation of an article containing advertising was lower when it appeared on the web than when it appeared in print, this result was not replicated. Examination of two subgroups showed that results for the subgroup resembling the student sample were consistent with the original study. They propose conditions under which student samples are found to be appropriate.

Carol Kaufman-Scarborough (2001), stated that successful advertising must attract attention, communicate clearly, and ideally be memorable for optimum impact. The basic processes of encoding and decoding underlie successful communication, but advertisers often neglect to test for accessibility by visually-disabled persons. The present paper presents a framework for detecting information-processing problems and illustrate the use of this framework by analyzing the responses of color-deficient consumers.

Dahlen and *et al.*, (2001), this article examines the impact of brand familiarity and internet user experience on banner- advertisement effectiveness. The results from a large empirical study show that there are major differences between the performances of banner advertisements for familiar and unfamiliar brands. Advertisements for familiar brands tend to wear out quickly, whereas banner advertisements for unfamiliar brands need multiple exposures to wear in. Major differences are also found between novice and expert. Internet users regarding their susceptibility to web advertising. Novice users are more affected by banner advertisements than are expert users. Implications based on the findings are discussed.

Andrew L. Mendelson and *et al.*, (2002), traditional hierarchy-of-effects models of advertising state that advertising exposure leads to cognitions, such as memory about the advertisement, the product and or the brand; which in turn leads to attitudes, such as product liking and attitude toward possible purchase; which in the end leads to behaviors, such as buying the advertised product (Albion & Farris, 1981). One issue that has not been raised in this area of research is what happens to a consumer who is not able to carry out the desired behavior because of lack of economic resources. Research has suggested that people of lesser economic means are particularly harmed by constant media messages of consumerism because they have no way to relieve the created consumerist wants and desires (West, 1994). It is possible that the inability to pursue wants and desires evoked by advertisement for luxury products could lead to differential patterns of emotional cognitive responding during processing of an advertisement. This study investigates differences in emotional and cognitive responses as revealed through physiological responses (heart rate, skin conductance, and facial EMG) for young college students of different socio-economic levels.

Cornelia Pechmann and *et al.*, (2002), ninth graders were randomly exposed to one of eight slice of life videotapes showing stimulus advertising (cigarette, antismoking, both, neither) and unfamiliar peers who either did or did not smoke cigarettes. The findings indicate that the cigarette advertising primed positive smoker stereotypes, which caused subjects to seek out favorable information about the peers shown smoking. Subjects' beliefs and intentions about cigarette consumption were thereby enhanced by the joint effects of advertising and peers. However, an antismoking advertisement shown in conjunction with cigarette advertising made salient negative smoker stereotypes, evoked unfavorable thoughts about peers shown smoking, and prevented cigarette advertising from promoting smoking.

Hudson S and *et al.*, (2002), the article focuses on a study which investigated the effectiveness of using cross-national standardized television advertisements targeted at Chinese Canadians in Canada. A quasi-experiment was conducted on two subject groups, Chinese people in Hong Kong and Chinese Canadians in Canada. Two advertisements by an investment company that were aired on the Chinese-language television channel were used. Both advertisements employed an implicit message and had the same underlying theme spelled out at the end of the advertisements. The authors were interested in determining if there would be a difference in attitude based on national environment.

Jones and *et al.*, (2002), discusses the effectiveness of advertisements featuring local business owners. The role of advertising in defining a company and giving it character; The consumers' response to advertisement featuring company owners; Companies that have created advertisements featuring their chief executive officers are studied and discussed.

Michael Volkov and *et al.*, (2002), stated that an advertising expenditure has risen globally and in Australia there has been a 2.7-fold increase in the last ten years. It is suggested that some advertisements may be "unacceptable", that is, unfair, misleading, deceptive, offensive, false or socially irresponsible. This research is concerned with consumer behaviour and consumer complaint behaviour specifically in the area of advertising in Australia. The findings indicate that complainants are significantly different from the population at large. This research explains that the regulatory bodies have a better understanding of the complaining public as well as on educating marketing communications strategists in effectively reaching their target markets.

Chang-Hoan Cho (2003), this study indicates that people who are highly involved with a product are more likely to click a banner advertisement than those with low product involvement. In addition, this study found an interaction effect of peripheral cues (advertisement size and animation) and level of product involvement on clicking of banner advertisements; i.e., the positive relationship between peripheral cues and banner clicking is found to be more pronounced among those with low, rather than high, product involvement.

Amitav Chakravarti and *et al.*, (2004), more than a billion dollars is spent annually on generic advertisements that promote the consumption of commodity goods. Generic advertising is designed to increase primary demand, or the "size of the pie," without affecting selective demand, or the "share of the pie." They found evidence to the contrary—generic advertising increases the consumer's sensitivity to changes in price and systematically alters brand preferences. These effects of generic advertising can be attributed to the tendency of generic advertisements to change the relative importance of the attributes used to evaluate the brands. The results have implications for the public policy issue of how to effectively implement generic advertising without differentially benefiting certain brands and the managerial issue of how to integrate generic and brand advertising in order to achieve product category and brand differentiation goals.

Gerard J Tellin (2004), he stated that an advertising can have a variety of effects on human thoughts, attitudes, feelings, and behavior, Researchers have used a variety of measures to assess advertising and its effects. To understand how advertising works, first need to describe all variables and understand how they relate to each other. It then describes how they relate to each other. Researchers have long suspected that the effects of advertising are related in a sequential chain so that response on one variable leads to response on another. Such a chain of sequential responses is called the hierarchy of effects. Hierarchy of effects provides a convenient framework to relate all the measures of advertising. The framework assumes that a relationship does in fact exist between the various effects of advertising. These various sequences constitute different sequences of variable in the framework. These various sequences constitute different models of the hierarchy of effects. This study presents a classification of the various measures for advertising. It then presents various hierarchies to relate these variables.

Howard and *et al.*, (2004), they did three field experiments examined an information processing explanation for the effectiveness of a direct wail persuasion technique. Respondents received an advertisement in the mail accompanied by a hand-written note of the form, "John, Try this. It works!" and signed using a common initial. In the first experiment, the technique increased (decreased) free sample requests when strong (weak) brand attributes were used. In a second experiment, the attribute quality interaction effect was found only for respondents who could not identify who sent them the advertisement. Those who knew the sender requested more free samples regardless of the attribute strength of the brand. A third experiment revealed that both the personalization and content of the note contribute to its effectiveness. Theoretical implications are discussed.

Jennifer Edson Escalas and *et al.*, (2004), research on mental simulation finds differential effects for process versus outcome focus. They manipulate the focus of participants' thoughts while viewing advertisements and find that under low to moderate involvement, argument strength has a greater effect on behavioral intentions when participants focus on the process versus the outcome of product use. This differential advantage of process focused thought reverses under conditions of high involvement. The apparent reason for the sensitivity of process focused thought to argument strength under low to moderate involvement is that a process focus leads to the relatively spontaneous formulation of a plan to purchase given strong, but not weak, advertisement arguments.

Kim Shyan Fam and *et al.*, (2004), have stated that a constantly changing and increasingly globalize world, religion still plays a significant role in influencing social and consumer behavior. This study analyzes what influence religion and intensity of belief has on attitudes towards the advertising of particular controversial products and services. A questionnaire was distributed to 1,393 people across six different countries and resulting in samples of four main religious groups. The results indicated some statistically significant differences between the groups, which can have important implications for global marketers.

Rama Yelkur and *et al.*, (2004), this study examines super bowl advertising effectiveness from the Hollywood movie industry's perspective. Results indicate that the average Super Bowl promoted film achieved twice as much first weekend, first week, and total U.S. box office revenue that it's average non-super Bowl promoted movie counterpart for the years 1998-2001. When all movies with production budgets of $ 35 million or more and U.S. release dates within 7 months of the 1998-2001 Super Bowls were considered, Super Bowl promoted moves grossed nearly 40 percent more that non-Super Bowl promoted movies. Conclusions are drawn and future research directions are outlined.

Turley, L.W and *et al.*, (2004), their study explored the effects of advertising in a sports arena on message recall, purchase intentions and actual purchase behavior. Overview of advertising recall; Presentation of the field study; Results and discussion.

Beattie and *et al.*, (2005), have stated that the design of effective communications depends upon an adequate model of the communication process. The traditional model is that speech conveys semantic information and bodily movement conveys information about emotion and interpersonal attitudes. But McNeill (2000) argues that this model is fundamentally wrong and that some bodily movements, namely spontaneous hand movements generated during talk (iconic gestures), are integral to semantic communication. But the increase of the effectiveness of communication using this new theory was questioned. Focusing on advertising they found that advertisements in which the message was split between speech and iconic gesture (possible on TV) were significantly more effective than advertisements in which meaning resided purely in speech or language (radio/ newspaper). They also found that the significant differences in communicative effectiveness were maintained across five consecutive trials. They compared the communicative power of professionally made TV advertisements in which a spoken message was accompanied either by iconic gestures or by pictorial images, and found the iconic gestures to be more effective. They hypothesized that iconic gestures were very effective because they illustrated and isolated just the core semantic properties of a product.

This research suggests that TV advertisements can be made more effective by incorporating iconic gestures with exactly the right temporal and semantic properties.

Demetrios Vakratasas and *et al.*, (2005), this study examines the long term effectiveness of multimedia advertising in a competitive setting and its implications for budget allocation decisions, using multivariate persistence methodology. Analysis of network TV, spot TV, and magazine advertising for the two major competitors in the U.S. SUV industry suggested that long-run advertising effectiveness differed considerably among media. These differences were attributed to the media lifespan, retrieval, and content of the message the convey. The authors purpose that budget allocation decisions should consider the long-run effectiveness of the different media employed to increase the productivity of advertising campaigns. They also conduct a simulation experiment to further investigate long-run scale effects of alternative allocation strategy scenarios.

Clow and *et al.*, (2005), they stated that because of the intangibility of services, producing effective advertisements challenges the creative ability of advertising creatives. Creating the right headline, the right copy, and the right visual are crucial to the effectiveness of an advertisement in terms of developing a positive attitude towards the brand and increasing the probability of making a purchase. The role of the visual element in creating such an effective advertisement, within the context of a service, was examined in this study. An experimental design was used to investigate the impact of four different visual strategies in combination with a generic creative message approach. Results indicate that when creative use a generic creative message strategy, an emotional visual creates the strongest results, especially in terms of attitude towards the visual element in the advertisement. Data analysis also indicated the visual element was a strong driver of attitude towards the advertisement, which in turn drove attitude towards the brand and purchase intentions. The impact of the visual is enhanced when creative choose a visual that is memorable and matches the written copy of the advertisement. These findings as well as other findings from the study are discussed in terms of current advertisement design and future research needs.

Janssens and *et al.*, (2005), the effects of advertisement and context type on the responses to advertisements for different brands of new and existing products were tested. In the first experiment (243 graduate students) a positive emotional advertisement and a non-emotional advertisement for a well-known and a new brand of printer were tested in a positive emotional context and a non-emotional media context. In the second experiment (206 graduate students) positive emotional and non-emotional advertisements for new brands of watches and healthy drinks were tested in an emotional and a non-emotional context. The type of context moderated the responses to advertisements for the well-known and new products: a positive emotional context led to a more positive attitude towards the advertisement and the brand and purchase intention for the well-known brand than for the new brand. A non-emotional context led to more positive responses for the new brand than for the well-known brand. In general, emotional advertisements led to more positive affective reactions and non-emotional advertisements led to more positive cognitive reactions. However, the type of advertisement did not have a moderating effect on the responses to advertising for the new or well-known brands or different product types. The studies illustrated the relevance of media context for advertising new versus existing products.

Lees and *et al.,* (2005), the objective of this research was to test the effect on click-through rates of a variation in the design of a web banner advertisement placed on a number of high-profile New Zealand websites. The variation involved the addition of a mouse pointer image next to the 'click here' message on the last frame of the advertisement. Previous studies had found that including a 'click here' instruction increased response to banner advertisements but in this study no such effect was found. However, click-through rates for the advertisement varied significantly across the sites examined. More research is therefore called for not only to identify whether a pointer image is able to increase click through rates in combination with other design elements, but also to further investigate the relationship between site content, visitorship and click-through rates.

Yoon and *et al.,* (2005), first objective of this study is to investigate whether consumers' advertisement preference is influenced by their degree of participation in, as well as their attitudes towards, sport. The relationships among preferences for advertisements and products and consumers' desire to purchase are also explored. Secondly, the study seeks to determine the role of product involvement in favouring particular advertisement types and increasing purchase intention. Thirdly, the practical implications for the use of athletes as models in advertisements in order to increase the effectiveness of sports advertisements are addressed. A survey was conducted of 200 college students from three universities in Seoul and Kyonggi-do. Pre-testing was used to validate the survey instrument and then experimental stimuli were prepared and tested against subjects. Sports participation, sports preference and lifestyle were found to affect advertisement preference. People with active lifestyles were more interested in sports advertisements than people with non-active lifestyles. Secondly, advertisement preference was found to influence product preference. Advertisements featuring products and athletes were found to be preferred to advertisements featuring products only. Thirdly, the product purchase intention was found to be influenced more when the advertisement featured both the product and an athlete, compared to when it featured the product only.

Chun-Tuan Chang (2006), statistical framing of product efficacy and graphic illustration were examined to explain the conditions under which messages would be more effective in a healthcare product advertisement. Using different health contexts (skin care and traveling) and statistical formats (percentage and frequency), two experiments investigate how consumers respond to positively and negatively framed messages with different forms but equivalent information about product efficacy. Framing effects were enhanced by graphic aids when statistics were presented in a percentage or a frequency with a small number size. The moderating role of graphic illustration on framing effectiveness was eliminated when statistics were presented in frequency with a large number size.

Fry and *et al.*, (2006),while overall road deaths in Australia have fallen since the late 1980's and the impact of road-safety advertising appears to be positive, alcohol-related road fatalities remain the leading cause of death among young Australian adults. Fatality and injury rates continue within this cohort despite increases in alcohol-related knowledge, continuing education efforts in the Australian school system, increased funding for police enforcement and high media presence of road safety advertising (Peder *et al.*, 2004). Notwithstanding advances in communication technologies, highly graphic, emotional, shock style television advertising remains the primary medium for road safety message dissemination. Rather than targeting those highest at-risk for drink driving, road safety advertisements typically target an undifferentiated general audience. To date understanding the process by which road safety advertising influences attitudes and behaviour has been the centre of fear arousal research. Nonetheless, there has been little examination of how young adults who differ in drink-driving risk-propensity (high versus low) respond to and process anti-drink driving advertisements designed to modify an avoidable behaviour. Taking a receiver oriented approach, the focus of this study examines how young adult, novice drivers who differ in 'need-for-sensation' (NFS) risk propensity respond to, and process, anti-drink driving advertisements that differ in arousal capacity (i.e. high, low sensation-value). The investigation was conducted in two stages: Study 1 (qualitative) and Study II (quantitative). Study I, the qualitative phase, explored by focus group interviews attitudes, perceptions, beliefs and experiences of sixty young adults aged 18 to 25 years towards alcohol consumption, drink-driving, and anti-drink driving advertising. The major qualitative finding is that young adults characterise drink-driving as a rational, deliberate, planned and accepted behaviour. Young adults were aware of the choices available for not drinking and driving and were aware of the health, social and physical (self and property) risks associated with alcohol consumption and associated behaviours. Nonetheless, the short-term personal experiences of revelry and group cohesion were more pertinent to them on an everyday basis. Alcohol consumption and drink-driving behaviour did not appear to differ between university and non-university students or gender, yet there were differences in attitudes and behaviour across the degree studied within the university cohort. Study II, the quantitative phase, was segmented into three sections. First, the study provides empirical support for NFS as a relevant a priori individual differences segmentation variable for differentiating between those more likely, versus less likely, to engage in responsible drink-driving behaviour. As expected low NFS individuals were more likely to not drink and drive. Second, findings support an interaction effect between an advertisement's sensation value and individual differences variable, NFS, on response outcomes. High NFS individuals engaged in higher levels of adaptive appraisal on the high sensation-value advertisement condition as compared to the low sensation value advertisement condition. Low NFS individuals did not discriminate across either advertisement condition. Adaptive appraisal was not counteracted by a corresponding increase in maladaptive appraisal. Both high and low NFS individuals viewed the high sensation-value advertisement condition with high levels of perceived threat and viewed the low sensation-value advertisement with higher levels of perceived efficacy. Yet, although high NFS individuals viewed the high sensation-value advertisement with high levels of threat they simultaneously viewed this advertisement with low levels of perceived efficacy. Third, NFS was not found to be a strong predictor moderating the relationship between message processing (cognitive, sensory, narrative) and response outcomes. The findings indicate strong support for a direct relationship between two modes of message processing: cognitive and narrative processing and response outcomes. Message recipients processed anti-drink driving advertisements via two routes to persuasion. There was stronger cognitive processing evident on advertisements possessing high arousal capacity, whereas stronger narrative processing was evident on low arousal capacity advertisements. This study suggests that those advertisements that possess high arousal capacity have the capability of facilitating attention to the central argument, the consequences of drinking and driving, as well as how drinking and driving may affect the message recipients' life. Alternatively, those messages that impart high levels of rational information have the capability of increasing attention to the peripheral cues in the message. It is also suggested that different styles of message processing, central versus peripheral, act in a synergistic way to influence response outcomes which indicates that there is no single route to persuasion. Individuals process messages in a complex manner attending to various signals in order to evaluate various components of the message. For road safety practitioners and social marketers the results of this study illustrates practical benefits for the design of anti-drink driving advertisements based on the segmentation variable NFS. The finding that high NFS individuals require advertisements that possess high levels of arousal capacity (i.e.: high in sensation-value) is an important development. Importantly, low NFS individuals do not discriminate in accepting the recommendations of advertisements that differ in arousal capacity clearly suggests that they accept messages regardless of their arousal capacity. This finding indicates that the goal of road traffic authorities, advertising agencies and social marketers should be directed towards targeting high NFS individuals who are more at risk for a drink-drive fatality. That message recipients process anti-drink driving messages via two routes to persuasion indicates that message designers need to consider the mix between the sensation-value of the message and consideration of the way message recipients' process the message, i.e. via central or systematic versus peripheral or heuristic components of the advertisement. Further investigation into the dual processing of anti-drink driving advertisements once individuals are exposed to the message is warranted to further understand the psychological processes influencing message processing. The findings of this research have important implications for both practitioners and academics. This research has provided an insight into the complexity of young adult's response outcomes and message processing of fear-based anti-drink driving messages.

Michael Fay (2006), stated that a tenet of the marketing and advertising communities that the claims and appeals contained in advertisements must reflect the behavior, aspiration or dreams of potential customers. Work undertaken in New Zealand challenged the received wisdom, suggesting that the content of advertisements exhibited marked cyclical patterns that had little to do with societal trends. This paper seeks to replicate and extend the earlier study in a larger and less derivative economic environment. For each year over the period 1950-2000, the levels of usage of 58 variables in a large sample of advertisements from major UK magazines were analysed. The patterns from the resulting data were examined to determine whether deviations around long-term secular trends were random, or whether cyclical tendencies were apparent. The findings confirm that the generally espoused view of advertising as a mirror of society may require substantial modification. Over time periods of five to 15 years the level of usage of various claims and appeals is cyclical, and the stage of the cycle is a far more important factor than the secular trend in understanding the changing levels of usage over operational time periods. Because the study is limited to advertising in UK magazines, further content analysis work is required using other media (TV) and other countries.

Nicholas Reading and *et al.*, (2006), the advent of Personal Video Recorders (PVRs) may alter existing patterns of television advertising viewing. Although much of this might be characterized by increased advertising avoidance, this article explores the potential for a new advertising model utilizing PVRs, "telescopic advertising," enabling viewers to access extended content associated with the advertisements for the same products using the traditional 30-second TV commercial format and the infomercial format. Across four product categories, using an Australian sample, telescopic advertisements achieved significantly higher attitude toward the advertisement, attitude toward the brand, and behavioral intentions.

Pechmann, Cornelia, *et al.*, (2006), they used a validated copy test method to examine the effectiveness of 8 types of antismoking advertisements representing health, counterindustry, and industry approaches. They tested the hypothesis that health advertisements about tobacco victims can lower most adolescents' intent to smoke if the advertisements elicit disgust and anti-industry feelings rather than fear. They hypothesized null effects for adolescents with conduct disorder because of their abnormally low empathy. Ninth-grade students from 8 California public schools (n = 1725) were randomly assigned to view 1 of 9 videotapes containing a TV show with advertisements that included either a set of antismoking advertisements or a set of control advertisements. Participants completed baseline measures assessing personality traits and post-exposure measures assessing smoking intent, feelings, beliefs, and advertisement evaluations. Results. Advertisements focusing on young victims suffering from serious tobacco-related diseases elicited disgust, enhanced anti-industry motivation, and reduced intent to smoke among all but conduct-disordered adolescents. Counterindustry and industry advertisements did not significantly lower smoking intention. Sponsors of tobacco use prevention advertisement campaigns should consider using advertisements showing tobacco-related disease and suffering, not just counterindustry advertisements. Advertisements should be copy tested before airing.

John Gabriel S. (2006), he stated that "Today's youth are no fools and are far more sophisticated than they were 20 years ago, when many of today's youth advertising guidelines were written", says Jerry Mc Gee who ran perhaps the largest advertising agency. Marketing to the youth is a delicate issue. Because of the combination of color, sound and action, television attracts more viewers than any other medium (with the exception of cinema). TV is perceived as a persuasive medium of communication. Moreover, the youth is treated 'special' audience. Besides these, gender-focus, gender-orientation are used as advertising techniques and strategies. These factors have pro0vided the motivation to write this research paper.

Shou-Shiung Chou (2006), the objective of this study was to evaluate the effectiveness of advertising rhetoric and trope. The "degree of advertising involvement," "familiarity of brand," and "degree of product involvement" acted as moderators. Two metrics, attitude toward the advertisement and attitude toward the brand, were used to measure the response to each design, while a conventional type of advertising rhetoric was used as comparative base. Likert's 7-scale was used in the questionnaire, and 227 effective questionnaires were collected. The internal consistency value (a) of both advertising attitude and brand attitude of the questionnaire were 0.83 and 0.85. Results indicated that the trope could generate better advertisement attitude than the normal type of advertisement only when it was applied to those people with lower advertising involvement. The trope could generate better advertisement and brand attitude for more familiar products than it could for less familiar products. The trope had inferior performance compared to the normal approach when it was applied to products with high degree of product involvement. The study allowed the conclusion that the trope had better performance when there was lower product involvement and lower advertising involvement but might cause more cognitive risk when the product was less familiar.

Smith and *et al.*, (2006), they stated that approximately five million children under the age of 18 will eventually die from smoking-related disease. However, antismoking advertisements directed to adolescents appear to be reducing the prevalence of smoking among youth. The reported study extends prior research using an experiment over time (N= 565) to test the influence of individual factors (grade level, gender, and ethnicity) on the effectiveness of two types of message content in antismoking advertisements. Predictor variables from prior research, such as beliefs about smoking and family and peer smoking, were included as covariates in the analysis. As expected, effectiveness was influenced by individual factors. Long-term health content was more effective among nonwhites, males, and high school students, while short-term content appeared to work better among junior high males.

Stewart and *et al.*, (2006), despite extensive research successfully using subliminal to affect individual attitudes, public understanding and public policy response reflect a lack of awareness of their effectiveness. This article attempts to redress this by presenting findings concerning the effectiveness of one class of subliminal stimuli, precognitive primes. It then considers the effect of the controversial 'RATS' subliminal political advertisement. Here the term 'RATS' appeared on screen for one frame, that is, one-thirtieth of a second, as part of an attack advertisement by the Republican National Committee criticizing presidential candidate Al Gore's prescription drug plan. An experiment carried out on Election Day 2000 presented the advertisement with or without the RATS frame, as well as a parallel Medicare advertisement by the Gore campaign, to subjects. Findings suggest that while evaluations and behavioral intentions were not significantly affected, attitudes toward Medicare, the political parties, and Al Gore were significantly affected by the subliminal stimulus. The experiment was small in scale, so the findings are far from definitive. But they suggest a need for further research on the topic.

Appiah and *et al.*, (2007), they tested the effectiveness of testimonial advertisements on black and white browsers' evaluations of a high-end product on a commercial website. The results demonstrate that, although white browsers in general respond no differently to a commercial site whether it features a black character testimonial advertisement, white character testimonial advertisement, or no testimonial advertisement, black browsers do respond differently to commercial sites based on the race of the character used in the testimonial advertisements. Specifically, the findings indicate that black browsers identified more strongly with black character testimonials, were more likely to believe a site was targeting them when the site contained black testimonials, and recalled more product information from a site that featured black character testimonials vis-à-vis a site with either white character testimonials or no testimonials. The theoretical and practical implications of these findings are discussed.

Decrop and *et al.*, (2007), they explained the context of overabundant advertisements and saturated consumers, message format is crucial in developing effective advertising campaigns. In this study, four major format components of print advertisements are considered: picture, logo, text and headline. The goal is to investigate the effectiveness of each of these components in triggering a response by the target audience. Three types of response are taken into account: knowledge (information), liking (attraction) and behavioural intention. Four series of hypotheses related to the influence of message format on the effectiveness of print advertisements are tested for an urban tourism destination through an experimental research design. Findings show that picture and text are the prevailing elements, while logo and headline are of marginal importance. Pictures are especially effective in attracting the consumer and arousing a behavioural intention, whereas text is most powerful in conveying information.

Hee-Sook Yoon and *et al.*, (2007), have explained that very low Click-Through Rates (CTR) raise serious questions about the effectiveness of banner advertisements. However, they believed that the effect of a banner advertisement is not limited by clicks. Banner advertisement information itself can be processed by the audience. They proposed that the exposure effect of a banner advertisement exists even when the banner is not clicked. The results of our experiments strongly support this effect. Analyses also revealed that a non-clicked banner advertisement can create as strong of an exposure effect as clicked banner advertisement. Also, audiences that are able to recall the existence of the banner advertisement on a web page develop stronger implicit memory than those who cannot. Researchers are invited to re-test these interesting findings in various cultures with differing levels of Internet penetration and experience.

Hoggard, and *et al.*, (2007), an experiment with 421 participants aged 18-45 was conducted to measure the effects of interactivity in an online movie advertising setting, and the effects of interactivity on consumer engagement and other brand metrics. Results from a post-test survey revealed insight into participants' perceived level of interactivity, and reflected varying levels of attitude towards advertisement messages, advertisement recall, mood, and factors in purchasing habits. Results suggested that while interactivity can sometimes hinder advertising recall rates, it can also increase positive attitudes toward the advertisement, click-through rate, intent to purchase, and mood. Practical implications and suggestions for further research are discussed.

Ioni Lewis and *et al.*, (2007), in their study threatening advertisements have been widely used in the social marketing of road safety. However, despite their popularity and over five decades of research into the fear-persuasion relationship, an unequivocal answer regarding their effectiveness remains unachieved. More contemporary "fear appeal" research has explored the extent other variables moderate this relationship. In this study, the third-person effect was examined to explore its association with the extent male and female drivers reported intentions to adopt the recommendations of two road safety advertisements depicting high physical threats. Drivers ($N = 152$) first provided responses on pre-exposure future driving intentions, subsequently viewed two advertisements, one anti-speeding and one anti-drink driving, followed by measurement of their perceptions and post-manipulation intentions. The latter measure, post-manipulation intentions, was taken as the level of message acceptance for each advertisement. Results indicated a significant gender difference with females reporting reverse third-person effects (i.e., the messages would have more influence on themselves than others) and males reporting classic third-person effects (i.e., the messages would have more influence on others than themselves). Consistent with such third-person effects, females reported greater intention not to speed and not to drink and drive after being exposed to the advertisements than males. To determine the extent that third-person differential perceptions contributed to explaining variance in post-manipulation intentions, hierarchical regressions were conducted. These regressions revealed that third-person scores significantly contributed to the variance explained in post-manipulation intentions, beyond the contribution of other factors including demographic characteristics, pre-exposure intentions and past behaviour. The theoretical and applied implications of the results are discussed.

Kara Chan and *et al.*, (2007), have examined how Chinese and German consumers react to print advertisements that are potentially offensive. Using culture theories about information context, individualism and feminine consciousness, the paper hypothesizes that Chinese consumers will be less accepting of the advertisements than German consumers. It also compares the dimensions of consumer perceptions for both countries and how consumer perceptions are related with intentions to reject the products and the brands because of the advertisements. A survey of 563 respondents aged 17-58 from urban China (Shanghai) and Germany was conducted in October 2005 and June 2006. A questionnaire with six print advertisements containing sexism and other themes was constructed. Data were collected through five universities. Findings on perceptions of the offensive advertisements among Chinese and German respondents were mixed. Overall, as expected, Chinese respondents were less accepting of offensive advertising, as they liked the advertisements less than German respondents. However, they were also more likely than German respondents to find the advertisements convincing and informative. Results showed that Chinese respondents and German respondents had different dimensions of advertising perceptions. The two print advertisements that received the most negative perceptions both contained sexually oriented body images. The study also found that advertising perceptions had a significant impact on consumers' intentions to reject the products and the brands. The city surveyed in China is highly advanced in terms of economical and advertising development when compared with all other Chinese cities. Consumer responses were derived from a student sample. Only the "manner" of offensive advertising was studied, and the "matter" as well as "media" were not covered.

Kim-Shyan Fam and *et al.*, (2007), to examine likeable executional techniques in advertising across five Asian countries and their impact on purchase intentions. There is not a specific likeable executional technique that influences a purchase in four of the five countries. India is the only country where significant but weak overall model fit observed. These results demonstrate that, while there are differences among the countries, people in the same cohort broadly share the same values. For product categories, our findings demonstrate that product nature may moderate cultural influence on advertising effectiveness. International advertisers who are vying for a share of the largely-untapped Asian market can benefit by understanding the target country's cultural values and using it as a guideline for creating effective executional techniques in advertising.

Wim Janssens and *et al.*, (2007), the purpose of this research is to study the moderating role of the personality trait Discomfort With Ambiguity (DWA) on the processing of mixed emotions in advertising. Two experiments were conducted. In the first experiment, the emotions between the medium context and the embedded advertisement were mixed. In the second experiment, the emotions in an advertisement were mixed by manipulating emotions in the text and picture. Results indicate that DWA, being a proxy for how well people are able to deal with mixed emotions, has a moderating effect on advertising processing. Individuals having a high DWA appear to respond less positively to mixed emotions.

DeRosia and *et al.*, (2008), they investigated the effectiveness of nonverbal symbolic signs and rhetorical metaphors in advertisements. Hypotheses are made based on appeals to both interpretive and psychological theoretical perspectives. In contrast to previous research that has assumed nonverbal advertisement elements are effortlessly and automatically processed, it is proposed here that consumers must devote a nontrivial level of cognitive effort if they are to comprehend nonverbal symbolic signs and metaphors. The hypotheses suggest boundary conditions for the effectiveness of nonverbal elements in advertising. An experiment is conducted as a test of the hypotheses, and the observations support the hypotheses.

Kathleen Mortimer, (2008) to identify the components that make up an effective service advertisement. The majority of advertisements utilise emotional appeals for not only experiential but also utilitarian services. They also provide physical representation of the service and an illustration of the service encounter. The level of documentation in all the advertisements is low. The findings provide practitioners with an analysis of service advertising campaigns that have been recognised for their effectiveness. It is possible to identify common characteristics in these advertisements which should be considered when creating service advertisements in the future.

Lewis I and *et al.*, (2008) drawing upon the multiple roles of affect posited by Elaboration Likelihood Model, the current paper examines the *effectiveness* of message-relevant affect. Specifically, humourous and fear-evoking anti-drink driving messages are examined in terms of perceptions of relative influence on self and others (i.e., the third-person effect) and their performance on a range of persuasion outcomes. The influence of involvement, response efficacy, and gender on persuasion outcomes is also examined. Participants (N =201) viewed two *advertisements* and completed two questionnaires: the first, assessed pre-exposure attitudes and behaviour and immediate-post exposure attitudes and intentions; the second, 2–4 weeks later, assessed attitudes and behaviour. The results revealed, as predicted, interactions of the key variables and evidence of the greater persuasiveness of negative appeals immediately after exposure whilst greater improvement of positive appeals over time. The findings highlight the importance of continuing the exploration of positive appeals as a persuasive alternative to negative appeals.

Mark Loughney and *et al.,* (2008), the ABC Television Network has undertaken a series of research projects to understand the effectiveness of advertising in online streaming of TV episodes on ABC.com. The results of the current study suggested that the single sponsorship model of the ABC Full Episode Player yielded a level of advertising effectiveness that exceeded historical benchmarks for TV. Average unaided sponsorship recall was nearly two and a half times that of typical advertising recall on TV. In addition, present and posttest comparisons showed substantial increases in top of mind brand awareness and positive effects on brand attributes. The results of the study will be discussed with regard to implications for online video advertising generally, with suggestions for future research to clarify issues not specifically addressed in this study.

Mathew Joseph and *et al.,* (2008), explained the purpose of this paper is to examine consumer attitudes toward direct-to-consumer (DTC) advertising and whether consumer attitudes regarding these types of advertisements differ based on income. A sample of 168 consumers completed the survey on-site at a pharmacy while waiting for their prescription(s) to be filled. The findings indicated that low-income consumers were more likely than higher income customers to: report being persuaded by DTC advertising to ask for an advertised drug; go to the doctor based on symptoms described in DTC advertising; and to prefer branded medication over generic alternatives. The results provide useful information to policy makers and drug companies. The finding that these advertisements appear to impact lower income consumers to a greater extent than their higher-income counterparts has both positive and negative implications. On the positive side, these advertisements appear to influence unhealthy, low-income consumers to seek medical treatment. The negative implication concerns the effectiveness of DTC advertising in persuading low-income consumer to prefer more expensive, branded drugs over generic alternatives.

Mortimer and *et al.,* (2008), they identified the components that make up an effective service advertisement. This is achieved by examining a sample of service advertisements that have been recognised for their success. The advertisements are analysed with reference to two areas of discussion; the use of rational and emotional appeals and the presence of three executional tools, i.e. physical representation, documentation and showing the service encounter or provider. The methodology uses a combination of case study approach and a content analysis of effective service advertisements. The appeals are classified utilising the Pollay (1983) list of advertising appeals. The three executional tools are taken from an overview of the main conceptual frameworks. The majority of advertisements utilise emotional appeals for not only experiential but also utilitarian services. They also provide physical representation of the service and an illustration of the service encounter. The level of documentation in all the advertisements is low. The research is based on a small sample of UK TV advertisements. Practical implications - The findings provide practitioners with an analysis of service advertising campaigns that have been recognised for their effectiveness, It is possible to identify common characteristics in these advertisements which should be considered when creating service advertisements in the future. A study of real-life service advertisements that have been classified as "effective" has not previously been undertaken. The findings are therefore of value to advertising academics and practitioners in that they contribute to our understanding of how advertising works.

Samu and *et al.*, (2008), they investigated the effects of direct and indirect sources of anti-smoking messages. Specifically, it examines the direct influence of advertised messages and the indirect effect of the subsequent discussion. Two studies examine the role of: (i) Source characteristics (i.e., messages disseminated through mass media and subsequently via discussion by friends or strangers); (ii) Message characteristics (i.e., messages that induce either log, or high fear); (iii) Individual characteristics (i.e., gender based differences within the target audience) in attitude formation towards smokers, the act of smoking, propensity to smoke, and the likelihood of being influenced. Message efficacy is found to vary by gender, type of advertisement appeal, as well as group membership of advertisement discussants. Implications for design of anti-smoking campaigns are derived.

Shin Yi Chou and *et al.*, (2008), have explained the Childhood obesity is an escalating problem around the world that is especially detrimental as its effects carry on into adulthood. In this paper they employed the 1979 Child–Young Adult National Longitudinal Survey of Youth and the 1997 National Longitudinal Survey of Youth to estimate the effects of television fast food restaurant advertising on children and adolescents with respect to being overweight. A ban on these advertisements would reduce the number of overweight children ages 3–11 in a fixed population by 18 percent and would reduce the number of overweight adolescents ages 12–18 by 14 percent. The elimination of the tax deductibility of this type of advertising would produce smaller declines of between 5 and 7 percent in these outcomes but would impose lower costs on children and adults who consume fast food in moderation because positive information about restaurants that supply this type of food would not be completely banned from television.

Fotini Patsioura and *et al.,* (2009), present an effectiveness conceptual framework to evaluate the overall performance of corporate advertising web sites towards the multiple advertising, promotional and relationship marketing objectives of their establishment. Specifically, communication, feedback and customer support policies are examined in order to identify their contribution in creating or influencing advertising "effects". Findings reveal significant dimensions of the participants' behaviour based on their actions, activities, preferences and intentions. Also, the outcomes show a great impact of the relationship marketing qualitative factors in question on specific advertising effectiveness indicators. The paper introduces a new conceptual framework to support the contribution and significance of relationship marketing factors on the overall performance of corporate advertising web sites. This should be a useful approach for both academic researcher and practitioners.

Jay (Hyunjae) Yu and *et al.,* (2009), as new technologies (e.g. online, mobile and interactive TV) develop worldwide, numerous types of personalized advertising, in which companies use an individual's name and or other types of personal information, have become more popular in many countries. Using many types of information about specific individuals, personalized advertising is designed to convey a customized message at the right time to the right person using diverse media. However, despite its universally increased use, few academic studies have explored the effectiveness of personalized advertising and consumers' response to it. This exploratory study focused on consumers' perceptions of personalized advertising delivered online (e-mail) and offline (letter and telephone call). The results show that consumers generally have negative perceptions of personalized advertising, regardless of how it is delivered, with the strongest negative reaction to telephone calls.

Zhang and *et al.,* (2009), there is much evidence that the presence of a feature *advertisement* can increase the sales and market share of the featured product. However, little is known about how feature advertisement characteristics (e.g., size, color, and location of the *advertisement*) affect the sales outcomes and how the effects take place. Prior research has predicted that feature *advertisements* lead to behavioral outcomes through their effect on consumers' attention. Building on this idea, the authors propose a Bayesian statistical model to study how feature advertisement characteristics affect sales of the featured products and the mediating role of attention in these relationships. They use data from eye-tracking tests of feature *advertisements,* aggregated and matched with sales data at the level of the feature *advertisement.* Their approach accounts for endogeneity in the key variables involved and overcomes limitations of standard mediation analyses. They show that the gaze duration on a feature *advertisement* affects sales of the featured product beyond the mere presence of the *advertisement* and that a standard mediation analysis that does not accommodate endogeneity produces biased estimates of the effects of feature advertisements characteristics on sales. Their proposed methodology is widely applicable to mediation analyses. The findings imply that attention data collected in lab tests can help marketers compare the relative sales outcomes of different feature advertisements designs and improve the *effectiveness* and efficiency of feature adverting decisions.

Measurement of Effectiveness of Advertisement

Franzen and *et al.,* (1942), in their conference paper concerned with the validity of advertising effectiveness *measurements* is presented. The author notes that the *measurements* in question are not geared toward the visibility of *advertisements,* but rather their effectiveness in creating in the consumer an association with the product being advertised.

William T. Moran (1951), in order to avoid weaknesses felt to exist in previous methods of measuring exposure to advertisements, Moran conducted a study based on certain assumptions and using a mathematical equation developed to provide the proportion of a sample which has been exposed to an advertisement. Results are presented to show how this new method compares with another one, derived from a proposal by Lucas. Heller raises a number of criticisms, the chief one concerning what he sees as an inconsistency in the method proposed. In the "reply," Moran defends his original position, and presents an example to show why the inconsistency which Heller referred to does not, in practice, exist.

Clarence E. Eldridge (1958), stated that Advertising continues to play an important role in our national economy. Therefore, the effectiveness of advertising is of great concern both to society and to the individuals who comprise our society. In spite of the progress that advertising has made over the years, there are two vital respects in which further improvement is needed: in its effective-ness, and in the evaluation of its effectiveness. There are five indispensable ingredients of good advertising. Their presence in any advertisement gives as much assurance as can be given before the fact that the advertisement is a good one. Also, the author believes that by his suggested after-the-fact appraisal, the ultimate effectiveness of the advertising in advancing the objectives for which it was designed can be measured. The author makes no extravagant claims for his method. He does not suggest that it is the last word, or that it provides a definitive solution to all the problems of improving and evaluating advertising. He merely hopes that it will provide one further modest step on the road to better advertising.

Christian and *et al.,* (1965), in their article presents an analysis of the importance of logotype in an *advertisement.* An experiment was done by the Philips Company in the Netherlands. Philips set up a split-run test with two identical *advertisements,* each with a different logotype. The study found that the well-known brand name got four times more "action" scores, two-and-a-half times the score on aided recall *measurement,* and a rating five times higher on unaided recall as the alternative *advertisement.* In a similar experiment, an *advertisement* was sent out as a direct-mail survey with the advertisers name and logotype blocked out. Most consumers were still able to correctly identify the advertiser.

Herbert e. Krugman (1966), the author suggested that the processes of attitude change underlying mass communication impact are of two kinds: with low involvement to persuasive stimuli one might look for gradual shifts in perceptual structure, aided by repetition, activated by behavioral choice situations, and followed at some time by attitude change, while with high involvement one could look instead for the classic and familiar conflict of ideas at the level of conscious opinion and attitude that precedes changes in behavior. The present paper describes the development and application of a workable tool to measure this involvement, a necessary step if the study of communication impact along these lines is to proceed further.

Christian and *et al.,* (1967), in their article focuses on the *measurement* of advertising effectiveness. The author asserts that a knowledge of markets, media and communication techniques is crucial to effective advertising. The value of research lies in predicting, identifying, and defining the market and audience at which an *advertisement* is directed. Several methods of identifying markets are discussed, including sales and market analysis techniques. The influence and effect of consumer education and income on advertising methods are also discussed.

Orenstein and *et al.,* (1967), have reviewed several monographs regarding marketing including "Attempts at Measuring the Effectiveness of Advertising," "Do People Really Read Advertisements?" and "How to Choose Between Major Categories of Media," by Marcel Marc.

Kuehl and *et al.,* (1977), the FTC's use of corrective advertising remedies to counteract misinformation in the marketplace has stimulated an emerging consumer behavior research tradition in this public policy issue in recent years. This study extends knowledge about the FTC's corrective advertising policy by reporting experimental findings on the viability of using brand beliefs for measuring the effectiveness of deceptive and corrective advertisements within the context of Gardner's "normative belief technique".

Subhash C . Jain and *et al.,* (1978), have explained through a sample of adult men and women was exposed to both comparison and individual brand advertisements under controlled conditions. Recall measurements were made for the brands being advertised on an immediate basis and twenty-four hours after exposure to the advertisements. Since different product classifications were promoted in the study, several implications are possible concerning the recall effectiveness of each type of advertisement and product brand.

Hanssens and *et al.,* (1980), have explained the relationships between 24 print advertisement characteristics and recall, readership, and inquiry-generation measures of effectiveness are examined for 1160 industrial advertisements. Both recall and readership are strongly related to format and content characteristics of industrial advertisements. The relationship between inquiry-generation and advertisement characteristics is significant but weaker. Some characteristics, such as advertisement size and position in the magazine, are consistently related to effectiveness across product categories and effectiveness measures. The effects of other characteristics, such as the use of four colors and attention-getting techniques, are specific to the product category and effectiveness measure. In addition to these, substantive findings, methodological issues in model development and testing are presented.

Patzer and *et al.,* (1980), behavioral science research strongly suggests that the appearance of an individual affects the perception of and reactions to the individual. This study attempts to determine the influence of one aspect of appearance— sexiness—upon marketing communications. Advertisement mock-ups with a female communicator were presented to male and female receivers. Attitude measures of advertisement effectiveness, perceptions of the product, and perceptions of the communicator were assessed. The results are discussed in terms of several theoretical explanations and implications for the marketing practitioner.

Bagozzi and *et al.,* (1983), have recalled and recognition of people for 95 print advertisements were examined with an aim toward investigating memory structure and decay processes. It was found that recall and recognition do not, by themselves, measure a single underlying memory state. Rather, memory is multidimensional, and recall and recognition capture only a portion of memory, while at the same time reflecting other mental states. When interest in the advertisements was held constant, however, recall and recognition did measure memory as a unidimensional construct. Further, an examination of memory over three points time showed considerable stability. The findings are interpreted from the perspective of recent research in cognitive psychology as well as current thinking in consumer behavior and advertising research. Managerial implications are considered as well.

Leigh and *et al.,* (1984), have stated that an umbrella advertisement, which involves promoting several products linked by way of a common theme, represents an attempt to achieve efficiency and or impact of a firm's advertising expenditures. Based on knowledge-assembly theory of cognitive structure, the approach may be better suited for certain conditions than for others. A 4x3 (branding policy by number of products) full-factorial laboratory experiment was conducted to determine if family branding policies are more inherently suited for use of the approach than individual policies and if the number of included products has an impact. Results provided general support for the conceptual structure formulated. Implications and directions for research are given.

Gates and *et al.,* (1986), study was designed to test the performance of two types of recognition measures (i.e., true-false vs. multiple choice questions) for assessing miscomprehension and to explore the effect of type of ad appeal (i.e., cognitive vs. affective) on miscomprehension *measurement.* Results indicated that multiple choice questions are somewhat easier for subjects to answer correctly. However, significant miscomprehension occurred with both question formats, and the performance of the two types of questions depended, to some extent, on the nature of the stimulus.

Surendra N and *et al.,* (1986), recognition tests are a very popular means of assessing the memory effectiveness of advertisements. Unfortunately the recognition scores obtained by current methods reflect both the memory for an advertisement and the response biases of the respondents. The authors introduce the theory of signal detection (TSD) which can be used to secure independent estimates of memory and response bias in recognition tests. They discuss how TSD can be used to improve advertisement recognition testing.

Muehling and *et al.,* (1990), have investigated a relatively new and unresearched advertising phenomenon: the 15-second advertisement. The effects of various claim-types (factual and evaluative), musical backgrounds (positive, negative, neutral, and no music), and advertisement attention or involvement levels (high and low) on brand attitudes were examined in a 15-second television advertising format. The results provide some interesting insights into the dynamics of the 15-second advertisement. It appears that an advertiser's choice of narrative (factual versus evaluative) in a 15-second format can have a significant influence on brand attitudes. The findings suggest, however, that the impact of narratives may be moderated by music, with factual narratives being most persuasive when coupled with favourable (or no) music, and evaluative narratives being most persuasive under neutral music conditions. The moderating effects of consumer involvement levels, while less pronounced, were also demonstrated under certain advertising claim or music conditions. Implications for future research are also discussed.

Grønhaug and *et al.,* (1991), have examined how a variety of factors including the size of an advertisement, the number of colors used, the product advertised, and characteristics of the audience, may influence recognition of advertisements. Advertisements are costly, goal-directed activities, whereby advertisers aim at influencing target groups and at creating changes in attitudes, preferences, and propensity to purchase their products. It was said that marketers, government agencies, institutions and even individuals are using advertising as a means of communication. Several factors cause difficulties in assessing the direct sales effects including a delay in time between exposure of the advertisement and purchase, use of multiple information sources by the buyer in purchase decision, and the spread of advertisement message through word-of-mouth communication.

Boles and *et al.*, (1992), have examined the role of feelings and judgments evoked by television *advertisements* through the use of large batteries of rating scales. In this study, free elicitations of feelings and judgments about advertisements are compared to scale responses. Some potential problems pertaining to the use of large batteries of items to measure feelings and judgments are illustrated, and complementary aspects of the two *measurement* approaches suggest some advantages of the concurrent use of both in gauging responses to advertisements. Results across both approaches confirm the importance of assessing feelings in models of the antecedents of attitude toward the advertisement and suggest that feelings explain about as much variance in advertisement as do judgments.

Finn and *et al.*, (1992), have applied the two-step approach to structural equation modeling to the PARM data studied by Bagozzi and Silk (1983) results in quite different conclusions as to the psychometric properties of recall and recognition scores. The data they analyzed are more consistent with a simple, alternative *measurement* model, which has different implications for the dimensionality questions Bagozzi and Silk raised. After controlling for random error, recall and recognition scores for print advertisement are highly correlated and yet discriminable. So, while recall and recognition have considerable common variance, the unidimensionality hypothesis is rejected. Either recall or recognition (or both) contains a significant amount of specific variance. Taking reader interest scores into account does not change the conclusion; reader interest scores are best accounted for as a lower reliability indicator of recognition.

Norris and *et al.*, (1992), have tested the hypothesis that depth of involvement in a magazine article is inversely related to subsequent recall and recognition of accompanying advertisements. Subjects read magazine articles interspersed with unfamiliar advertisements for common product types. Results showed that the more deeply the subjects were involved in the articles, the less they remembered about the accompanying advertisements. Articles about recipes were rated least interesting, enjoyable, and absorbing, and they elicited less attention and concentration from the readers than fiction and feature articles, but subjects who read the recipes remembered the advertisements best and subjects who read the fiction article remembered the advertisements worst.

Joel J. Davis (1993), he considered reasons why consumer response has, at best, been mixed with regard to "Green" marketing. Proposes reasons why consumer response has not been overwhelmingly positive and then, based on a review of key research findings, presents guidelines for the development of three components of environmental product advertising: the specificity of the environmental claim, the level of emphasis given the environmental claim and the context for presenting the claim.

Paul M. Fischer and *et al.*, (1993), evaluate the effectiveness of the mandated Surgeon General's warning on cigarette advertisements in comparison to new warnings developed using standard advertising techniques. Adolescent subjects were exposed in a controlled setting to slide images of advertisements including a Marlboro cigarette advertisement containing either mandated or newly developed warnings. Setting - Subjects were recruited from, and testing was completed in, high schools from the area of Augusta, Georgia (USA). A convenience sample of 220 subjects ranging in age from 13 to 19 years. Controlled exposure to either a currently mandated warning or one of three newly developed warnings placed within a cigarette advertisement. Main outcome measures - Post-exposure recall, masked recall, and aided recognition tests were used to evaluate the effectiveness of the warnings' communication. These are standard market re search methods that are frequently employed to evaluate print advertisements. The mandated warning per formed poorly as a communication device. It was identified as a health advisory, but failed to communicate more specific risk information. Only 15 per cent of subjects recalled the warning's health concept in the masked recall test. In contrast, newly developed warnings were more effective in communicating specific health information: 66% recalled the health message. The major elements of the cigarette advertisement were quickly noted and frequently recalled. The median cumulative exposure time required to identify the advertisement as a Marlboro cigarette advertisement was only 0.03 seconds. The currently mandated warnings on cigarette advertisements fail to communicate specific health risk in formation effectively. Warnings which are novel, targeted, and developed through a creative process function more effectively as communicating devices.

D'Souza and *et al.*, (1995), have stated that would regular users of established brands be susceptible to the influence of *advertisements* that are repeated more than the competition, even if they have heard the *advertisements* before? The authors conducted an experiment to find out. They paid careful attention to ecological validity and accurate preference *measurement,* designing an experiment to measure the incremental effect of advertising repetition on awareness, preference shifts, and brand choice. They discuss the results of the experiment in terms of implications for managers, further research on advertising repetition, and theory development.

Gitav Enkataramani Johar (1995), has revealed that consumers highly involved in processing an advertisement are likely to make invalid inferences from incomplete-comparison claims at the time of processing and, hence, be deceived. Less involved consumers may be induced to complete such claims at the time of measurement, which makes it appear that they also were deceived by the advertisement. Experiment 2 then demonstrates that deception depends on the processing demands of the advertising claim. Only less involved consumers are deceived by inconspicuous-qualification claims, which require detailed processing of the advertisement for non-deception. The author discusses the implications of these findings for advertisers and public policy.

Zhao and *et al.*, (1995), have investigated the influence of political *advertisements* and television news on voters' political knowledge. Use of exposure and attention to measure television watching; Impact of *measurements* and control strategies on magnitude of independent-dependent correlation.

France and *et al.*, (1997), in their paper investigates the impact of program-elicited affective valence formed at different levels of cognitive appraisal on the processing and evaluation of embedded advertisements. The results indicate that at lower levels of cognitive appraisal, affective valence of the program has no impact on advertisement evaluations or processing. However, at higher levels of cognitive appraisal, the target advertisement is less effective in the negative program compared to the positive program. Thought-responses indicate that different processing mechanisms may be operating in the different program contexts.

Pirisi and *et al.*, (1997), have explained features the medical instrument Vision 2000, which measures a person's eye position. Advertising agencies' use of the instrument to measure visual *advertisements'* ability to catch a person's eye; Medical applications of the instrument.

Thomas and *et al.*, (1997), have offered advice for heating and ventilation companies on maximizing the benefits of *advertisements.* Reason why media advertising's potential is unrealized; Three types of research affecting media advertising; *Measurements* to be considered for inclusion in advertising tracking questionnaire.

Robert J. Fisher and *et al.*, (1998), the significance of volunteering for both individuals and society has lead to numerous studies on this behavior across the social sciences. However, virtually no prior research has evaluated how and to what extent organizations can effectively encourage individuals to contribute time to a worthy cause. The present research uses a social norm perspective to examine the conditions under which promotional appeals based on group need and promises of recognition affect volunteerism. The perspective suggests that norm compliance can be expected only when the prescribed behavior is both important to the group's welfare and subject to group mediated rewards. Consequently, they hypothesize that promotional appeals based on group need and promised recognition are effective only when they are used in combination. Results of a laboratory and a field experiment are consistent with this hypothesis and provide insights into the process by which the appeals affect individuals' decisions to help. The results also have implications for understanding and promoting other socially desirable behaviors such as recycling, energy conservation, litter reduction, and the purchase of "green" products.

Tina M. Lowrey (1998), explained through three experiments investigated the effects of syntactic complexity on the persuasive-ness of advertising. Experiment 1 showed that, in a broadcast advertising context, syntactic complexity affects recall and recognition but not the persuasiveness of the advertising. However, Experiment 2 indicated that, in a print context, persuasiveness of an advertisement is affected by syntactic complexity. Finally, Experiment 3 demonstrated that motivation to process information interacts with syntactic complexity to determine the persuasiveness of print advertising. These results imply that the impact of syntactic complexity on advertising effectiveness is more complicated than previously thought.

Abhilasha Metha (1999), Concept Convergence Analysis (CCA) provides a framework to use psychological variables such as self-concept to better assess advertising performance. Segmenting audiences based on their self-concept can provide valuable insight into the effectiveness of advertising in influencing consumers. Additionally, the convergence of consumer self-image and perceived brand image can be an important mediating variable in consumer decisions regarding the advertised brand: Purchase intent was found to be stronger for respondents whose self-image and perceived brand image are congruent. Through the application of CCA, a new technique using psychological profiles based on self-concept, it is shown how copy research results could be better profiles based on self-concept, it is shown how copy research results could be better utilized for actionable decision making. The case of a fragrance brand is presented.

Appiah-Adu and *et al.*, (1999), in their study assessed the effectiveness of print based travel agency advertisements. A systematic method was developed to evaluate the comparative effectiveness of different creative strategies employed in three travel agency print advertisements. Based on a questionnaire which focused on emotional, aesthetic, rational and personal dimensions of the advertisements, subsequent responses were analysed through a linear principal component analysis technique. The process critically examined the creative strategies employed and highlighted the most effective advertisement. To conclude, implications of the findings for the development of effective travel agency print advertisement strategies as well as future research directions are discussed.

Christine Communal and *et al.*, (1999), have looked at the relationship between national culture and management through an examination of the messages conveyed by a sample of British, French, and German advertisements for management positions. The results from the study show that there are clear differences in management philosophy and practice, as perceived from the literature and the messages conveyed by a sample of advertisements in the UK, France and Germany.

Jourdan and *et al.*, (1999), the purpose of this article is to propose a new classification scale for *advertisements* based on the individual perception of the informational or emotional intent of the advertisement. After a review of the literature, we adopt the creation of a *measurement* scale based on induced affective and cognitive reactions. The method of creation and validation follows Churchill's Paradigm to achieve a scale with 2 distinct constructs and 9 items. A classification of 10 different advertisements based on the scale grades illustrates by example the diagnostic value of the instrument. Caveats and managerial applications are also discussed. Work in advertising research is primarily concerned with *measurement* of persuasive capacity and explanation of its antecedents. In this respect, the numerous models which have been developed concentrate on the roles of sender and receiver. Numerous studies have indeed tried to characterize the objective informational or emotional content of an advertisement. Few however have turned on the way the receiver perceives subjectively the advertiser's intent to persuade him through either informational or emotional cues. The objective of this article is therefore to construct a classification scale for advertising according to their perceived informational or emotional characteristics. After a short review of the existing literature, they adopt a definition for the constructs on which the generated items of the scale are based. They briefly presented Churchill's paradigm used as the validation method and afterwards summarized the results. Finally, a cluster analysis of 10 *advertisements* illustrates the diagnostic value of the scale use for advertising practitioners.

Lau and *et al.*, (1999), have examined the effects of negative political advertisements on the United States political system via meta-analysis, a systematic, quantitative review of the literature. Effectiveness of negative political advertisements; Impact of television's increasing dominance of political campaigns; Influence of negative advertisements on participatory democracy.

George S. Low and *et al.*, (2000), have tested empirically a conceptualization of brand associations that consists of three dimensions: brand image, brand attitude and perceived quality. A better understanding of brand associations is needed to facilitate further theoretical development and practical measurement of the construct. Three studies were conducted to: test a protocol for developing product category specific measures of brand image; investigate the dimensionality of the brand associations construct; and explore whether the degree of dimensionality of brand associations varies depending upon a brand's familiarity. Findings confirm the efficacy of the brand image protocol and indicate that brand associations differ across brands and product categories. The latter finding supports the conclusion that brand associations for different products should be measured using different items. As predicted, dimensionality of brand associations was found to be influenced by brand familiarity.

Mark Uncles (2000), paper argues that simple, common-sense ideas of how to measure change in marketing settings can often result in ambiguous (and possibly incorrect) conclusions being drawn. To illustrate the conceptual model of change advanced in this paper, a hypothetical. This paper has two objectives. First, to introduce a new conceptualisation of change to marketing researchers. This framework has been used in organisational research to interpret the effects of various types of interventions to change people's attitudes and behaviors. When applied in marketing contexts, it provides a logical, integrated framework to: (a) search for different types of change; and equally importantly (b) to report these changes. The second objective is to apply this more extensive conceptualisation of change to the very popular service quality measure of service quality developed by Parasuraman, Zeithaml and Berry.

Mike Glanville (2000), recently ran a campaign that included display advertisements and banners on content advertising. They measured the results, and found that banners advertisements were nine times more effective than text only advertisements. They created a simple excel spreadsheet and recorded the start and end date of each week. On the landing page where the PPC advert sent customers to, they added a Site Meter - for these free meters could be searched on the web, and used to check how many customers reach their landing page. They recorded from Google, how much they spent in the week on advertising. They then divided the cost by the number of clicks to see how much each click cost. Google show these stats on the PPC summary page, but what they don't show how many enquiries they actually get. The results can be quite staggering. If Pay Per Click advertising is trial, they are not to be carried away with the number of clicks they get back, the real test is how many enquiries they receive.

Miller and *et al.*, (2000), have stated that the formulation and validation of a multidimensional scale designed to measure the properties of *advertisement*-evoked mental imagery. The scale was developed using (1) procedures suggested by psychometrics researchers, (2) three separate subject samples and (3) 55 *advertisements* drawn from print, radio and television media. The scale designed to measure imagery vividness, quantity, valence and sensory modality, exhibited reliability as well as discriminant, nomological and criterion validity. The analyses revealed that the dimensionality of the scale is stable whether the advertising medium is print, radio or television.

Katherine Gallagher and *et al.*, (2001), they replicate, using adult web users, a study comparing advertising effectiveness and content evaluation in print and on the web (Gallagher, Foster, and Parsons, 2000). As in the original study involving students, the replication found that advertising was equally effective in the two media. However, while the original study found that evaluation of an article containing advertising was lower when it appeared on the web that when it appeared in print, this result was not replicated. Examination of two subgroups showed that results for the subgroup resembling the student sample were consistent with the original study. They propose conditions under which student samples are appropriate.

Pradeep Korgaonkar and *et al.*, (2001), have studied on the liaison between America Online and Hispanic Publishing Corporation to launch an interactive area called HISPANIC Online attests to the growing importance of the Hispanic consumers to US corporations. Still, little published research exists documenting the evaluation and usage of Web advertising by this growing segment of the US population. Applying Pollay and Mittal's seven-factor advertising beliefs model, the authors explore the Hispanic Web users' beliefs, attitudes, and use of Web advertising. The seven belief factors regarding Web advertising, as well as attitudes and demographic factors, of the Hispanic respondents were studied in three usage contexts of Web advertising: the attention subjects paid to Web advertisements; the frequency of subjects clicking on Web advertisements; and the frequency of subjects leaving Web sites. Multivariate discriminant analysis suggests that the seven belief factors and the attitude factor, along with age and income levels, are significantly correlated with the three usage contexts of Web advertising. The study results and implications for Web advertisers are discussed.

Shen and *et al.*, (2002), this study reports finding from a survey of media directors of interactive advertising agencies regarding how they price, evaluate, and pretest banner advertisements. Results suggest that more than 90 per cent of the responding agencies used cost per thousand frequently to price banner advertisements, whereas about 33 per cent used click-throughs. In addition, a majority of the agencies used click-throughs and outcomes (e.g., inquires, purchases) rather than exposures to gauge banner advertising effectiveness. Although few agencies pre-tested their banner advertisements on a regular basis, most perceived the lack of *measurement* standards and independent auditing of Web sites as major problems facing Internet banner advertising. Findings from this study provide benchmarks for future research on the topic and help facilitate the process of developing viable pricing and *measurement* standards on the Internet.

Utpal M and *et al.*, (2002), have stated that the Self generated validity research has demonstrated that responding to survey questions changes subsequently measured judgments and behavior. They examined the scope and persistence of the effect of measuring satisfaction on customer behavior over time. In a field experiment conducted in a financial services setting, they hypothesize and find that measuring satisfaction (*a*) changes one time purchase behavior, (*b*) changes relational customer behaviors (likelihood of defection, aggregate product use, and profitability), and (*c*) results in effects that increase for months afterward and persist even a year later. These results raise questions concerning the design, interpretation, and ethics in the conduct of applied marketing research studies.

Arch G and *et al.*, (2003), have described a meta-analysis of advertising conversion research findings that includes examining the influence of question framing on key output measures of advertising effectiveness. The article summarizes findings for 32 tourism-advertising studies. Two hypotheses are tested: (H1) the response rate to questionnaires mailed to sampled advertisement inquirers is lower when the brand sponsoring the study is identified versus not identified; and (H2) the estimated buyer/inquirer conversion rate is higher when the brand sponsoring the study is identified versus not identified. The findings support H1 and strongly support H2. They framed a study and questions to persons sampled by referencing these persons' prior known requests for information about a given brand is likely to reduce interest in responding among non buyers of the stated brand and bloat estimates inquiry-to-purchase conversations for the brand. To confirm and estimate the size of such distortions, they recommend designing-in context manipulations in planning surveys to measure the effectiveness of inquiry or generating advertisements.

Boonghee Yoo and *et al.*, (2003), over the last several decades, advertising effects on sales have been studied without appropriately taking into consideration competitors' advertising activities. As a result, advertisers often instinctively match competitors' parity approach is that they implicitly assume zero-sum competition only. This study identifies a variety of competitive conditions under which better budgeting strategies can be formulated. Specifically, four types of competition are conceptualized based on how an advertiser and its competitors affect each other's sales according to level of media advertising spending. In addition, appropriate strategies for setting advertising budgets to deal with each situation are discussed. A mathematical method is developed to measure advertising effectiveness for both the advertiser and competitors on sales of a focal brand. The method computers current and carryover effects, identifies in which type of competition the advertiser is operating, and, accordingly, determines which budgeting strategy best suits the situation. In an empirical illustration, the method was applied to date collected monthly over eight years. The analyzed product was Scotch whisky sold in Thailand.

Chandon and *et al.*, (2003), debated about which media metric efficiently measures the effectiveness of a web-based advertisement, such as banners, is still alive and well. Nonetheless, the most widely used measure of effectiveness for banner advertisements is still the click-through rate. The purpose of this article is to review the measures currently used to measure effectiveness in web advertising and to empirically determine the factors that might contribute to observed variations in click-through rates based on an actual sample of advertising campaigns. The study examined the complete set of all advertising insertions of 77 customers of a large advertising agency over a one-year period. A resulting sample of 1,258 placements was used to study the effect of banner formats and exposure levels on click-through rates using analysis of variance. Results suggest that the strongest effect on click-through rates comes from the use of trick banners (172 = 0.25) and that other factors such as size of the advertisement, motion, use of "click here," and "online only" type of announcers all have a significant impact of click-through rates. Implications of these findings as well as limitations of the current study are discussed and directions for future research agendas proposed.

Jennifer Edson Escalas Barbarab and *et al.*, (2003),in their research examines differences in consumers' sympathy and empathy responses to televised drama commercials. The research frame work is multidiscip-linary, for constructed definition from humanities disciplines (aesthetics and philosophy) grounds the empirical testing of sympathy and empathy responses to advertising. Valid and reliable measurement instruments are developed to test relationships between sympathy and empathy as responses to classical and vi-gentle advertising dramas. Results of two experiments indicate that sympathy responses mediate the effect of a drama advertisement's form on empathy responses, with both sympathy and empathy directly enhancing positive attitudes to an advertisement.

Elizabeth Cowley and *et al.,* (2004), have recently been demonstrated that exposure to advertising after consumption can change consumers' memory such that they remember tasting a better product. This research investigates whether advertising can change consumers' memory such that they remember tasting a different product. Less familiar consumers who tasted grapefruit juice and then saw advertisements claiming the brand was orange juice were somewhat more likely to remember that they tasted an orange grapefruit juice blend. More familiar consumers were significantly less likely to remember tasting an orange grapefruit juice blend after seeing the misleading advertisements. The results suggest that the more familiar consumers use the misleading advertisements to help them remember exactly what product was consumed.

Pablo Briñol and *et al.,* (12004), two studies tested the notion that the confidence consumers have in their cognitive responses to an advertisements can increase or decrease the favorability of product attitudes. Increasing confidence in positive thoughts enhanced advertisement effectiveness. Increasing confidence in negative thoughts reduced advertisement effectiveness. These self validation effects occurred regardless of the type of product and regardless of whether thought confidence was measured or induced through an experimental manipulation. The present research also demonstrated that source credibility can influence consumer attitudes by affecting thought confidence. Finally, thought confidence was distinguished from other potentially related thought dimensions. Antecedents, moderators, and consequences of self validation effects are described.

Melewar T.C. and *et al.,* (2004), have reviewed the standardization debate in international advertising strategy. First, the paper identifies the standardization, adaptation and compromise schools of advertising including their advantages and disadvantages and then presents some of the contingency models with special focus on variables related to products, customer segments and organization. Then, a number of deficiencies in the academic literature as a whole are presented. The conclusion is that the preferred school of advertising is the compromise school, but that the continuum perspective is of little use to practitioners as they want to know what variables determine the position on the standardization continuum in their sector and whether the level of standardization is increasing or decreasing.

David S. Waller and *et al.,* (2005), have explained the purpose of this paper was to determine attitudes towards the advertising of certain controversial products or services and reasons for being offensive across four different countries, Malaysia, New Zealand, Turkey and the UK. This was achieved by analyzing the responses to a questionnaire that was distributed to a convenience sample of university students in the four countries. A total of 954 were sampled for this study. The results indicated that geography is not a major determinant of attitudes, and that religious and historical factors play a very important role. Of the 17 products presented, 11 resulted in similar answers for New Zealand and the UK, and seven were similar for Malaysia and Turkey. However, it was apparent that the two countries mostly populated by Muslims had some differences as Malaysia has a multicultural society that must make some allowances for other ethnic groups. It also appears that racism and racist images are of concern to all those sampled.

Fortin and *et al.*, (2005), in their article measures the effects of various levels of interactivity and vividness of a message on attitudes and behavioral intentions within a web-based advertisement. As a conceptual foundation, the study introduces the multi-step model of the impact of interactivity on advertising effectiveness. The model is termed multi-step because of the hierarchy of direct and indirect effects. A 3 × 3 interactivity by vividness between-subjects factorial design tests the model. A total of 360 responses were collected through an online web interface. Data were analyzed by means of individual analysis of covariance (ANCOVA) procedures. The multi-step model was also tested with path analysis to verify the significance of the interrelationships between constructs in a simultaneous equations procedure. Results indicate moderate effects of interactivity and vividness on social presence and, indirectly, involvement that in turn have strong effects on traditional advertising effectiveness measures. The findings suggest that the effects of interactivity reach a "plateau" at medium and high levels, indicating a diminishing returns effect. Conversely, the impact of vividness appears to be linear with a steady increase across low, medium, and high levels. No interaction effect was found between the two treatments. The study also provides some insights on using the web as a gateway for experimental research and data collection.

*Hyunjoo Oh (2005) t*o develop and validate a new scale for affective reactions to print apparel advertisements. The confirmatory factor model supported that unipolar categories of warm, negative, upbeat, sensual, and bored feelings effectively represent affective reactions to apparel advertisements. Evidence was established for reliability and validity. The major limitation of this study was the reliance on student subjects for scale development and testing. It limits the generalizability of the results to other populations. Further research is recommended to test the scale by using different samples and stimuli. This paper fulfils needs for the scales that measure emotional aspects of clothing behaviors. Scholars could use the scale developed in this study to investigate how the specific categories of affective reactions influence subsequent information processing and attitude formation for advertised products or brands.

Julie Verity (2005), have explained the purpose of this study in between 1997 and 2002, Shell changed the way it organised its advertising activity, switching from a local approach to a global organisation. The transition was significant, given the group's long history of decentralisation. It was also very successful. This paper explores how this transition was made by applying the theoretical lenses of the Resource-Based View (RBV) and Dynamic Capability View (DCV). Qualitative data were collected in 2002 from key executives in Shell and J.W. Thompson from which observations were made about Shell's transition and the change process. These observations are then explored further by applying the theoretical lens of the RBV and its natural extension, the DCV, testing what could be learned from the practical application of these theories. A dynamic capability is identified as a significant reason for Shell's success. A second important factor was that Shell did not attempt to copy an organisation with an apparent superior capability.

Schweidel and *et al.*, (2006), presented a feature-based statistical model and subsequently explores the degree to which similarity perceptions between two advertisements can be decomposed and explained by a "weighted-and-summed" distance measure, computed on the advertisements' executional elements, after controlling for familiarity and viewers' attitudinal responses toward the advertisements. Furthermore, the authors obtain empirical findings in two major areas: First, variation in similarity ratings can be explained by the advertisements' features, a finding of potential importance for advertisement construction. Second, some, but not all, executional elements that have been shown (in the literature) to drive recall and persuasion are effective at driving perceptions of similarity. This is of practical importance because managers want their advertisements not only to be liked and remembered but also (possibly) to be perceived as similar (or dissimilar) to those for other products. In particular, an understanding of which items drive which constructs (recall and persuasion, or similarity) can contribute to a more effective overall marketing strategy.

Jim Novo (2007), explained that marketing mix modeling (time series analysis) is so important a tool in the chest of a marketing Analytics group: a good model can estimate the contribution of each medium to the outcome (sales, click, calls, etc.). It can even account for non-traditional media such as sponsorships, endorsements, naming rights, etc. and can do all that at an aggregate level, that is, without resorting to client level data. A well crafted brand advertisement campaign may have a long term positive result without necessarily driving sales. The results coming out of Marketing Mix Modeling also point to the fact that "brand" spending either contributes to the top line in a month or two at most, or not at all. "Brand" investments work in synergy with more direct vehicles, and tend to strengthen the effectiveness of the latter, but are very ineffective when called to drive sales on their own. Marketing Mix Modeling can measure the effectiveness and can do it now without resorting to expensive investments in database technology.

Lohtia and *et al.,* (2007), have presented an approach for measuring the efficiency of banner advertisements. Their approach, using data envelopment analysis (DEA), accommodates multiple inputs and multiple outputs and estimates a relative measure of efficiency. In an illustrative example, the authors evaluate the efficiency of banner advertisements using click-through data and respondent recall and attitude data.

Rick T and *et al.,* (2007), using a large-scale database, they present, test, and refine a model for Direct-To-Consumer (DTC) advertising effectiveness via structural equation modeling. Results suggest that consumers who are greatly involved in their healthcare and possess positive attitudes toward DTC advertising appear to be more likely to contact a doctor about the prescription drug after viewing a DTC advertisement. While individuals that are poor in health and or holds more favorable attitudes toward the healthcare system do appear to respond to DTC advertising, the effect is quite small. The results of this study provide a comprehensive overview of DTC advertising's effect on behavior.

AnjaZurcher Wray and *et al.,* (2008), the purpose of this paper is to examine the importance of cognitive-versus chronological-age factors in activewear apparel *advertisements* targeting female baby boomers in the USA. A total of 50 female participants aged 41-65 were asked to view two print *advertisements:* one showing activewear apparel worn by a cognitive-age model and the other by a chronological-age model. Participants then responded to a four-part questionnaire that included a *measurement* of cognitive age, physical activity, response to the *advertisements,* and purchase intent. The responses indicated that the participants view themselves as younger than their chronological age and were more inclined to respond favorably toward the *advertisement* using the cognitive age model. Although this study focuses on only one consumer group - US baby boomers - it reveals their current attitudes toward *advertisements* of activewear apparel as well as their motivations for purchasing activewear apparel. More research on this age demographic and the impact of cognitive age vs. chronological age on their perceptions of advertising is needed. Currently one of the largest age demographics in the USA, baby boomers are known for having higher amounts of disposable income as compared to other age cohorts and for their interest in physical fitness and leading active lifestyles. The results of this study point to the need to understand the age-related perceptions of this consumer group in order to successfully market activewear apparel products directly to them.

David Szetela (2008), described methods for how to compare the effectiveness of text advertisements in your PPC campaigns. Testing and improving advertisements copy is essential to optimizing overall PPC campaign performance. Improving advertisements text leads to better CTR and quality score, which means it can help drive the CPC down, and or let consumers buy more clicks per dollar. So it has a direct impact on the campaign's ability to increase the number of profitable sales.

Mark Robertson (2008), in his article describes the real promise of online video - to drive more effective results for advertisers. Citing a study done by Double Click from last year, Mark puts traditional banner advertisements (GIF and JPEG) to the test against in banner video advertisements and notes that, hands down, the video advertisements perform much better than traditional banner advertisements at driving higher CTR. More than that, however, Mark talks about the inherent differences between traditional banner advertisements and video based banner advertisements. With traditional banner advertisements there is only one objective - to drive click throughs - and to immediately take viewers away from the page they are on to another site.

Minamizawa, (2009), provide an advertisement effect measurement device for making it possible to measure an effect in the case where inquiries about advertisement put on a webpage are carried out by telephone. When a reception terminal device receives an access necessary for a user to inquire an advertisement from a user terminal through a data communication network together with a telephone number of the user including an advertisement identifier corresponding to the advertisement, a call between an advertiser telephone and the user telephone is set up through a telephone network and a history of the access is recorded, so that it is possible to measure the history as an advertisement effect in response to the inquiry from the user by telephone. Further, since a call between a user telephone number and an advertiser telephone number is set up by a third party call control unit when a caller is responsible for expenses in the telephone network the user is not required to bear a telephone charge.

WoonBong Na and *et al.*, (2009), have explained the purpose of this paper is to report the use of Decision System Analysis (DSA) mapping the streams of communications (i.e. interactions), thoughts, actions and decisions involved for advertising agencies as executives in these firms gain client approval, and design creative, promotional and media strategies. This study uses DSA. This little-used technique requires protocol analysis, interviews and observation before transcription of the organizational decision processes into flow charts. The research first identifies four models, describing four specific decision types, then derives a general model from them. Executives from four agencies not in the

original sample later confirms the models. The models generally confirm the existing knowledge base, with a few minor exceptions. This qualitative technique suffers the common malady of the researchers losing objectivity because of their immersion in the case-companies. Wherever possible the research employs quantitative techniques to verify observational judgments. The "thick description" and the summary charts of the advertising agency decision processes have the potential to aid agency decision makers to better structure their decision processes.

United States Patent 5991734, (2009) this invention relates to a method for measuring the creative value added to a communication, such as an advertisement in the media of print, television or radio. In a preferred embodiment, the invention provides a quantitative measure of the creative value added to a communication. To this end, a communication test sample is compared to a creativity neutral control which is a communication which intentionally lacks any creativity.

Pre-test Measurement of Effectiveness of Advertisement

Adams H.F (1915), tested the assumption that advertisements brought in a relative amount of business, on 69 men and 92 women. The Ss were handed a series of advertisements of the American Collection Service, 4 half page and 10 full page advertisement; a quarter-page advertisements of Saturday Evening Post size of the Burroughs Adding Machine Co. Data was in terms of the number of insertions, total number of inquiries, advertising cost, cost per inquiry and profit or loss. Results of the Ss and business tests were compared and it was concluded that the order of merit test was not an adequate laboratory method for testing the business value of advertisements and that where it was possible to obtain accurate business measurements, the laboratory test was inadequate, but, where it was impossible to secure accurate business measurements, the laboratory test was adequate.

Starch and *et al.*, (1923), have discussed the importance of testing advertisements, and examines some of the methods used to do so. The author points out that many advertisements are not as effective as others that cost the same amount, and as such is the case, it is of great concern to an executive to test the effectiveness of an advertisement before it is implemented. The five elements of a successful advertisement are presented as well as a general method for testing the effectiveness of the advertisement with respect to these elements. Lastly, the author analyzes data from some of the methods to show how the data can be interpreted and which methods of testing are most accurate.

Stocks J. M. B (1965), described various approaches to the validation of television advertisement testing which have been undertaken by one particular company during the last twelve years. There is no one specific answer to the problem of validation with a measure of this kind because of the complex nature of the situation in which advertising works. Before and after exposure to the test advertisements within a programme respondents are asked to choose from a list of brands the one they would like to win in a draw held immediately after the decision is made. This technique purports to measure the effect of television commercials upon market behavior rather than upon attitudes or opinion. It does this by isolating the television commercial from the other influences which contribute towards a market decision (package design, displays, discounts, supply, storekeepers' recommendations, prior experience, personal influence). It might be argued that the isolation of the television commercial from all these other influences inhibits the normal interplay of advertising and these influences. There is no doubt that the technique sets up an artificial marketing situation, the significant query is whether this laboratory set-up provides an accurate guide to the role played by television advertising in bringing about actual market decisions.

William H.Antrin (1978), stated that an advertising is important for the success of a business but it carries a hefty price tag. Before you purchase your media plan, it is wise to test your advertisement(s) first. The role of pre-testing is to help companies identify the best possible advertising concepts to drive the sales results they want. Insightrix typically conducts pre-testing via online surveying and or focus group testing. Measuring advertising effectiveness is an important part of the advertising research process. It can provide information on the advertisement's performance as well as on the success of your media plan. Insightrix' Ad Tracking Service called AdTracker™ is a proven methodology of measuring advertising effectiveness. Our approach is based on experience and a sophisticated measurement model. The features of our model include measurement of claimed recall, proven recall, prompted recall, and linkage to the company's brand. These features combine to provide clients with "added value" and ensure sound decision-making on creative and media issues.

P. Vanden Abeele and *et al.,* (1981), have looked at the opinions and attitudes of advertisers and agencies with regard to pre-testing and pre-test methods in a small market like Belgium. Evaluates the criteria of the study into four components: motivation and or behaviour; attitude and attitude change; visual impact and recall; and information transfer. It reveals that the importance attached to the criteria increases in the same order. Concludes that the respondents are relatively favourable to message ratings, but have a negative attitude to forced exposure ratings.

Day and *et al.,* (1990), have explored the validity of using rough or unfinished material in pre-testing the on-air effectiveness of television commercials. Importance of psychological construct in message communication; Creation of positive feelings towards the advertised brand; Persuasion of the consumer.

Stephen R. McDaniel and *et al.,* (2000), there is growing concern over commercial promotions of products that are unhealthy or unsafe. In some cases, policy recommendations have called for restrictions on promotional activities, such as event sponsorship, when used to promote products like alcohol, tobacco, and fast ("junk") foods. This study utilises variations of fast-food and tobacco print advertisements containing sport sponsorship themes in a test of Fiske's theory of schematriggered affect. Using a pretest or posttest experimental design, print advertisements manipulations were developed which involved pairing a known brand of fast-food and a known brand of cigarettes with three different sport events. MANCOVA analyses largely supported existing research on schematriggered affect, and run counter to some of the arguments for regulating tobacco sponsorships. Sponsorship ad manipulations were found to impact subjects' perceptions of advertisements schema congruence as well as their subsequent attitudes towards the sponsorship advertisements. However, advertisement congruence effects were not observed in terms of significant differences between treatment groups' mean brand attitudes or purchase intentions.

Post-test Measurement of Effectiveness of Advertisement

William H. Antrim and *et al.,* (1978), have compared the records of sales for the months before the campaign with the sales during and after the campaign. Their records showed that their sales increased during the campaign and continued to maintain at a higher level after it. By comparing the sales before, during, and after a campaign, the researcher was used two methods namely pre-test and post-test for measuring the effectiveness of their advertisements. In post test method the recognition test and recall test are commonly used to measure the effectiveness of advertisement.

Earl and *et al.,* (1980), full disclosure in advertising has become a concept of major concern to public policy decision makers and advertising practitioners. Comparative advertising, two-sided messages, and the use of performance tests results are three techniques used to help consumers become better informed and more knowledgeable about products. Yet, little empirical testing has been done to determine whether use of these techniques actually increases the informativeness of advertisements. This article reports the results of a factorial-designed experiment regarding the effects of comparative messages, message sidedness, and the use of performance test results in print advertisement on two dimensions of informativeness the reader's perception of advertisement informativeness and the reader's awareness of product features.

William, H.Bolen (1984), manufacturers should pre-test their advertisements to predict as accurately as possible whether their campaigns will be effective in the market place. Measurement of the effectiveness of the tested commercial is determined by comparing the audience preference for the brand after the program with their preference before the program. The Different methods of pre-testing are used to test the advertisement copy. They are Checklist method, Portfolio test, Mock magazine test, Perceptual Meaning Studies (PMS): The post-testing methods are give us an idea about the actual performance of the advertisements in terms of exposure, perception, communication and sales effect. They could assess the credibility and comprehension of the advertisements. The methods of post tests are: Recall tests, Recognition test: Triple association test, Sales effect tests, Sales results tests, Enquires test, Attitude test. The DAGMAR process (Defining Advertising Goals for Measured Advertising Result), is an important element in the measurement of effectiveness of advertisements. According to the DAGMAR approach, the communication task of the brand is to gain: Awareness, Comprehension, Conviction, Image , Action.

Doyle and *et al.*, (1990), study aims to incorporate ANN for measuring advertisement effectiveness. Specifically, its aim is to discover important factors that influence the advertisement effectiveness in Indian environment using ANN. Advertising will only survive and grow if it focuses on being effective. Strategy, creativity, and execution are the three broad dimensions that characterize effective advertising. Therefore, effective advertisements must connect these three elements. TV is considered to be the most glamorous and prestigious media. A pilot survey was conducted on TV advertising and viewers attitudes. TV advertisements in the form of film are most popular among the viewers. Viewers gave three major reasons for monotony while viewing TV advertisements:(i) large number of advertisements is being shown; (ii) repetitive advertisements; (iii) exaggerated claims made in the advertisements. In this study, the following 13 factors are considered for measuring advertisement effectiveness: 1.Affectative 2.Attention 3.Attraction, 4.Changes 5.Desire 6.Economics 7.Emotions 8.Exposure 9.Influence,10.Persuasion 11.Psychological 12.Senses 13.Social. ANNs are intelligent systems that are related in some way to a simplified biological model of the human brain. Neural networks have self learning capability, are fault tolerant and noise immune, and have applications in system identification, pattern recognition, classification, speech recognition, image processing, etc, the post processing can be achieved by reverse process of preprocessing. Back propagation ANNs are used for the analysis and forecasting of advertising and promotion impact. In this paper, the back propagation training algorithm is used to adjust the weights such that the neural network produces the required output for the given input data. The four layer feed forward ANN model used for advertisement effectiveness. Finally they concluded that the back propagation algorithm is an efficient method for measuring the advertisement effectiveness.

Edward Rosbergen and *et al.*, (1997), they proposed a methodology to study the effects of physical advertisements properties on consumers' visual attention to advertising that accounts for heterogeneity in these effects across consumers. In an illustrative experiment, they monitored consumers' eye movements during naturalistic exposure to a consumer magazine, in which experimentally designed advertisements are inserted. A latent class regression model accounting for heterogeneity across consumers through unobserved segments is used to analyze the eye movement data in detail. Three consumer segments are identified that exhibit distinct patterns of visual attention as well as different profiles of product involvement, brand attitude, and advertising recall. Implications for visual attention theory and for advertising research are discussed.

Michael J Baker (1998), the process of measuring the effectiveness of an advertisement or an advertising campaign. Measurements can be carried out before the advertising finally runs (pre-test) or after the campaign has started (post-test), on a sample of the eventual target audience. Many of the established testing techniques are applicable to both situations; some are specific to one or the other. Ideally, measurement of effectiveness should be a straightforward matter of comparing actual performance with specific criteria derived from predetermined objectives. Practice is seldom ideal, however, because practitioners - both advertising agencies and advertisers - fail to articulate objectives which are usable for the purpose: see advertising objectives. The vacuum left is filled by ready-made, general-purpose test methods. There is no doubt about the range and sophistication of advertising testing procedures available, but it should be understood that they are not as a rule 'bespoke' tests, specific to the peculiar circumstances of a given advertising campaign. Furthermore, it is not always easy to recognise the surrogate criterion they are actually measuring. It can be argued that the standard procedures are in fact implicitly based on a hierarchy-of-effects model of how advertising works, widely used as the conceptual framework for the literature of advertising in general. The six 'levels' or steps of this hierarchy provide the substitute objectives and hence the criteria of effectiveness. The result is that an advertisement is required to 'pass a test', rather than to demonstrate its effectiveness by satisfying specific criteria derived from specific objectives. The relationship of such a test to real effectiveness may be no stronger than that of the standard driving test to driving ability: it measures only what it measures. Space does not permit one-by-one description of the substantial number of advertising tests available today. Instead, the most commonly encountered are separately described in their alphabetical turn, each time explicitly related to the relevant level in the hierarchy-of-effects. See especially attitude measurement, laboratory tests, reading-and-noting, recall testing. Authors have remarked on a surprising tendency among practitioners not to test advertising campaigns at all, which is not what the interested but non-expert outsider would expect. Possible reasons are: the cost of making any modifications which a pre-test might indicate; reluctance on the part of advertising agencies to risk an unflattering pre-evaluation; the over-and-done-with syndrome, where post-testing is concerned; reluctance on the part of clients to discover an unwelcome truth; and vested interest in general. However, it would be improper to close without reiterating that no one doubts the skill and sophistication of British advertising researchers, whose reputation is high in the world, nor the breadth of their techniques. It is the conceptual underpinning of the tests which is questionable.

Robert J. Fisher and *et al.*, (1998), the significance of volunteering for both individuals and society has lead to numerous studies on this behavior across the social sciences. However, virtually no prior research has evaluated how and to what extent organizations can effectively encourage individuals to contribute time to a worthy cause. The present research uses a social norm perspective to examine the conditions under which promotional appeals based on group need and promises of recognition affect volunteerism. The perspective suggests that norm compliance can be expected only when the prescribed behavior is both important to the group's welfare and subject to group mediated rewards. Consequently, they hypothesize that promotional appeals based on group need and promised recognition are effective only when they are used in combination. Results of a laboratory and a field experiment are consistent with this hypothesis and provide insights into the process by which the appeals affect individuals' decisions to help. The results also have implications for understanding and promoting other socially desirable behaviors such as recycling, energy conservation, litter reduction, and the purchase of "green" products.

Kathryn A. Braun (1999), this research suggests that marketing communications create expectations that influence the way consumers subsequently learn from their product experiences. Since post experience information can also be important and is widespread for established goods and services, it is appropriate to ask about the cognitive effects of these efforts. The post experience advertising situation is conceptualized here as an instant source forgetting problem where the language and imagery from the recently presented advertising become confused with consumers' own experiential memories. It is suggested that, through a reconstructive memory process, this advertising information affects how and what consumers remember. Consumers may come to believe that their past product experience had been as suggested by the advertising. Over time this post experience advertising information can become incorporated into the brand schema and influence future product decisions.

Anand Kumar (2000), the effectiveness of advertisements has been an issue of great concern to marketers, especially with the rapid increase in the number of marketing communications that the average consumer receives every day. Prior research has examined the impact of verbal interference on consumers memory for different elements of the advertisement that is, interference caused by similar verbal elements in advertisements for brands in the same product category. This study examined the impact of similar contextual or background stimuli on consumers' memory for different elements of the advertisement. Consumers were exposed to print advertisements for products in different product categories. The similarity of contextual cues-that is, background scenes-was manipulated (similar vs. dissimilar).U sing a 2 (contextual cues interference: low and high) × 2 (processing goal: ad and brand) x 3 (cues: brand name, ad photo, product class) between-subjects design, it was found that exposure to advertisements with similar contextual elements reduced individuals' ability to recall not only contextual or background elements but also brand name from a target advertisement.

Shanker Krishnan H. and *et al.*, (2003), they report two studies that examined how the strength of humorous advertising executions and their relevance to the brand claims in the advertisement influence consumer memory for the claims. They inferred the underlying memory processes by testing claims memory using recall, recognition, and indirect tests following incidental exposure to advertisements manipulating humor strength and claims relevance. Memory for the humor component was checked as corroborating evidence. They also validated these inferences by contrasting these effects on claims and humor memory with those under instructed elaboration. Study 1 shows that for humor of low claims relevance, brand claims memory is an inverted U-shaped function of humor strength. Compared to both non humor and high strength humor, moderate humor facilitates both encoding and retrieval of the claims. The patterns of humor memory and instructed elaboration effects suggest that low-relevance humor is not spontaneously linked to the claims even when processing resources are available. Study 2 shows that when strong humor is made more relevant, brand claims memory improves even during incidental exposure. Corresponding humor memory and instructed elaboration effects imply that relevance encourages the formation of humor-claims links that facilitate encoding and retrieval of the claims. The results show that although strong humor inhibits the processing received by the brand claims, enhancing its claims relevance can compensate for such inhibition.

Bruce F. Hall (2004), Posttests of Print Advertisements Inquiry tests measure the effectiveness based on inquires generated from Advertisements appearing in various print media Informal inquiry of customers, prospect Advertisements in successive issues, same medium Split-run tests, different Advertisements, same medium Runs of same Advertisement, different media Posttests of Print Advertisements Recognition tests (Starch Readership Report) Noted Score – percentage of readers who remember seeing the Advertisement Seen-associated score – percentage of readers who recall seeing or reading any part of the Advertisement identifying the brand Read-most score –percentage who report reading at least half of copy portion of Advertisement Purports to measure . . . Pulling power of elements of the Advertisements Effectiveness of competitors' Advertisements Comparison of alternative executions of Advertisements Readership score indications of involvement Critics identify potential problems . . . False claiming of recognition Interviewer sensitivities and biases Low reliability and validity of scores. Posttests of Print advertisements Gallup-Robinson Magazine Impact Research Service - Magazines placed in homes and respondents are asked to read them. A telephone interview is conducted a day later. Measures: Proven Name registration – percent who can accurately recall the advertisement idea communication – number of sales or copy points they can recall Favorable buying attitude – extent of favorable purchase reaction to brand or company Posttests of Broadcast Commercials Day after recall tests Diagnostic Tests Test marketing Single Source Tracking Studies Ipsos-ASI Offers a Comprehensive Testing Measure :Factors that Make or Break Tracking Studies 1. Properly defined objectives 2. Alignment with sales objectives 3. Properly designed measures 4. Consistency through replication of the sampling plan 5. Random samples 6. Continuous interviewing, not seasonal 7. Evaluate measures related to behavior 8. Critical evaluative questions early to eliminate bias 9. Measurement of competitors' performance 10. Skepticism about questions asking where advertisement was seen or heard 11. Building of news value into the study 12. "Moving averages" used to spot long-term

13. Data reporting relationships rather than as isolated facts

14. Integration of key marketplace events with tracking results.

Jason C. G. Halford and *et al.*,(2004), explained the impact of television (TV) advertisements (commercials) on children's eating behaviour and health is of critical interest. In a preliminary study they examined lean, over weight and obese children's ability to recognise eight food and eight non-food related adverts in a repeated measures design. Their consumption of sweet and savoury, high and low fat snack foods were measured after both sessions. Whilst there was no significant difference in the number of non-food adverts recognised between the lean and obese children, the obese children did recognise significantly more of the food adverts. The ability to recognise the food adverts significantly correlated with the amount of food eaten after exposure to them. The overall snack food intake of the obese and overweight children was significantly higher than the lean children in the control (non-food advert) condition. The consumption of all the food offered increased post food advert with the exception of the low-fat savoury snack. These data demonstrate obese children's heightened alertness to food related cues. Moreover, exposure to such cues induce increased food intake in all children. As suggested the relationship between TV viewing and childhood obesity appears not merely. a matter of excessive sedentary activity. Exposure to food adverts promotes consumption.

Rohini Ahluwalia and *et al.,* (2004), based on recent theories of persuasion knowledge and rhetorical figures in advertising, our model delineates conditions under which rhetoricals are likely to enhance argument elaboration (low salience of the rhetorical) and those under which they are likely to direct attention on the message source (high salience of the rhetorical format). Two experiments support the model and suggest that salience of rhetorical figures has the potential to influence not only the direction of message processing but also the effectiveness of various advertisement executions.

Spike Cramphorn (2004), created a model to measure the effectiveness of Business- to-Business Advertising which should include both pre-test and post-test measures and measure the effectiveness of the money, message and media. The products being advertised for are industrial machines and the advertising is largely done in trade guides and the print media. He needs techniques and methods which may be useful in measuring the effectiveness of such type of advertising.

Garcia and *et al.,* (2006), investigates the effects of cultural values on cross-cultural consumer responses to sex appeals in advertising. Special emphasis is placed on examining how consumers uncertainty avoidance index (UAI) influences their responses to sexual appeals in advertising. The study employs a 2 × 2 factorial between-subject, *post-test* only experimental design to study these relationships. Results from MANOVA analysis demonstrate that there are main effects of sexual appeals and consumers' UAI on their attitudes toward the advertisement (Aad).The interaction effect between UAI and sexual appeals is also statistically significant. The usefulness of consumer cultural values in predicting cross-national consumer responses to advertising is discussed. Implications and extensions into other cross-cultural settings are suggested for future research.

Pei-Luen Patrick Rau and *et al.,* (2006), stated that the development of mobile telecommunication has made breakthrough advances in recent years. Compared to the Internet, mobile telecommunications has anywhere, anytime and always online characteristics. As growth in the Internet advertising market continues, mobile advertising has attracted attention. In this research, the effectiveness of two types of mobile message advertisements, watermarks and music are studied and compared. Two experiments were carried out to test four proposed hypotheses. The independent variable in experiment 1 was the watermark transparency (20%, 40% and 60%). The independent variable in experiment 2 was the music format with five levels: no music, vocal and instrumental version at high volume, vocal and instrumental version at low volume, instrumental version at high volume and instrumental version at low volume. The results showed that the watermarks transparency and format were effective in mobile advertising. The 60% watermark was found better than the 20% and 40% watermarks. The 40% watermark was found better than the 20% watermark for advertisement recall only. Music and vocal/ instrumental music versions were effective in mobile advertisements. The vocal music version was found effective in mobile advertising. Music with both vocal and instrumental versions was more effective in advertisement recall than instrumental music for mobile device users.

Celebreties/Models/Endorsors in Advertisements

Friedman and *et al.*,(1976), four groups of students were presented with identical advertisements for sangria wine, attributed to one of four different types of endorsers: a celebrity, student, professional expert, and company president. A fifth group serving as a control was presented with the same advertisement, but it was not attributed to an endorser. Subjects were asked to rate the wine on three scales: expected selling price, probable (anticipated) taste and intent-to-purchase. In addition, the advertisements were rated on their believability. While endorsers did not significantly affect the expected selling price or believability, they had an effect on probable taste and intent-to-purchase. The authors conclude that it is probably worthwhile for an advertiser to use an endorsement for his product, rather than utilize a similar advertisement without an endorsement.

Bush and *et al.*, (1979), have reported the results of a 2 × 3 factorial experiment which measures high and low prejudice white consumers' evaluations of advertisements for which models' race is manipulated. The study disconfirms the results of a previous study which differ substantially from those of the general body of literature on the effects of black models. The response of consumers to black models is found to be consistent with previous research findings.

Richard E. Petty and *et al.*, (1983), stated that undergraduates expressed their attitudes about a product after being exposed to a magazine advertisement under conditions of either high or low product involvement. The advertisements contained either strong or weak arguments for the product and featured either prominent sports celebrities or average citizens as endorsers. The manipulation of argument quality had a greater impact on attitudes under high than low involvement, but the manipulation of product endorser had a greater impact under low than high involvement. These results are consistent with the view that there are two relatively distinct routes to persuasion.

Lynn R. Kahle and *et al.,* (1985), three factors were manipulated in an advertisement for disposable razors: celebrity-source physical attractiveness, celebrity-source liability, and participant product involvement. Attitudes and purchase intentions changed due to celebrity-source attractiveness, and the results were interpreted as supporting social adaptation theory.

Grant McCracken (1989), this article offers a new approach to celebrity endorsement. Previous explanations, especially the source credibility and source attractiveness models are criticized, and an alternative meaning transfer model is proposed. According to this model, celebrities' effectiveness as endorsers stems from the cultural meanings with which they are endowed. The model shows how meanings pass from celebrity to product and from product to consumer. The implications of this model for our understanding of the consumer society are considered. Research avenues suggested by the model are also discussed.

Michael A. Kamins and *et al.,* (1989), study examines celebrity endorsements in advertising using a two-sided framework, in terms of the internalization and identification processes of social influence as discussed Kelman (1961). The two-sided execution was designed to increase a viewer's perception of advertiser credibility including a discussion of a limitation of the advertised service. Results show that when compared to a traditional one-sided celebrity endorsement, the two-sided communication elicited significantly higher advertising credibility and effectiveness ratings, higher evaluation of the sponsor in terms of perceived overall quality of service, as well as a significantly greater intention to use the advertised service. These findings suggest that the use of a celebrity appeal in a two-sided form is an effective advertising strategy.

Michael A. Kamins (1990), this study represents a supportive test of the attractiveness aspect of the "match-up" hypothesis of celebrity / product congruence discussed in depth by Kahle and Homer (1985). The hypothesis implies that the physical attractiveness of a celebrity endorser may only enhance both product-and advertisement-based evaluations if the products characteristics "match-up" with the image conveyed by the celebrity. Empirically, it was found that for an attractiveness-related product, use of a physically attractive celebrity (Tom Selleck) was observed to significantly enhance measures of spokesperson credibility and attitude toward an advertisement, relative to use of a physically unattractive celebrity (Telly Savalas). Alternatively, the physically attractive celebrity was found to have no effect on various spokesperson-, product-and advertisement-based dependent measures relative to the physically unattractive celebrity for an attractiveness-unrelated product. Implications of these findings for advertising strategy are discussed, and directions for future research are outlined.

Tom and *et al.*,(1992), have stated that the frequent use of spokespersons in advertisements is an indication of the widespread belief in their effectiveness. The use of celebrity spokespersons, in particular, has been gaining popularity. According to a recent survey by Video Storyboard Tests, Inc., more television viewers today (22 percent) have very positive feelings about celebrity spokespersons than in 1987 (16 percent). Moreover, almost twice as many viewers as in 1987 indicated that celebrity spokespersons made the advertisement more memorable (39 percent today versus 22 percent in 1987).

Jagdish Agrawal and *et al.*, (1995), Celebrity endorsement has become a prevalent form of advertising in the United States. Despite extensive literature on the effects of celebrity endorsements on consumers' brand attitudes and purchase intentions, little is known about the economic value of these endorsements. Research on this topic has typically focused on theories explaining how celebrity endorsements influence consumers' attitudes and intentions. The authors assess the impact of celebrity endorsement contracts on the expected profitability of a firm by using event study methodology. Their approach assumes that the announcement of a celebrity endorsement contract, usually widely publicized in the business press, is used as information by market analysts to evaluate the potential profitability of endorsement expenditures, thereby affecting the firm's expected return. Announcements of 110 celebrity endorsement contracts were analyzed. Results indicate that, on average, the impact of these announcements on stock returns is positive and suggest that celebrity endorsement contracts are generally viewed as a worthwhile investment in advertising.

Goldsmith and *et al.*, (2000), have stated that the advertisers frequently use endorsers or spokespersons as credible sources to influence consumers' attitudes and purchase intentions. Corporate credibility—the reputation of a company for honesty and expertise—is another type of source credibility that can influence consumer reactions to advertisements and shape brand attitudes. The present study assessed the impact of endorser and corporate credibility on attitude-toward-the-advertisements, attitude-toward-the-brand, and purchase intentions. They surveyed 152 adult consumers who viewed a fictitious advertisement for Mobil Oil Company. They rated the credibility of the advertisement's endorser, the credibility of the company, and attitude-toward-the-advertisement, attitude-toward-the-brand, and purchase intentions. Path analysis confirmed that endorser credibility had its strongest impact on advertisement while corporate credibility had its strongest impact on AB. The findings suggest that corporate credibility plays an important role in consumers' reactions to advertisements and brands, independent of the equally important role of endorser credibility.

Chung-kue Hsu and *et al.,* (2002) stated that celebrity endorsement advertising is a prevailing advertising technique. Some marketers choose to utilize multiple celebrities to promote their products or brands. Nevertheless, it is surprising that so little research has focused on this phenomenon. This research discussed advantages and potential concerns of multi-celebrity endorsement advertising and documented the actual use of multiple celebrity endorsers in the milk mustache campaign in the USA. They analyzed the content of the 50 milk mustache advertisement appearing on the http://www.whymilk.com Web site on a list of celebrity- or product-related dimensions. Overall, they found that these milk mustache advertisements have matched their celebrities' gender, age and type of milk attributes in appealing to their female or male, teen or adult consumers. The results support that fit between the endorsed product and various celebrities is a key factor for using multiple celebrity endorsers in advertising.

Marla Royne Stafford and *et al.,* (2002), recent growth in the U.S. economy has been in the service sectors, and increased understanding of the marketing and advertising of services is critical to sustaining this growth. This paper investigates issues related to the advertising of common retail services. Results from an empirical study into the relative effectiveness of four types of spokespersons for a hedonic and a utilitarian retail service indicate that a created character fits well with the hedonic service but not with the utilitarian service. The celebrity spokesperson performed well for both types of services, but effects varied across service type. The hypothesized contingency relationship between spokesperson type and service type was supported.

David H. Silvera (2004), examines whether consumers infer that celebrity endorsers like the products they endorse, and presents a model using these inferences and other characteristics of the endorser to predict attitudes toward the endorsed product. Participants in two experiments examined written endorsement advertisements and were asked to infer the extent to which the endorser truly liked the advertised product and to rate the endorser's attractiveness, similarity to themselves, and knowledge of the product.

Attitudes toward the advertisement, the endorser and the product were also measured. The resulting model indicated that product attitudes were predicted by inferences about the endorser's liking for the product and by attitudes toward the endorser.

Peck and *et al.,* (2004), a variety of negative consequences for girls and women have been associated with women's and men's viewing unrealistic portrayals of women in advertising. However, research on the positive consequences of presenting larger-sized women in advertisements, and the conditions under which they are effective, has been lacking. The present research examined such positive effects and found that larger-sized female models in advertisements were rated as more attractive when an instructional frame activated nontraditional beliefs (a new women's magazine that features larger-sized models) than when it activated traditional beliefs (a traditional women's magazine). These effects were more pronounced for women than for men, and particularly for women who scored higher in their need for cognition. The degree to which women generated positive thoughts about themselves in response to the advertisements tended to correspond with their ratings of increased attractiveness of the models in the advertisements. Implications of findings for using positive larger-sized female models in advertisements are discussed.

Silvera and *et al.,* (2004), examined whether consumers infer that celebrity endorsers like the products they endorse, and presents a model using these inferences and other characteristics of the endorser to predict attitudes toward the endorsed product Participant in two experiments examined written endorsement advertisements and were asked to infer the extent to which the endorser truly liked the advertised product and to rate the endorser's attractiveness, similarity to themselves, and knowledge of the product attitudes toward the advertisement, the endorser and the product were also measured The resulting model indicated that product attitudes were predicted by inferences about the endorser's liking for the product and by attitudes toward the endorser.

Mark R. Forehand and *et al.,* (2005), an experiment reveals that the relationship between celebrity attitude and attitude toward brands paired with the celebrity's voice is moderated by identification of the celebrity but only when attitude is measured explicitly. Using explicit measures, celebrity attitude was positively (negatively) related to brand attitude change when the evaluator could not (could) identify the celebrity. This finding is attributed to "resetting," a correction of the perceived influence from irrelevant cues. On implicit measures, a positive relationship between celebrity and brand attitude was observed regardless of celebrity identification. The disassociation between the explicit and implicit results suggests that resetting requires explicit evaluation.

Baird and *et al.*, (2006), have examined the effect of exposure to male models in advertisements on men's body satisfaction. Participants were 173 college males that were recruited from introductory psychology courses. Participants were assessed using the Body Assessment (BA), Magazine Advertisement Questionnaire (MAQ), and one of two sets of magazine advertisements that consisted of either clothing or. cologne products, or those same products featured with a male model. Participants who viewed advertisements with male models showed an increase in body dissatisfaction, while those who viewed only products demonstrated no change in body dissatisfaction. The importance of this finding is that the body dissatisfaction experienced through exposure to idealized images of men in the media is only the beginning of possible outcomes such as anabolic steroid use, eating disorders, and muscle dysmorphia. Limitations and suggestions for continued research are discussed.

Beomjoon Choi and *et al.*, (2008), have stated that blacks are nearly 13% of the population in the U.S and they have substantial buying power. Consequently, advertisers have a real interest in attracting this market segment, and cannot fail to include Black models in their advertising messages. But given the relatively low frequency of Black models featured in commercials (Wilkes & Valencia, 1989; Williams, Qualls, & Grier, 1989), it appears that advertisers may be hesitant to use Black models. It is likely that advertisers may have real concerns about how White consumers may react to non-White models in their advertisements. This is especially a concern for high-value goods other than cars, in whose advertisements Blacks are highly unlikely to appear (Bailey, 2006). Why arc there so few Black models in commercials, given that the research literature suggests that race has not been found to have an impact on viewers' responses (e.g., Whittler, 1989)? Although the research seems to indicate that Whites do not evaluate advertisements featuring Blacks differently from those featuring Whites, it may be that practitioners have found that advertisements featuring Black models are less effective in attracting consumers to buy their products-a result they have refrained from publishing, if not acting upon. In this article, they used a more subtle technique for demonstrating racial bias than has been typically used by marketing researchers for the assessment of models in advertising. Most of the early research shows that White consumers do not respond negatively to advertisements or promotional materials featuring Blacks (Bush, Gwinner, & Soloman, 1974; Schilinger & Plummer, 1972; Solomon, Bush, & Hair, 1976; Bush, Hair, & Solomon, 1979; Tolley & Goett, 1972). In a long series of studies in marketing and social psychology, many studies have found little bias against Black by White participants, and often a bias in favor of Black targets (e.g., Devine, Plant, Amodio, Harmon-Jones & Vance, 1991 Whittler & DiMeo, 1991 But one must ask where the source of this apparent indifference lies. Is it because there is little or no prejudice affecting these decisions, or is it because White responses to advertisements with a Black model are carefully controlled, with prejudice and discrimination suppressed? They suggested that evaluations of Black models in advertisements are determined by a complex mix of positive and negative feelings characterized by ambivalence. Crandall and Eshleman (2003) have proposed the Justification-Suppression Model (JSM) of the expression of prejudice. They argue that racial prejudice is usually suppressed, resulting in lower overt expressions of prejudice than is genuinely felt. However, because affect has motivational properties, people will seek a way to express prejudice, and justifications will allow overt discrimination. A justification is any process that can allow the expression of prejudice, without suffering sanctions, whether external or internal. There are many different kinds of justification, and they appear in many guises. One particular justification of prejudice expression is "legitimacy credits." Legitimacy credits are the memory of previous non-prejudiced behavior, which can be called upon to offset a subsequent release of prejudice. Legitimacy credits can be acquired by engaging in any overtly non-prejudiced behavior-by behaving positively toward a group, by having friends from the group, by smiling at group members on the bus, by buying a piece of art from a group member, or even by evaluating the group positively on a rating scale. In the present study, they investigated how the acquisition of legitimacy credits affects the evaluation of the advertisements featuring Black and White models, by providing people a chance to gain legitimacy with a positive evaluation of a high quality advertisement featuring a Black model. Then, they measured people's evaluation of the subsequent mediocre advertisement with another Black model.

Chan and *et al.*, (2008), materialism is an important issue, especially among young people, and especially in a Chinese context. Based on a theoretical model of the endorsement of materialistic values among Chinese youth, the objectives were to examine the influence of interpersonal communication on social comparison, and the influence of advertising viewing on imitation of celebrity models. In turn, the study examined how both social comparison and imitation of celebrity models contribute to young people's endorsement of materialistic values. A mall intercept survey of 631 young people aged 15--24 in Hong Kong revealed that peer communication and susceptibility to peer influence had strong positive relationships to engagement in social comparison. Motivation for viewing advertisements had a strong positive relationship to imitation of celebrity models. In turn, both social comparison and imitation of celebrity models were positive predictors of materialism.

Johnson, G.D. (2009), since the end of the apartheid regime, the number of advertisements casting actors from different racial backgrounds simultaneously has significantly increased. Comments about this development are multi-faceted. While some observers praise this technique as the ideal social mirror of the "new" South Africa, others criticize it as a pervasive commercial tactic. Consistent with this debate, it is important for brands to understand consumers' perceptions of multi-racial advertising. Indeed, these perceptions are also assumed to influence consumers' attitude towards the advertised brand. Based on the attribution theory, this study investigates whether South African companies, by integrating a multi-racial feature in an advertisement, create the perception amongst consumers that their advertisement is socially responsible and, in so doing, increase their brand equity. The empirical results of this study support that consumers' attitude towards a brand is significantly influenced by the extent to which they attribute a social responsibility to its advertisements. Nevertheless, it is also found that using multi-racial advertising is a necessary but not sufficient condition to generate this social attribution.

Luther and *et al.,* (2009), the primary objective of this study was to examine advertisement-inspired social comparison behavior among Japanese female and male teenagers. It was found that both females and males compared themselves with models in advertisements, although females engaged in the behavior more than males. Significant associations were also found between advertisement-inspired comparison behavior and the importance placed on physical attractiveness in social roles as well as the acceptance of artificial means of enhancing appearance. Public self-consciousness was the primary psychological construct found to be driving advertisement-inspired social comparison behaviour.

Micu and *et al.,* (2009), their research in the developing market economy of Romania employs in-depth interviews and an advertising-trial experiment to examine the effects of attractiveness in advertisements on product evaluations and self-judgments. Our qualitative data indicate that attractive (versus average-looking) models yield favorable advertisement and product evaluations, but generate both negative and positive self-judgments. Our post--advertisement exposure experimental data corroborate immediate positive product evaluations and negative self-judgments. The subsequent two-week trial equalizes product evaluations across model conditions (attractive versus average-looking versus no model) and mitigates the negative effect of attractiveness on women's satisfaction with their own attractiveness. Moreover, women who use products advertised by attractive models report more favorable self-attractiveness and self-confidence.

Ethical Values in Advertisements

Henry Petroski and *et al.,* (1986), it appears to be a matter of fashion, if not one of etiquette, that today's trade book does not make its debut without wearing a dust jacket. Though it may be gaudy (a loud, bleeding madras straight off the rack) or conservative (a tasteful blazer from Books Brothers), a jacket must be worn. It is as if bookstores, paraphrasing their restaurant neighbors, display this sign in their windows: Books Must Wear Jackets. The dust jacket, also known as the book jacket, dust cover and dust wrapper - this last term to be eschewed, lest it be confused with the bookseller's usage of "wrappers" for paper covers - dates at least from 1832, according to John Carter, the bibliophile. Since 19th-century jackets were considered ephemera, mere wrapping paper to be discarded by the purchaser of the book, few examples of that period survive.

Bush and *et al.,* (1994), recently, an increased number of advertisements have been questioned as being potentially unethical. Because of complaints from academicians, special interest groups, competitors, and broadcasters, certain advertising campaigns have been pulled from the media. The fact that potentially unethical advertisements are reaching the market-place suggests that current methods of advertisement evaluation may be inadequate for some of today's controversial or innovative campaigns. The authors introduce the narrative paradigm as a possible solution or tool for discerning potentially unethical aspects of advertisements. A narrative approach to the evaluation of advertisement messages can reveal inconsistencies between the advertisement and the intended or influential audiences before the damaging effects of inappropriate campaigns occur.

Anusorn Singhapakdi and *et al.,* (1999), given the ever-increasing globalization of economies, growing numbers of marketing firms are expecting more of their profits to be derived from international sales. Global competition is ferocious; thus, developing long-term partner relationships often becomes a significant competitive advantage. Corporate ethics are of pivotal importance in global business, though globalization also complicates ethical questions, because an individual's culture affects his or her ethical decision making. Failures to account for the effects of differences in consumers' culturally-based ethical values will hinder a marketer's efforts to expand internationally. Compares consumers from Malaysia and the USA in terms of their perceptions of marketing ethics situations, their attitudes toward business and salespeople, and their personal moral philosophies. The survey results reveal some significant differences between the consumers from these two countries.

David S. Waller (1999), as society becomes more complex, as they become more aware of the harmful effects of some products and as agencies try to become more creative to "cut through the clutter" to gain awareness, there will be more advertisements which the general public perceive as "offensive". Analyses the responses to a survey of attitudes towards the advertising of particular products and reasons for being offensive. The attitudes are examined by means of a survey which presents a series of potentially controversial or offensive products. The study can be used by advertising agencies to develop an understanding of which advertising is perceived by some people as offensive, and a list of potentially controversial clients.

Kim Shyan Fam and *et al.*, (2004), in a constantly changing and increasingly globalized world, religion still plays a significant role in influencing social and consumer behavior. This study will analyze what influence religion and intensity of belief has on attitudes towards the advertising of particular controversial products and services. A questionnaire was distributed to 1,393 people across six different countries and resulting in samples of four main religious groups. The results indicated some statistically significant differences between the groups, which can have important implications for global marketers.

Svante Andersson and *et al.*, (2004), in this study, violent advertising is discussed. An empirical study, using picture analysis, is carried out. The intent of the advertisers' message is compared with the interpretation of a male and a female consumer group. It is concluded that the consumers' interpretations not are the ones that the advertisers had intended. The violence was interpreted in a much more negative way than expected. It is also concluded that there are differences in interpretations between men and women.

Deborah Y. Cohn (2005), stated that Taxonomies (e.g., classification schemes) are valuable in that they clarify and create conceptual and theoretical frameworks to integrate a large variety of research (Brinkmann, 2002; Crie, 2003). In addition, taxonomies draw attention to the importance of a subject and provide a framework for organizing what they know and what they have yet to explore (Berenbaum, Raghavan, Le, Vernon, & Gomez, 2003). This article develops a taxonomy to explore the ethical considerations of advertising professionals. A netnographic study was conducted and the results are presented. A taxonomy is developed in which advertising practitioner concerns are classified into four categories: (1) societal impact, (2) industry norms and rules, (3) my ethical dilemmas, (4) others' behavior, and (5) industry responses. This research supports and extends previous academic research into advertising ethics.

Robert J. Fisher and *et al.*, (2005), two studies examine gender differences in responses to advertising with emotional content that varies on agency-a fundamental component of the male, but not female, stereotype. As hypothesized, males reported a less pleasant viewing experience and a less favorable attitude toward the advertisement when a low agency emotion (i.e., stereotype incongruent) advertisement was viewed with another male, while their responses were not affected by the presence of another person when they were exposed to a high agency emotion (i.e., stereotype congruent) advertisement. Males' and females' private responses were not significantly different, and females' responses were invariant across social contexts and type of advertisement.

Kyoko Fukukawa and *et al.*, (2006), they examined why ordinary people engage in Aberrant Consumer Behavior (ACB), and pays particular attention to the extent to which consumer perceptions of corporate 'unfairness' lead to a response in kind. The study examines five ethical scenarios including insurance claim exaggeration and software piracy, using data from 344 UK consumers. Ajzen's Theory Of Planned Behavior (TPB) provides an initial analytical framework. The study also adopts an additional variable, perceived unfairness, referring to the extent to which an actor is motivated to redress an imbalance perceived as unfair. In comparison to TPB, the study reveals different components of ACB. Furthermore, analysis of variance indicates that consumer perceptions of unfairness by insurance companies provide a significant reason for claim exaggeration. This suggests that ACB is one form of market response to unfair corporate performance. Thus it is argued that an examination of ACB will not only help to understand which ethical aspects of corporate performance might be perceived as unfair, but also to evaluate the extent to which it contributes to a negative perception of particular industries and corporations. The closing discussion considers how a consumer negative response to corporate performance might relate to pricing, product attributes and customer relationships.

McMenemy and *et al.*, (2006), focused on the significance of ethical values in librarianship. The author reflects that values and ethics in librarianship encompasses not just from the performance of responsibilities and service but throughout the different stages of a librarian's career. The researcher summarizes the set of core values and ethics in librarianship in simple terms which include giving the rights of every individual access to information, freedom of speech, unbiased service, excellence in organization of materials, the protection of intellectual property. The researcher opines that deprofessionalism in the frontline of librarianship is the biggest threat to the library profession and suggests that the solution to this concern is the strength of ethical values and philosophy in the practice of librarianship.

Gunne Grankvist and *et al.*, (2007), the purpose of this article is to study whether preference for a product increased, or decreased, as a consequence of information that the product was either eco- or fair trade labelled. An additional purpose was to investigate associations between importance attached to values and preference for eco- and fair-trade labelled food products. Effects of information that orange juice was either eco- or fair trade labelled were studied in an experimental setting, with a sample of Swedish students. Importance attached to values was measured with the List of Values (LOV) scale. Taste preference was the evaluated aspect. No significant effects of the experimental manipulation were observed. Attaching greater importance to the value "warm relationships with others" was associated with a more favourable rating of the taste of both eco- and fair-trade labelled juices. The value "security" was positively associated with an increased taste preference for the group exposed to the fair trade, but not the eco, label.

Jakob Nielsen (2007), reported on the ethical aspects of Internet advertising. The author reports on a study undertaken by website usability expert Jakob Nielsen. Nielsen found that the less an advertisement on a web page actually looked like an advertisement, the more likely people were to pay attention to it. Nielsen considers this unethical because it blurs the distinction between paid advertisement and the site's content. The author states that this distinction is a key aspect professional ethical element of journalism.

S.Mercia Selva Malar, (2008), seeks to emphasise the importance of firms being responsible to society. The paper examines firms' omissions and commissions in the various functional areas of management while they focused on profit. Examples of such omissions and commissions are also discussed. Support from businessmen and authors who share such a viewpoint is mentioned. In the long term, firms that are socially responsible are successful. Practising social responsibility consciously, firms can make the world a better place for all people. It can be beneficial for the entire society. Omissions and commissions arising out of being profit-focused are the author's original contribution. The paper is of value to researchers and practitioners of corporate social responsibility and business ethics. Firms need to understand that they cannot succeed and excel for long if they neglect stakeholders other than shareholders.

Terje I. Vaaland and *et al.*, (2008), aims to develop an integrating overview of the present status of the theory of Corporate Social Responsibility (CSR) applied in the marketing context and asks whether, to what extent and how the discipline of marketing has addressed CSR. After clarifying core concepts and proposing a new definition of CSR, 54 articles in leading marketing journals between 1995 and 2005 are analyzed in terms of publication characteristics, research design, variables, sampling, level of analysis, issues raised, and key findings. Recommendations include a broadened perspective in empirical research to address CSR in its entirety, expand the focus beyond consumers, include a broader range of samples and conduct more inductive, exploratory empirical studies. These steps will contribute to a multidimensional view of the future customer. Given the veritable explosion in CSR research in the recent years, there is a genuine need for the field to take stock of what has been learned so far and what that implies in terms of where researchers should be headed.

Gerard Prendergast and *et al.*, (2009), the aim of the research reported in this paper was to identify for which types of products and services consumers find the advertising to lack credibility and in which media this effect is most serious. The association between self-esteem and skepticism towards advertising was also explored. Using a structured questionnaire, 200 Hong Kong shoppers were surveyed in mall intercept interviews. The results showed that advertisements for weight-loss products were considered the least credible. The broadcast media (radio, broadcast television and cable television) were considered the most credible advertising media, while direct mail and the internet were considered the least credible. Self-esteem was found to be positively related with skepticism towards advertising. By recognizing the credibility of their advertisements and the media in which they are placed, and the influence of self-esteem on advertising skepticism, the findings are of use to advertisers in formulating their strategies. The findings also provide information of value for policy makers trying to combat non-credible and deceptive advertising.

REFERENCES

1. Schleifer, Stephen, Dunn, S. Watson (1968), "Relative Effectiveness of Advertisements of Foreign and Domestic Origin", *Journal of Marketing Research (JMR)*, 5(3) 296-299.
2. David Corkindale (1976), "Setting objectives for advertising", *European Journal of Marketing*, 10(3) 109 – 126.
3. V.Kanti Prasad (1976), "Communications-Effectiveness of Comparative Advertising: A Laboratory Analysis", *Journal of Marketing Research*, 13(2) 128-137.
4. Stephens, Nancy (1982), 'The Effectiveness of Time-Compressed Television Advertisements With Older Adults", *Journal of Advertising*, 11(4) 48-76.
5. Alpert, Mark L., Golden, Linda L., Hoyer, Wayne D (1983), "The Impact of Repetition on Advertisement Miscomprehension and Effectiveness", *Advances in Consumer Research*, 10(1) 130-135.
6. Lana Hall and Ingrid Foik(1983), "Generic versus Brand Advertised Manufactured Milk Products: The Case of Yogurt" *North Central Journal of Agricultural Economics*, 5 (1) 19-24.
7. Kilbourne, William E, Painton, Scott, Ridley, Danny (1985), "The Effect of Sexual Embedding On Responses to Magazine *Advertisements", Journal of Advertising*, 14 (2) 48 56.
8. Bruce A. Austin (1986), "Cinema Screen Advertising: An Old Technology With New Promise For Consumer Marketing", *Journal of Consumer Marketing*, 3 (1) 45 – 56.
9. Burton, Scot, Lichtenstein, Donald R (1988), "The Effect of Ad Claims and Ad Context on Attitude Toward the Advertisement", *Journal of Advertising*, 17(1) 3-11.
10. Loken, Barbara, Howard-Pitney, Beth (1988), 'Effectiveness of Cigarette Advertisements on Women: An Experimental Study", *Journal of Applied Psychology*, 73 (3) 378-382.
11. Mazursky, David, Schul, Yaacov (1988), "The Effects of Advertisement Encoding on the Failure to Discount Information: Implications for the Sleeper Effect", *Journal of Consumer Research* , 15(1) 24-36.
12. Okechuku, Chike, Gongrong Wang (1988), "The effectiveness of Chinese print advertisements in North America", *Journal of Advertising Research*, 28(5) 25-34.

13. Pamela M. Homer and Lynn R. Kahle (1990), "Source Expertise, Time of Source Identification, and Involvement in Persuasion: An Elaborative Processing Perspective", *Journal of Advertising*, 19(1), 30-39.
14. David W. Lloyd, Kevin J. Clancy (1991), "Television program involvement and advertising response: some unsettling implications for copy research", *Journal of Consumer Marketing*, 8 (4) 61 – 74.
15. Stephen Ansolabehere and Shanto Iyengar (1994), "Riding the Wave and Claiming Ownership Over Issues: The Joint Effects of Advertising and News Coverage in Campaigns", *The Public Opinion Quarterly,* 58(3) 335-357.
16. Yang, Chung-Chuan Ken (1995), "Screen-Based Interactive Advertisements and Their Effectiveness: An Exploratory Study of Cross-National Computer Users", *Journal of International Business Studies,* 26 (4) 910-910.
17. France Leclerc and John D. C. Little (1997), "Can Advertising Copy Make FSI Coupons More Effective?", *Journal of Marketing Research*, 34 (4)473-484.
18. Yong Zhang, James P. Neelankavil, (1997) "The influence of culture on advertising effectiveness in China and the USA: A cross-cultural study", *European Journal of Marketing*, 31 (2), 134 - 149.
19. Charles F. Hofacker, Jamie Murphy (1998) "World Wide Web banner advertisement copy testing", *European Journal of Marketing,* 32 (7/8) 703 – 712.
20. Quester, Pascale G (1998), "Antecedents of Anti-Smoking Advertisements' Effectiveness: A Bi-Cultural Study", *Journal of International Consumer Marketing*, 10(4) 29.
21. Rae, Nathan; Brennan, Mike(1998), "The relative effectiveness of sound and animation in Web banner advertisements", *Marketing Bulletin,* 9 76.
22. Deborah Roedder John(1999), "Consumer Socialization of Children: A Retrospective Look At Twenty Five Years of Research", *Journal of Consumer Research*, 26 68-77.
23. Mark Ritson, Richard Elliott (1999), "The Social Uses of Advertising: An Ethnographic Study of Adolescent Advertising Audiences" *Journal of Consumer Research,* 26 79-86.
24. Chanthika Pornpitakpan; Tan, Tze Ke Jason(2000), "The Influence of Incongruity on the Effectiveness of Humorous Advertisements The Case of Singaporeans", *Journal of International Consumer Marketing,* 12(3), 27-45.
25. Elizabeth S. Moore, Richard J. Lutz (2000), "Children, Advertising, and Product Experiences: A Multi method Inquiry", *Journal of Consumer Research,* 27, 98-109.
26. Kumar, Anand(2000)," Interference Effects of Contextual Cues in Advertisements on Memory for Ad Content", *Journal of Consumer Psychology (Lawrence Erlbaum Associates),* 9(3)155-166.
27. Katherine Gallagher, Jeffrey Parsons and K.Dale Foster, (2001), " A tale of two studies: Replicating "Advertising Effectiveness and content evaluation in print and on the web" *Journal of Advertising Research,* July-August, 71-81.
28. Carol Kaufman-Scarborough (2001), "Accessible advertising for visually-disabled persons: the case of color-deficient consumers", *Journal of Consumer Marketing,* 18(4) 303 – 318.

29. Dahlen, Micael, (2001), "Banner Advertisements through a New Lens", *Journal of Advertising Research,* 41(4), 23-30.
30. Andrew L. Mendelson, Paul D. Bolls(2002), "Emotional effects of advertising on young adults of lower socio-economic status" *Journal of Marketing,* 59 (3) 53-62.
31. Cornelia Pechmann, Susan J. Knight (2002), "An Experimental Investigation of the Joint Effects of Advertising and Peers on Adolescents' Beliefs and Intentions about Cigarette Consumption", *Journal of Consumer Research,* 29, 101-125 .
32. Hudson, S, Hung, C. L, Padley, L(2002), "Cross-national standardisation of advertisements: a study of the effectiveness of TV advertisements targeted at Chinese Canadians in Canada", *International Journal of Advertising,* 21 (3)345-366.
33. Jones, Lara(2002), "Are advertisements featuring local business owners effective or detrimental", *Enterprise/Salt Lake City,* 31 (31) 1.
34. Michael Volkov, Debra Harker, Michael Harker (2002), "Complaint behaviour: a study of the differences between complainants about advertising in Australia and the population at large" *Journal of Consumer Marketing,* 19 (4) 319-332.
35. Chang-Hoan Cho (2003), "The Effectiveness of Banner Advertisements: Involvement and Click-through", *Journalism & Mass Communication Quarterly,* 80 (3)623-645.
36. Amitav Chakravarti, Chris Janiszewski (2004), "The Influence of Generic Advertising on Brand Preferences", Journal of Consumer Research, 30, 25-38.
37. Gerard J Tellin (2004), "Effective Advertising", Response Books, New Delhi.
38. Howard, Daniel J.; Kerin, Roger A(2004), "The Effects of Personalized Product Recommendations on Advertisement Response Rates: The "Try This. It Works!" Technique", *Journal of Consumer Psychology (Lawrence Erlbaum Associates),* 14 (3) 271-279.
39. Jennifer Edson Escalas, Mary Frances Luce (2004), "Understanding the Effects of Process Focused versus Outcome Focused Thought in Response to Advertising", *Journal of Consumer Research,* 31, 78-86.
40. Kim Shyan Fam, David S. Waller, B. Zafer Erdogan (2004), "The influence of religion on attitudes towards the advertising of controversial products", *European Journal of Marketing,* 38,(5/6) 537 – 555.
41. Rama Yelkur, Chuck Tomkovick, Patty Traczyk (2004), "Super Bowl Advertising Effectiveness: Hollywood Finds the Games Golden" *Journal of Advertising Research,* 56(8) 143-156. 126b.
42. Turley, L. W.; Shannon, J. Richard, (2004), "The impact and effectiveness of advertisements in a sports arena", *Journal of Services Marketing,* 14 (4/5) 323.
43. Beattie, Geoffrey, Shovelton, Heather(2005), "Why the spontaneous images created by the hands during talk can help make TV advertisements more effective", *British Journal of Psychology,* 96 (1)21-37.
44. Demetrios Vakaratsas and Zhenfeng MA, (2005), "A look at the long-run effectiveness of multimedia advertising and its implications for budget allocation decisions, *Journal of Advertising Research,* 17 (2), 241-255.

45. Clow, Kenneth E Berry, Christine T, Kranenburg, Kristine E, James, Karen E,(2005), "An Examination of the Visual Element of Service Advertisements", *Marketing Management Journal*, 15 (1), 33-45.
46. Janssens, Wim; De Pelsmacker, Patrick (2005), "Advertising for New and Existing Brands: The Impact of Media Context and Type of Advertisement", *Journal of Marketing Communications,* 11 (2) 113-128.
47. Lees, Gavin; Healey, Ben(2005), "A Test of the Effectiveness of a Mouse Pointer Image in Increasing Click through for a Web Banner Advertisement". *Marketing Bulletin*, 16, 1-6.
48. Yoon, Sung-Joon; Choi, Yong-Gil(2005), 'Determinants of successful sports advertisements: The effects of advertisement type, product type and sports model", *Journal of Brand Management*, 12 (3) 191-205.
49. Chun-Tuan Chang (2006), "Is a Picture Worth a Thousand Words? Influence of Graphic Illustration on Framed Advertisements", *Advances in Consumer Research,* 33 (1) 104-112.
50. Fry, Marie-Louise (2006), "Message processing of fear-based anti-drink driving advertisements" *Message processing of fear-based anti-drink driving advertisements.*
51. Michael Fay (2006), "Cyclical patterns in the content of advertisements: Replication, confirmation, extension and revision", *European Journal of Marketing,* 40 (1/2) 198 – 217.
52. Nicholas Reading, Steven Bellman, Duane Varan, Hume Winzar (2006), "Effectiveness of Telescopic Advertisements Delivered via Personal Video Recorders" *Journal of Advertising Research,*.41(6) 217-225. 126a.
53. Pechmann, Cornelia; Reibling, Ellen T(2006), "Antismoking Advertisements for Youths: An Independent Evaluation of Health, Counter-Industry, and Industry Approaches", *American Journal of Public Health*, 96(5) 906-913.
54. S John Gabriel (2006), "The Impact of Television Advertisements on Youth: A Study", *The ICFAI journal of Marketing Management*, V, (3) 71-79.
55. Shou-Shiung Chou(2006), "Effects of Trope Advertisement on Chinese Consumers", *Journal of American Academy of Business, Cambridge*, 9 (1) 229-232.
56. Smith, Karen h.; Stutts, Mary Ann(2006), "The Influence of Individual Factors on the Effectiveness of Message Content in Antismoking Advertisements Aimed at Adolescents", *Journal of Consumer Affairs*, 2006, 40 (2), 261-293.
57. Stewart, Patrick A.; Schubert, James N (2006), "Taking the "Low Road" with Subliminal Advertisements: A Study Testing the Effect of Precognitive Prime "RATS" in a 2000 Presidential Advertisement", *Harvard International Journal of Press/Politics*, 1 (4) 103-114.
58. Appiah, Osei(2007), "The Effectiveness of "Typical-User" Testimonial Advertisements on Black and White Browsers' Evaluations of Products on Commercial Websites: Do They Really Work?" *Journal of Advertising Research,* 47 (1), 14-27.
59. Decrop, Alain(2007), ".The influence of message format on the effectiveness of print advertisements for tourism destinations" *International Journal of Advertising,* , 26(4), 505-525.

60. Hee-Sook Yoon, Doo-Hee Lee(2007), "The Exposure Effect of Unclicked Banner Advertisements", *Advances in International Marketing*, 18(12) 211-229.

61. Hoggard, Jesse T (2007), "Moving towards a Very Long Engagement: The Effects of Interactivity on Prolonging Engagement with Online Movie Advertisements" , *Master's Thesis.*

62. Ioni Lewis, Barry Watson, Richard Tay(2007), "Examining the effectiveness of physical threats in road safety advertising: The role of the third-person effect, gender, and age", *Transportation Research Part F: Traffic Psychology and Behaviour* 10(1), 48-60.

63. Kara Chan, Lyann Li, Sandra Diehl, Ralf Terlutter, (2007) "Consumers' response to offensive advertising: a cross cultural study", *International Marketing Review*, 245 606 – 628.

64. Kim-Shyan Fam, Reinhard Grohs, (2007) "Cultural values and effective executional techniques in advertising: A cross-country and product category study of urban young adults in Asia", *International Marketing Review*, 24(5), 519 – 538.

65. Wim Janssens, Patric De Pelsmaker, et al (2007), "The moderating role of the personality trait discomfort with ambiguity", *Journal of Marketing Communication,* 9(3)110-125.

66. DeRosia, Eric D(2008), "The effectiveness of nonverbal symbolic signs and metaphors in advertisements: An experimental inquiry", *Psychology & Marketing,* 25 (3) 298-316.

67. Kathleen Mortimer (2008), "Identifying the components of effective service advertisements", *Journal of Services Marketing,* 22(2), 104-113.

68. Lewis, I, Watson, B, et al (2008), "An examination of message-relevant affect in road safety messages: Should road safety *advertisements* aim to make us feel good or bad", *Transportation Research*, 11 (6) 403-417.

69. Mark Loughney, martin Eichholz, Michelle Hagger (2008), "Exploring the Effectiveness of Advertising in the ABC.com Full Episode Player" Journal of Advertising research, 25 (5) 322-328.

70. Mathew Joseph, Deborah F. Spake, Zachary Finney (2008), "Consumer attitudes toward pharmaceutical direct-to-consumer advertising: An empirical study and the role of income" *International Journal of Pharmaceutical and Healthcare Marketing,* 2, .(2)117 – 133.

71. Mortimer, Kathleen(2008), "*Journal of Services Marketing,* 22, (2/3) 104-113.

72. Samu, Sridhar; Bhatnagar, Namita(2008), "The efficacy of anti-smoking advertisements: the role of source, message, and individual characteristics", *International Journal of Nonprofit & Voluntary Sector Marketing,* 13 (3) 237-250.

73. Shin Yi Chou, Inas Rashad, Michael Grossman (2008), "Fast Food Restaurant Advertising on Television and Its Influence on Childhood Obesity", *The Journal of Law and Economics*, vol. 51, 114-119.

74. Fotini Patsioura, Maro Vlachopoulou, Vicky Manthou, (2009) "A new advertising effectiveness model for corporate advertising web sites: A relationship marketing approach", Benchmarking: *An International Journal*, 16(3), 372 – 386.

75. Jay (Hyunjae) Yu; Cude (2009), "Hello, Mrs. Sarah Jones! We recommend this product!' Consumers' perceptions about personalized advertising: comparisons across advertisements delivered via three different types of media", *Brenda. International Journal of Consumer Studies*, 33, 4, 503-514.
76. Zhang, Jie, Wedel, Michel, Pieters, Rik (2009), "Sales Effects of Attention to Feature *Advertisements:* A Bayesian Mediation Analysis", *Journal of Marketing Research (JMR)* , 46 (5)669-681.
77. Franzen, Raymond (1942), "Inequalities Which Affect Scores of *Advertisements", Journal of Marketing,* 6 (4)128-132.
78. William T. Moran (1951), "Measuring exposure to advertisements", *Journal of Applied Psychology*, 35(1) 72-77.
79. Clarence E. Eldridge (1958), "Advertising Effectiveness: How Can It Be Measured?", *The Journal of Marketing,* 22 (3) 241-251.
80. Christian, Richard C (1965), "How Much Does an Industrial Logotype Add to the Effectiveness of an *Advertisement?", Journal of Marketing,* 29 (2)57-59.
81. Herbert E. Krugman (1966), "the Measurement of Advertising Involvement" *Public Opinion Quarterly,* 30 (4)583-596.
82. Christian, Richard C, Gordon, Howard L (1967) "Yes, Virginia, Research Helps Better *Advertisements", Journal of Marketing,* 31 (1)64-66.
83. Orenstein, Frank E (1967), "Attempts at Measuring the Effectiveness of Advertising / Do People Really Read Advertisements?/ How to Choose Between Major Categories of Media", *Journal of Marketing Research (JMR),* 4 (4) 409-410.
84. Kuehl, Philip G, Dyer, Robert F (1977), "Application of the "Normative Belief" Technique for Measuring the Effectiveness of Deceptive and Corrective Advertisements", *Advances in Consumer Research,* 4.(1) 204-212.
85. Subhash C. Jain and Edwin C. Hackleman(1978), "How Effective Is Comparison Advertising for Stimulating Brand Recall?", *Journal of Advertising,* 7 (3)20-25.
86. Hanssens, Dominique M., Weitz, Barton A (1980), "The Effectiveness of Industrial Print Advertisements Across Product Categories", *Journal of Marketing Research (JMR),* 17 (3) 294-306
87. Patzer, Gordon L (1980), "A Comparison of Advertisement Effects: Sexy Female Communicator Vs Non-Sexy Female Communicator", *Advances in Consumer Research,* 7 (1)359-364.
88. Bagozzi, Richard P, Silk, Alvin J (1983), "Recall, Recognition, and the *Measurement* of Memory for Print *Advertisement", Marketing Science,* 2(2) 95.
89. Leigh, James H (1984), "Recall and Recognition Performance for Umbrella Print Advertisements", *Journal of Advertising,* 13 (4) 5-30.
90. Gates, Fliece R (1986), "Further Comments on the Miscomprehension of Televised *Advertisements", Journal of Advertising,* 15(1) 4-9.
91. Surendra N. Singh and Gilbert A. Churchill (1986), "Using the Theory of Signal Detection to Improve Ad Recognition Testing", *Journal of Marketing Research,* 23(4) 327-336.

92. Muehling, Darrel D, Bozman, Carl S (1990), "An Examination of Factors Influencing Effectiveness of 15-Second Advertisements", *International Journal of Advertising,* (4) 331-344.

93. Grønhaug, Kjell, Kvitastein, Olav, Grønmo, Sigmund (1991), "Factors moderating advertising effectiveness as reflected in 333 tested advertisements", *Journal of Advertising Research,* 31 (5) 42-50.

94. Boles, James, Scot Burton (1992), "An Examination of Free Elicitation and Response Scale Measures of Feelings and Judgments Evoked by Television *Advertisements", Journal of the Academy of Marketing Science* , 20 (3) 225.

95. Finn, Adam (1992), "Recall, Recognition and the *Measurement* of Memory for Print *Advertisements:* A Reassessment", *Marketing Science,* 11, (1) 95

96. Norris, Claire E.; Colman, Andrew M(1992), "Context Effects on Recall and Recognition of Magazine Advertisements", *Journal of Advertising,* Vol. (21) (3) 37-46.

97. Joel J. Davis (1993), "Strategies for environmental advertising", *Journal of Consumer Marketing,* 10(2) 19 – 36.

98. Paul M. Fischer, Dean M. Krugman, James E. Fletcher, Richard J. Fox, Tina H. Rojas (1993), "An Evaluation of Health Warnings in Cigarette Advertisements Using Standard Market Research Methods: What Does It Mean to Warn?", *Tobacco Control,* 2 (4) 279-285.

99. D'Souza, Goes, Rao, Ram C (1995), "Can repeating an *advertisement* more frequently than the competition affect brand preference in", *Journal of Marketing,* 59 (2) 32.

100. Gitav Enkataramani Johar (1995), "Consumer Involvement and Deception from Implied Advertising Claims", *Journal of Marketing Research,* 32 (3) 267-279.

101. Zhao, Xinshu, Bleske, Glen L (1995), "*Measurement* effects in comparing voter learning from television news and campaign *advertisements", Journalism & Mass Communication Quarterly,* 72 (1) 72-83.

102. France, Karén Russo; Park, C. Whan(1997) "The Impact of Program Affective Valence and Level of Cognitive Appraisal on Advertisement Processing and Effectiveness", *Journal of Current Issues & Research in Advertising,* 19 (2) 1-21.

103. Pirisi, Angela (1997), "Eye-catching *advertisements" Psychology Today,* 30 (1) 14.

104. Thomas, Jerry W (1997), "Looking for results? Track your *advertisements", Air Conditioning Heating & Refrigeration News,* 200 (4), 76.

105. Robert J. Fisher, David Ackerman (1998), "The Effects of Recognition and Group Need on Volunteerism: A Social Norm Perspective", *Journal of Consumer Research,* 25, 13-21.

106. Tina M. Lowrey (1998), "The Effects of Syntactic Complexity on Advertising Persuasiveness", *Journal of Consumer Psychology,* 7 (2) 187-206.

107. Abhilasha Metha (1999), "Using Self-Concept to Assess Advertising Effectiveness" Journal of Advertising Research, 32 (8) 81-88.

108. Appiah-Adu, Kwaku(1999), "Assessing the Effectiveness of Travel Agency Print Advertisements", *Journal of International Marketing & Marketing Research,* Vol. 24, no. 3, p. 145-160.

109. Christine Communal, Barbara Senior (1999), "National culture and management: messages conveyed by British, French and German advertisements for managerial appointments", *Leadership & Organization Development Journal*, Vol 20, no.1, P 26 – 35.
110. Jourdan, Philippe (1999), "Creation and Validation of an Advertising Scale Based on the Individual Perception of the Emotional or Informational Intent of the *Advertisement*", *Advances in Consumer Research*, 26 (1) 504-512.
111. Lau, Richard R.; Sigelman, Lee(1999), 'The effects of negative political advertisements: A meta-analytical assessment", *American Political Science Review*, 93 (4) 851.
112. George S. Low, Charles W. Lamb Jr (2000), "The measurement and dimensionality of brand associations", *Journal of Product & Brand Management*, 9 (6) 350 – 370.
113. Mark Uncles(2000), "The Alpha, Beta, Gamma Approach to Measuring Change and its use for Interpreting the Effectiveness of Service Quality Programs",*.A transcript of record.*
114. Mike Glanville(2000), "Measuring the effectiveness of Pay Per Click" http://affiliate-school.blogspot.com/ .
115. Miller, Darryl W, Hadjimarcou, John, Miciak, Alan (2000), "A scale for measuring *advertisement*-evoked mental imagery", *Journal of Marketing Communications*, 6,(1), 1-20.
116. Katherine Gallagher, Jeffrey Parsons, K. Dale Forster (2001), "A Tale of Two Studies: Replicating Advertising Effectiveness and content Evaluation in Print and on the Web", Journal of Advertising Research, vol.48 (9) 150-162.
117. Pradeep Korgaonkar, Ronnie Silverblatt, Bay O'Leary (2001), "Web advertising and Hispanics", *Journal of Consumer Marketing,* 18 (2) 134 – 152.
118. Shen, Fuyuan (2002), "Banner *Advertisement* Pricing, *Measurement,* and Pretesting Practices: Perspectives from Interactive Agencies", *Journal of Advertising*, 31(3) 59-67.
119. Utpal M. Dholakia,Vicki G. Morwitz(2002), "The Scope and Persistence of Mere Measurement Effects: Evidence from a Field Study of Customer Satisfaction Measurement", *Journal Of Consumer Research,* 29 57-68.
120. Arch G. Woodside, Chris Dubelaar, (2003), "Increasing quality in measuring advertising effectiveness: A meta-analysis of question framing in conversion studies", *Journal of Advertising Research,* March, 78-84.
121. Boonghee Yoo, Rujirutana Mandhachitara (2003), "Estimating Advertising Effects on Sales in Competitive Setting" *Journal of Advertising Research,* 28 (3) 310-319.
122. Chandon, Jean Louis, Chtourou, Mohamed Saber; Fortin, David R (2003), "Effects of Configuration and Exposure Levels on Responses to Web Advertisements", *Journal of Advertising Research*, 43(2) 217-229.
123. Jennifer edson escalas barbarab . stern (2003), ". Sympathy and Empathy: Emotional Responses to Advertising Dramas" *Journal of Consumer Research,* 294, 566-578.
124. Elizabeth Cowley, Eunika Janus (2004), "Not Necessarily Better, but Certainly Different: A Limit to the Advertising Misinformation Effect on Memory", *Journal of Consumer Research,* 31 55-63.

125. Pablo Briñol, Richard E. Petty, Zakary L. Tormala (12004), "Self Validation of Cognitive Responses to Advertisements", *Journal of Consumer Research*, 30, 45 -55.

126. T.C.Melewar, Claes Vemmervik (2004) "International advertising strategy: A review, reassessment and recommendation", *Management Decision*, 42 (7) 863-881.

127. David S. Waller, Kim-Shyan Fam, B. Zafer Erdogan(2005), "Advertising of controversial products: a cross-cultural study", *Journal of Consumer Marketing*, 22 (1) 6-13.

128. Fortin, David R.; Dholakia, Ruby Roy(2005), "Interactivity and vividness effects on social presence and involvement with a web-based advertisement", *Journal of Business Research*, 58 (3) 387-396.

129. Hyunjoo Oh, (2005) "Measuring affective reactions to print apparel advertisements: a scale development", *Journal of Fashion Marketing and Management*, 9 (3), 283 – 305.

130. Julie Verity (2005), "Interpreting the successful transformation of Shell's advertising activity 1997-2002", *Management Decision*, 43 (1) 72 – 85.

131. Schweidel, David A., Bradlow, Eric T., Williams, Patti (2006), "A Feature-Based Approach to Assessing Advertisement Similarity", *Journal of Marketing Research (JMR)*, 43 (2) 237-243.

132. Jim Novo(2007)., "Marketing Mix Modeling - Measuring the effectiveness of "Brand" Advertisement" *Marketing Modeling* -Permalink.

133. Lohtia,Ritu,Donthu,Naveen,Yaveroglu, Idil(2007), "Evaluating the efficiency of Internet banner *advertisements" Journal of Business Research,* Vol. 60 no 4, p365-370.

134. Rick T. Wilson, Brain D. Till (2007), "Direct-to-consumer Pharmaceutical Advertising: Building and Testing a Model for Advertising Effectiveness", Journal of Advertising Research, 38 (10) 270-280.

135. AnjaZurcher Wray Nancy Nelson Hodges (2008), "Response to activewear apparel *advertisements* by US baby boomers: An examination of cognitive versus chronological age factors", *Journal of Consumer Marketing,* 12 (1) 8-23.

136. David Szetela(2008), "Measuring a Text Ad's Effectiveness" *Search Engine Watch Webcast* 1, 10-15

137. Mark Robertson(2008), "Video Banner Ads vs. Traditional Banner Ads - Measuring Effectiveness" *International Journal of Advertising,* 9 (2) 15-22.

138. Minamizawa,(2009), "Advertisement Effect Measurement Device, Advertisement Effect Measurement Method Used In The Advertisement Effect Measurement Device And Advertisement Effect Measurement Control", *ITO, Naoko.*

139. WoonBong Na, Roger Marshall, Arch G. Woodside (2009), "Decision system analysis of advertising agency decisions", *Qualitative Market Research: An International Journal,* 12 (2) 153 – 170.

140. United States Patent 5991734, (2009) "Method of measuring the creative value in communications"- *ViscosityJournal.com*-24th-Sep-2009 at 11.05a.m.

141. Adams H.F. (1915), "The adequacy of the laboratory test in advertising", *Psychological Review*, 22(5), 402-422.

142. Starch, Daniel (1923), "Testing the Effectiveness of Advertisements", *Harvard Business Review*, 1(4)464-474.
143. Stocks, J. M. B (1965), "Validating Television Advertisement Tests", *Commentary: The Journal of the Market Research Society*, 7 (3) p. 159-165.
144. William H.Antrin(1978), "Advertising Effectiveness" *International Journal of Advertising*,19 (3), 299-315.
145. P.Vanden Abeele, P. Luysterman, (1981) "The Evaluation of Pre-tests by Advertising People: Results of a Survey in Belgium", *European Journal of Marketing*, 15(1) 48-57.
146. Day, Robert L(1990), "Revisiting the Rough/Finished Issue in Advertisement Pre-testing: A Practitioner's Viewpoint", *Marketing Research*, 2 (3) 22-29.
147. Stephen R. McDaniel, Gary R. Heald (2000), "Young Consumers' Responses to Event Sponsorship Advertisements of Unhealthy Products: Implications of Schema-triggered Affect Theory", *Sport Management Review*, 3 (2) 163-184.
148. William H. Antrin and Eugene L Dorr (1978), "Advertising", 2nd Edition, Mc-Graw Hill Company, New Delhi, p. 143-150.
149. Earl, Ronald L., Pride, William M (1980), "The Effects of Advertisement Structure, Message Sidedness, and Performance Test Results on Print Advertisement in formativeness", *Journal of Advertising*, Vol. 9, No. 3, pp. 36-46.
150. William H.Bolen(1984), "Advertising Effectiveness"-*www. science direct.com*-24th sep 2009, at 11.15a.m.
151. Doyle & Saunders, (1990), "Measuring advertisement effectiveness—a neural network approach" *Neuro-Fuzzy Laboratory* funded by A.I.C.T.E. (All India Council for Technical Education), New Delhi, Government of India.
152. Edward Rosbergen, Rik Pieters, Michel Wedel (1997), "Visual Attention to Advertising: A Segment Level Analysis", *Journal of Consumer Research*, 24, 78-87
153. Michael J Baker(1998), "*The Westburn Dictionary of Marketing*" Westburn Publishers Ltd 2002.
154. Robert J. Fisher,David Ackerman (1998), "The Effects of Recognition and Group Need on Volunteerism: A Social Norm Perspective", *Journal Of Consumer Research*, 25, 38-46.
155. Kathryn A. Braun(1999), "Post experience Advertising Effects on Consumer Memory", *Journal Of Consumer Research*, 25, pp57-68.
156. Anand Kumar (2000), "Interference Effects of Contextual Cues in Advertisements on Memory for Ad Content", *Journal of Consumer Psychology*, 9 (3) 155-166.
157. H. Shanker Krishnan and Dipankar Chakravarti (2003), "A Process Analysis of the Effects of Humorous Advertising Executions on Brand Claims Memory", *Journal of Consumer Psychology*, 13 (3) 230-245.
158. Bruce F. Hall(2004), "Measuring The Effectiveness Of The Promotional Program - Presentation Transcripty" *Mcgraw-Hill/Irwin*.
159. Jason C. G. Halford, Jane Gillespie, Victoria Brown, Eleanor E. Pontin, Terence M. Dovey (2004), "Effect of television advertisements for foods on food consumption in children", *Appetite*, 42 (2) 221-225.

160. Rohini Ahluwalia, Robert E. Burnkrant (2004), "Answering Questions about Questions: A Persuasion Knowledge Perspective for Understanding the Effects of Rhetorical Questions", *Journal of Consumer Research*, (31) 49-56.

161. Spike Cramphorn (2004), "Measuring Effectiveness Of Business-to-business Advertising" *Journal of advertising research*, 2, (3), 2-5.

162. Garcia, Eli, Yang, Kenneth C. C (2006), "Consumer Responses to Sexual Appeals in Cross-Cultural *Advertisements", Journal of International Consumer Marketing*, 19 (2) 29-52.

163. Pei-Luen Patrick Rau, Duye Chen (2006), "Effects of watermark and music on mobile message advertisements", *International Journal of Human-Computer Studies*, 64 (9) 905-914.

164. Friedman, Hershey H, Termini, Salvatore, Washington, Robert (1976), "The Effectiveness of Advertisements Utilizing Four Types of Endorsers", *Journal of Advertising*, 5 (3) 22-24.

165. Bush, Ronald F.; Hair Jr., Joseph F.; Solomon, Paul J (1979), "Consumers' Level of Prejudice and Response to Black Models in Advertisements" *Journal of Marketing Research*, 16 (3)341-345

166. Richard E. Petty, John T. Cacioppo, David Schumann (1983), "Cntral and Peripheral Routes to Advertising Effectiveness: The Moderating Role of Involvement", *The Journal of Consumer Research*, 10 (2) 135-146.

167. Lynn R. Kahle and Pamela M. Homer (1985), "Physical Attractiveness of the Celebrity Endorser: A Social Adaptation Perspective", *The Journal of Consumer Research*, Vol.11, (4) 954-961.

168. Grant McCracken (1989), "Who is the Celebrity Endorser? Cultural Foundations of the Endorsement Process", *The Journal of Consumer Research*, 16 (3) 310-321.

169. Michael A. Kamins, Meribeth J. Brand, Stuart A. Hoeke, John C. Moe (1989), "Two-Sided versus One-Sided Celebrity Endorsements: The Impact on Advertising Effectiveness and Credibility", *Journal of Advertising*, 18 (2)4-10.

170. Michael A. Kamins (1990), "An Investigation into the "Match-up" Hypothesis in Celebrity Advertising: When Beauty May Be Only Skin Deep", *Journal of Advertising*, 19 (1)4-13.

171. Tom, Gail, Clark, Rebecca, Elmer, Laura, Grech, Edward, Masetti Jr., Joseph, Sandhar, Harmona,(1992), "The Use of Created Versus Celebrity Spokespersons in Advertisements", *Journal of Consumer Marketing*, 9 (4)45.

172. Jagdish Agrawal and Wagner A. Kamakura (1995), "The Economic Worth of Celebrity Endorsers: An Event Study Analysis", *The Journal of Marketing*, 59 (3) 56-62.

173. Goldsmith, Ronald E.; Lafferty, Barbara A.; Newell, Stephen J.(2000), "The Impact of Corporate Credibility and Celebrity Credibility on Consumer Reaction to Advertisements and Brands", *Journal of Advertising*, 29 (3)43-54.

174. Chung-kue Hsu, Daniella McDonald, (2002) "An examination on multiple celebrity endorsers in advertising", *Journal of Product & Brand Management*, 11(1), 19 – 29.

175. Marla Royne Stafford, Thomas F. Stafford (2002), "A Contingency Approach: The Effects of Spokesperson Type and Service Type on Service Advertising Perceptions", *Journal of Advertising*, 31 (2) 17-35.

176. David H. Silvera, Benedikte Austad, (2004) "Factors predicting the effectiveness of celebrity endorsement advertisements", *European Journal of Marketing*, 38 (11/12), 1509 – 1526.
177. Peck, Joann; Loken, Barbara (2004), "When Will Larger-Sized Female Models in Advertisements Be Viewed Positively? The Moderating Effects of Instructional Frame, Gender, and Need for Cognition", *Psychology & Marketing*, 21 (6) 425-442
178. Silvera, David H.; Austad, Benedikte(2004), "Factors predicting the effectiveness of celebrity endorsement advertisements", *European Journal of Marketing*, 38 (11/12), 1509-1526
179. Mark R. Forehand,Andrew Perkins(2005), "Implicit Assimilation and Explicit Contrast: A Set/Reset Model of Response to Celebrity Voice Overs", *Journal Of Consumer Research*, 32 45-56.
180. Baird, Amy L.; Grieve, Frederick G (2006), "Exposure to Male Models in Advertisements Leads to a Decrease in Men's Body Satisfaction", *North American Journal of Psychology*,Vol.8, no.1, p115-121
181. Beomjoon Choi, Crandall, Christian S (2008), "Permission to be Prejudiced: Legitimacy Credits in the Evaluation of Advertisements with Black and White Models", *Advances in Consumer Research - North American Conference Proceedings*, 35, 724-725
182. Chan, Kara; Prendergast, Gerard P. (2008), "Social comparison, imitation of celebrity models and materialism among Chinese youth." *International Journal of Advertising*, 27(5) 799-826.
183. Johnson, G. D.(2009), "The social dimension of multi-racial advertising: Its impact on consumers' attitude", *South African Journal of Business Management*, 40 (2) 45-52.
184. Luther,Catherine A (2009), "Importance Placed on Physical Attractiveness and Advertisement-Inspired Social Comparison Behavior Among Japanese Female and Male Teenagers.", *Journal of Communication*, 59 (2) 279-295.
185. Micu, Camelia C, Coulter, Robin A, Price, Linda L (2009), "How Product Trial Alters the Effects of Model Attractiveness", *Journal of Advertising*, 38 (2) 69-81.
186. Henry Petroski; Henry Petroski (1986), "Dress For Success: The Dust Jacket As Art, Advertisement And Nuisance", *New York Times Book Review*, 21.
187. Bush, Alan J.; Bush, Victoria Davies (1994), "The Narrative Paradigm as a Perspective for Improving Ethical Evaluations of Advertisements", *Journal of Advertising*, 23 (3) 31-41.
188. Anusorn Singhapakdi, Mohammed Y.A. Rawwas, Janet K. Marta, Mohd Ismail Ahmed (1999), "A cross-cultural study of consumer perceptions about marketing ethics", *Journal of Consumer Marketing*, 16 (3) 257-272.
189. David S. Waller (1999), "Attitudes towards offensive advertising: an Australian study", *Journal of Consumer Marketing*, 16 (3) 288 – 295.
190. Kim Shyan Fam, David S. Waller, B. Zafer Erdogan (2004), "The influence of religion on attitudes towards the advertising of controversial products" *European Journal of Marketing*, 38 (5/6) 537 – 555.
191. Svante Andersson, Anna Hedelin, Anna Nilsson, Charlotte Welander (2004), "Violent advertising in fashion marketing", Journal of Fashion Marketing and Management, 8 (1)96 – 112.

192. Deborah Y. Cohn (2005), "Current Ethical Dilemmas of Advertising Professionals", *Research in Ethical Issues in Organizations*, 6, 149 – 168.

193. Robert J. Fisher, Laurette Dubé (2005), "Gender Differences in Responses to Emotional Advertising: A Social Desirability Perspective", *Journal of Consumer Research*, 31,107-114.

194. Kyoko Fukukawa, Christine Ennew, Steve Diacon (2006), "An Eye for an Eye: Investigating the Impact of Consumer Perception of Corporate Unfairness on Aberrant Consumer Behavior", *Research in Ethical Issues in Organizations*, 7 187-221.

195. McMenemy, David (2006), "What Would You Do?: Reflecting on the Importance of Ethical Values in Librarianship", *Journal of the Career Development Group*, 9 (4) 71-73.

196. Gunne Grankvist, Hans Lekedal, Maarit Marmendal (2007), "Values and eco- and fair-trade labelled products", *British Food Journal*, 109 (2) 169 – 181.

197. Jakob Nielsen (2007), "Ethical Aspects of Internet Advertising", *Library & Information Update*, 6 (11) 10-10.

198. S.Mercia Selva Malar, (2008), "The "ethics" of being profit focused", *Social Responsibility Journal*, 4 (1/2) 136 – 142.

199. Terje I. Vaaland, Morten Heide, Kjell Grønhaug (2008), "Corporate social responsibility: investigating theory and research in the marketing context", *European Journal of Marketing*, 42 (9/10) 927 – 953.

200. Gerard Prendergast, Po-yan Liu, Derek T.Y. Poon (2009), "A Hong Kong study of advertising credibility", *Journal of Consumer Marketing*, 26 (5) 320 – 329.

3

Profile of the Study Area

History of Tiruchirappalli District

Woraiyur, a part of present day Tiruchirappalli, was the capital city of Cholas from 300 B.C. onwards. This is supported by archaeological evidences and ancient literatures. There are also literary sources which tell that Woraiyur continued to be under the control of Cholas even during the days of Kalabhra interregnum (A.D. 300 - 575).

Later, Woraiyur along with the present day Tiruchirappalli and its neighboring areas came under the control of Mahendra Varma Pallava I, who ascended the throne in A.D. 590. Till A.D. 880, according to the inscriptions, this region was under the hegemony of either the Pallvas or the Pandyas. It was in A.D. 880, Aditya Chola brought a downfall to the Pallava dynasty. From that time onwards Tiruchirappalli and its region became a part of Greater Cholas. In A.D. 1225 the area was occupied by the Hoysulas. Afterwards, it came under the rule of later Pandyas till the advent of Mughal Rule.

Tiruchirappalli was for some time under the Mughal rule, which was put to an end by the Vijayanagar rulers. The Nayaks, the Governors of Vijayanagar empire, ruled this area till A.D. 1736. It was Viswanatha Nayaka who built the present day Teppakulam and the Fort. The Nayak dynasty came to an end during the days of Meenakshi.

The Muslims ruled this region again with the aid of either the French or the English armies. For some years, Tiruchirappalli was under the rule of Chanda Sahib and Mohamed Ali. Finally the English brought Tiruchirappalli and other areas under their control. Soon after the area was ceded to East India Company as per the agreement at the eve of the Karnatic war, Tiruchirappalli district was formed under the Collectorship of Mr. John (Junior) Wallace in 1801. The district was then under the hegemony of British about 150 years till the day of independence of India.

Geographical Position		
	North Latitude	Between 10′ to 11-30′
	East Longitude	Between 77-45′ to 78-50′
Area and Population		
(i)	**Area (Sq.Km.)**	**4,403.83**
	2001 Census	
(ii)	**Population**	**24,18.366**
	(*a*) Male Population	12,08,534
	(*b*) Female Population	12,09,832
	(*c*) Rural Population	12,79,204
	(*d*) Urban Population	11,39,162
(iii)	**Density (Sq.km)**	**549**
(iv)	**Literates**	**16,73,478**
(v)	**Main Workers**	
	(*a*) Total Workers	10,64,521
	(*b*) Male Workers	6,87,814
	(*c*) Female Workers	3,76,707
	(*d*) Rural Workers	6,71,320

List of Educational Institutions in Trichy

Being considered as an educational city, Tiruchirapalli has schools and colleges that are hundreds of years old. College Road in Chatram has three colleges and five schools. It is worthwhile to note that the 'Former President of India' Dr. A.P.J. Abdul Kalam and writer Sujatha Rangarajan (Rangarajan) studied at St. Joseph's College in the city. Also, another 'Former President of India' R. Venkataraman studied at National College here.

Universities

- Anna University, Trichy
- Bharathidasan University
- National Institute of Technology, Trichy
- Prist University, Trichy Campus
- Periyar Maniammai University, Trichy Campus
- SRM University, Trichy Campus
- SASTRA University, Thanjavur- Trichy Border

Engineering colleges

- M.A.M. College of Engineering
- C.A.R.E. School of Engineering

- Cauvery College of Engineering and Technology
- Imayam College of Engineering
- Indra Ganesan College of Engineering
- J.J. College of Engineering and Technology
- Jayaram College of Engineering and Technology
- Kurinji College of Engineering and Technology
- K.Ramakrishnan College of Engineering
- Kongunadu College of Engineering and Technol
- Anna University, Trichy (Formerly Bharathidasan Institute of Technology)
- M.A.M. College of Engineering & Technology
- Mount Zion College of Engineering and Technology
- M.I.E.T Engineering College
- Mookambigai College of Engineering
- National Institute of Technology, Trichy(Formerly known as REC - Regional Engineering College)
- Oxford Engineering College
- Paventhar Bharathidasan College of Engineering and Technology
- Pavendar Bharathidasan Institute of Information Technology
- Prist University, Trichy Campus
- SRM University, Trichy Campus(From 2009)
- Saranathan College of Engineering
- Shri Angalamman College of Engineering & Technology
- Sudharsan Engineering college
- SASTRA University
- School of Advanced Engineering and Information Technology
- Shivani Engineering College
- Shivani Institute of Technology
- Samboorna Institute of Engineering and Technology
- The Selvam Women Excellence Engineering Technology
- Trichy Engineering College
- Trichy Institute of Engineering and Technology
- Vetri Vinayaha College of Engineering and Technology

Arts & Science Colleges

- Aiman College of Arts and Science for Women
- Bishop Heber College
- Cauvery College for Women

- Chettinad College of Arts and Science
- Chidambaram Pillai College of Women
- Christhu Raj College
- Government Arts college
- Holy Cross College
- Jamal Mohamed College
- Kalai Kaviri College of Fine Arts
- Kurinji Arts and Science College
- M.I.E.T. College of Arts and Science
- National College
- Nehru Memorial College
- Pavendar Bharadhidasan Arts and Science College
- Periyar E.V.R. College
- School of Quality Management
- Seethalakshmi Ramaswami College
- Shrimathi Indira Gandhi College
- Sri Sankara School of Management and Comp. Science
- Srimad Andavan Arts and Science College
- Srimad Andavan Sanskrit College
- St. Josephs College
- SRM University, Trichy Campus(From 2009)
- Tranquebar Bishop Manickam Lutheran (T.B.M.L) College
- Urumu Dhanalakshmi College

Management Colleges

- Indian Institute of Management (IIM),Trichy {From 2010}
- Bharathidasan Institute of Management(BIM)
- DoMS,NIT,TRICHY
- Anna University,Trichy
- Bharathidasan University
- Hall Mark B School
- Jamal Institute of Management
- Bishop Heber College
- St.Josheph Institute of Management
- Saranathan College
- JJ College of Engg & Technology
- And Trichy has nearly 38 institutes offering MBA programme

Polytechnic Colleges

- Dhanalakshmi Srinivasan Polytechnic College, Perambalur
- Government Polytechnic College
- Infant Jesus Polytechnic College
- Lalgudi Co-operative Polytechnic College
- M.A.M Polytechnic College
- M.I.E.T. Polytechnic College
- N. Ramasamy Iyer Memorial Polytechnic College.trichy
- Sri Adhisankarar Polytechnic College
- Seshasayee Institute of Technology
- Shivani Polytechnic College (Formerly JJ Polytechnic)
- Trichi Selvom's women Polytechnic College
- Thanthai Roever Institute of Polytechnic College, Perambalur.
- Periyar Centenary Polytechnic College, Vallam, Thanjavurdistrict

Medicine Colleges

- K.A.P.V. Govt. Medical College(TAMILNADU DR.MGR UNIVERSITY)
- Chennai Medical College Hospital and Research Centre (CMCH&RC)(dr.mgr medical university)

Dental Colleges

- Rajas dental college (Sofia dental college)

Nursing Colleges

- Child Jesus College of Nursing
- Dr.G.Sakunthala College of Nursing
- Dhanalakshmi Srinivasan College of Nursing, Perambalaur
- Indira College of Nursing
- Nehru College of Nursing
- Sardar Rajas College of Nursing
- Servite College of Nursing
- Thanthai Roever College of Nursing, Perumbalur
- Periyar College of Nursing

Pharmacy Colleges

- Periyar College of Pharmaceutical Sciences for Girls
- Trichy college of Pharmacy
- GVN Institute of Paramedical Sciences
- Periyar Maniyammai Paramedical College

Physiotherapy Colleges

- Thanthai Roever College of Physiotherapy , Perambalur
- Kamalam Viswanathan College of Physiotherapy, Trichy.
- Government College of Physiotherapy (GCP)

Ophthalmology Colleges

- St. Joseph's Institute of Ophthalmology

Agriculture Colleges

- Anbil Dharmalingam Agricultural College and Research Institute
- Agricultural Engineering College and Research Institute

Hotel Management Colleges

- Arasan Institute of Hotel Management and Catering Technology
- JENNEYS ACADEMY
- Sree Balaji Institute of Hotel Management and Catering
- SRM Institute of Hotel Management
- Sri Adhisankarar Institute of Hotel Management and Catering Technology
- State Institute of Hotel Management and Catering Technology
- V.J.P. College of Catering and Hotel Management

College of Legal Studies

- The Government Law College, Tiruchirapalli, founded in 1979.

Schools

The Notable ones include:

- Alpha Cambridge international school (ICSE)
- Alpha Plus Matriculation School
- Alpha Wisdom Vidyashram, KK Nagar (CBSE)
- A.K.K.V.Aarunadu matriculation school.
- Arockiyamatha matriculation school
- Aurobindo Public School
- BHEL Matriculation School
- Bishop Heber College higher secondary School, Teppakulam
- Bishop Heber College higher secondary School, Puttur
- Boiler Plant Boys Higher Secondary School
- Boiler Plant girls Higher Secondary School
- Brindavan Vidyalaya - ICSE School
- Campion Anglo-Indian Higher Secondary School
- Cauvery matriculation school

- Chinmaya vidhyalaya (CBSE)
- Crea academy School
- Dhanalakshmi Srinivasan matriculation school
- E.R. Higher Secondary School
- Good Shepherd matriculation school.
- Government Girls Hr. Sec. School
- Government Industrial Training Institute
- Government School for Boys and Girls
- Holycross higher secondary school
- Infant Jesus Middle School,Kajamalai
- Jaihind Internationl School (IGCSE)
- Jayendra matriculation school
- Jegen Matha matriculation school
- Jessie Matriculation Hr. Sec. School
- JMC AYESHA MATRICULATION SCHOOL for Girls.
- Joan of Arc international school (ICSE)
- Kajamian Higher Secondary School
- Kamakoti Vidyalaya (ICSE)
- Kamala Niketan school (CBSE)
- K.A.P. Vishwanatham higher secondary School (KAPV Higher Secondary School)
- Karpaga Vinayagar matriculation school
- Kendriya Vidhyalaya (CBSE)
- Khajamian higher secondaery school
- Mahatma Gandhi Higher Secondary School(CBSE)
- Monfort School(CBSE)
- National College higher secondary School
- Nehru matriculation School
- Orchard Matriculation School, KK Nagar
- Padmabhushan Sri N. Ramaswami Ayyar Memorial Polytechnic for Girls
- Periyar Centenary Memorial Matriculation Higher Secondary School
- Railway Mixed High School
- Rajaji Vidhyalaya, Thennur (CBSE)
- R.C. higher secondary school
- Rockfort Matriculation Higher Secondary School
- RSK Higher Secondary School (CBSE)

- Savithri Vidyasala Hindu Girls' Higher Secondary School
- SBIOA Higher Secondary school
- Seva Sangam girls higher secondary school
- Seventh-day Adventist Higher Secondary School
- Sri Akhilandeswari Secondary and Higher School (CBSE)
- Sri Akilandeswari Vidyalaya(CBSE)
- Srimathi Indira Gandhi College
- Higher Secondary School for Boys, Srirangam
- Srirangam Girls' Higher Secondary School
- Sri Renga matriculation School
- Sri Sivananda Balalaya (CBSE)
- St Anne's girls higher secondary school
- St Antonys Matriculation School
- St James Matriculation Hr. Sec. School
- St Johns Vestry Anglo Indian Higher Secondary School
- St. Joseph's Anglo-Indian Girls Higher Secondary School
- St. Little Flower Matriculation HSS
- SRV Matriculation Higher Secondary School Samayapuram
- SVV higher secondary school
- Tiny Tots Montessori School
- Tower Matriculation School
- Vaijaynti vidhyalaya (CBSE)
- Vailankanni Raj Matriculation Hr. Sec. School
- Y.W.C.A Matriculation School
- Sri Vageesha Vidhyashram, Srirangam. (CBSE)
- Sacred heart boys higher secondary school, Ponmalaipatti

Profile of Periyar E.V.R. College Trichy

In the year 1965, the Government of Tamilnadu Started Periyar EVR College in Tiruchirappalli. The first ever development of the college was marked by the immediate acquisition of additional land making it an expansive campus of 52.62 acres. Then came up gradually the classrooms, laboratories and hostel one after the other, consequent to the steadily swelling student strength.

Profile of St. Joseph's College (Autonomous)

The One hundred and sixty years old St Joseph's College, which was founded at Nagapattinam with one student in 1844 by the Fathers of Society of Jesus (The Jesuits) even before the establishment of the

University of Madras in 1858, was later shifted to Tiruchirappalli in 1883. The Jesuits are one among the many religious orders of the Catholic Church dedicated exclusively to the cause of Higher Education at a global level. The College is located in the central part of Tamil Nadu, easily accessible by road, rail and air, with the present strength of students numbering about 6000 studying in 12 under-graduate, 19 postgraduate and 12 research departments.

True to its motto, Pro Bono et Vero (for Good and Truth), the Sesquicentenarian St Joseph's College always upheld and radiated Goodness and Truth in its endeavour to impart qualitative higher education. This educational establishment has been instrumental in churning out thousands of truly educated men; not only physically fit, but intellectually well equipped; not merely cultured and refined but thoroughly schooled and disciplined. Thus this College stands for what is best in education as its ideal, crystallized in its glorious motto 'Pro Bono et Vero' - truly upholding the glory and honour it richly deserves, testified by time and history.

St Joseph's College has produced a number of rare and remarkable geniuses of whom the crown is the present President of India, His Excellency Dr A P J Abdul Kalam. St Joseph's takes genuine pride to place on record a few of the vast number of luminaries who had received their education in this College. Dr C V Narasimhan, former Under Secretary General, UNO, Dr K Venkatasubramanian, Member, Union Planning Commission, Government of India, Mr N Gopalasamy, Secretary, Ministry of Home Affairs, Government of India, Justice A R Lakshmanan, Supreme Court Judge, Most Rev. Dr Peter Fernando DD, Archbishop of Madurai, Most Rev. Dr M Casimir SJ, Former Archbishop of Madras-Mylapore also of Madurai, Rev. Dr M Amaladas SJ, Former General Assistant, Rome and Rev. Fr Julian Fernandez SJ, General Assistant, Rome, Mr A X Alexander IPS ADGP, Mr Vijaya Kumar IPS, Commissioner of Police, Chennai are some of the eminent dignitaries from this Alma mater. Freedom fighters, Ministers of the Centre and State, Members of the Legislative Councils, Army officers, Scientists, Journalists, Industrialists, Ambassadors, Advisors to the Government, Vice-Chancellors and Religious dignitaries form the illustrious alumni of this College. Shri Bala Gangathara Thilagar, Shri Rabindra Nath Tagore, Pandit Jawaharlal Nehru, Shri Rajagopalachariar, Smt Indhira Gandhi, Shri K Kamaraj, Shri C N Annadurai, were the popular visitors to this College among other notable persons from India and abroad.

St Joseph's College is affiliated First Grade College to Bharathidasan University, Tiruchirappalli. It celebrated its centenary in 1944, sesquicentenary in 1995, attained Autonomous status in 1978 and was accredited with Five Stars by NAAC in 2000. The College has excellent library and laboratory facilities and a well-connected Computer Centre with more than 200 systems. The campus is networked with Intranet facilities with the latest computers. The first department of St Joseph's recognized to carry out research leading to PhD degree was Chemistry in 1965, followed by Physics in 1971, Botany and Economics in 1976, English and History in 1982, Tamil in 1986, Human Resource Development in 1987, Mathematics in 1988, Computer Science in 1992, Commerce in 1998, and Statistics in 2001. At present, the College is offering full time research programmes leading to MPhil and PhD, both in arts and science subjects and so serving the society at large promoting research and development.

Holy Cross College (Autonomous)

Holy Cross College has a magnificent history. It was started for the benefit of the young girls of Trichy as early as 1923 when higher education for women was considered almost a transgression against the age-old respected customs and Indian ideas concerning higher education for girls. The College rose to its present position as a first grade College from humble beginnings.

Started as a primary school in 1901 in St. Mary's Thope, Tiruchirapalli.It became a lower secondary school in 1902. After a short while the School was shifted to Main Bazaar Road and raised to a High School in 1905. In the years that followed, there was a growing public demand for a college for Women in Trichy, as there was then no such institution in this part of the province, South of Madras City. In response to that demand it was raised to the status of a second grade College affiliated to the University of Madras in 1923. The College was elevated to the full status of a first grade College in 1933.

In 1964, the College was raised to the status of a post graduate college. With the birth of the Bharathidasan University in the year 1982, the College was separated from the parental University of Madras and was affiliated to the Bharathidasan University. This opened out avenues for the College to expand its dimensions. The college was proud of starting a Vocational Degree Course with Rehabilitation Science in 1983-84. The year 1983, the Diamond Jubilee Year saw the completion of 60 years of devoted and selfless work of the Sisters of the Cross of Chavanod, its Principals, staff and students and well-wishers.

In recognition of its services to the cause of women's education for over six decades, the college was granted autonomous status from June 1987. The attainment of autonomous status in 1987 ushered in a new era of academic freedom for Holy Cross College. Under autonomy the College expanded its scale of operation by commencing several new self-financed programmes and restructured some of the aided programmes to make the courses socially relevant and job oriented.

The college which started with five students and five staff members, has grown from strength to strength. Academic excellence, value based education, highly motivated teaching and supportive staff, well planned, socially oriented, extensive outreach programmes and outstanding performances in sports, games and fine arts are unique features of Holy Cross College.

The Platinum Jubilee year (1998) - the college is proud to have been accreditted with FIVE STAR, status by National Assessment and Accreditation Council.

In the new millennium as the College marches towards a century of its establishment the emphasis will be towards coping with international global trends in the field of Higher Education. As an accredited Institution the College will be for International linkages through student and staff exchange programmes to ensure that, the curriculum is being re-modified to accommodate a choice based credit system. A full-fledged and multidisciplinary research department in women studies and an extension department based on Sisters of the Cross of Society for Education and Development (SOC-SEAD) are being planned to meet the requirements of advanced centres of excellence.

On the sands of time, we have successfully completed 77 years of fruitful service to the cause of women's education. With a profound sense of gratitude to the Creator, the Originator of every great achievement, we march towards the new century.

Profile of Cauvery College for Women

Cauvery College for women one of the first self-financing colleges started in the year 1984-85 is run by Reddy Educational Trust which is a temple of learning and always provides a chance to grow in all spheres of life. Cauvery College is completing 25 academic years of its service to women's education and she realizes more than ever that, nothing meaningful can be achieved unless women receive a multifaceted training to prepare them, to take up their crucial role in the society. We march towards it, counting on the strength and sustenance of the Divine Guidance, with the vision and special concern of the members of the trust, spiritual strength and humanitarian support of all the parents as well as the well wishers of this college. The Trust members are 48 in number who are enlightened and interested citizens of Trichy District and have a philanthropic outlook with noble and progressive ideals. This prestigious institution aims for excellence in Education wherein we have opened our portals to many first generation learners and students from rural areas to varied branches of study.

Profile of Srimad Andavan College

This co-educational college was started on 26th Oct 1996 Dr. Shankar Dayal Sharma, former President of India and is affiliated to the

Bharathidasan University. Managed by a group of eminent educationalists and industrialists the institution constantly attracts a beeline of students by its innovative programmes, teaching and learning strategies. The Management, principal and the staff strive with a missionary zeal in making every individual exemplary and informative in his / her chosen field of study.

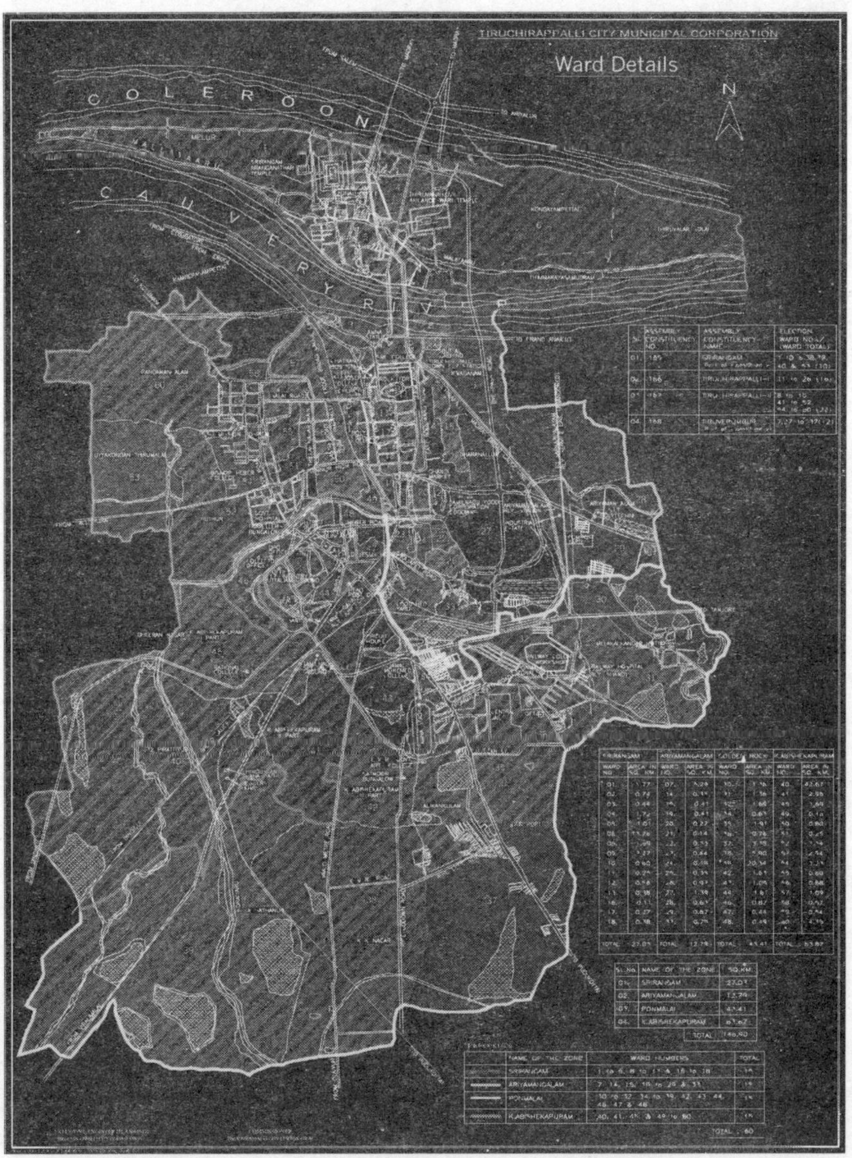

Tiruchirappalli Municipal Corporation Map

REFERENCES

1. www.trichy.co.in accessed on 2nd November 2009.
2. www.tn.co.in accessed on 2nd November 2009.
3. www.periyarevrcollege.org accessed on 15th November 2009.
4. www.sjctni.edu accessed on 15th November 2009.
5. www.holycrosscedu.org accessed on 8th January 2010.
6. www.cauverycollege.ac.in accessed on 8th January 2010.
7. www.andavancollege.ac.in accessed on 10th January 2010.

4

Analysis and Interpretation on Collected Data from the Opinion-Leaders

Table 4.1: Distribution of the Respondents by their Age

Sl.No.	Age group	Frequency	Percent
1.	18-20 years	1	1.3
2.	21-25 years	8	10.7
3.	26-30 years	14	18.7
4.	31-35 years	18	24.0
5.	36-40 years	7	9.3
6.	Above 40	27	36.0
	Total	75	100.0

Source: Primary Data

Among the 75 respondents, only one was belonging to the age group of 18 20 years, eight were belonging to 21-25 years, 14 were belonging to 26-30 years, 18 were belonging to 31-35 years, seven were belonging to 36-40 years and the remaining 27 were belonging to above 40 years of age.

In other words, one point three per cent of the respondent was belonging to the age group of 18-20 years, 10.7 per cent of the respondent were belonging to 21-25 years, 18.7 per cent of the respondent were belonging to 26-30 years, 24 per cent of the respondent were belonging to 31-35 years, nine point three per cent of the respondent were belonging to 36-40 years and the remaining 36 per cent of the respondent were belonging to above 40 years of age.

It was observed that majority (36 per cent) of the respondents were above 40 years of age.

Among the total respondents, 64 respondents were male and the remaining 11 respondents were female. In other words 85.3 per cent of the respondents were male and the remaining 14.7 per cent of the respondents

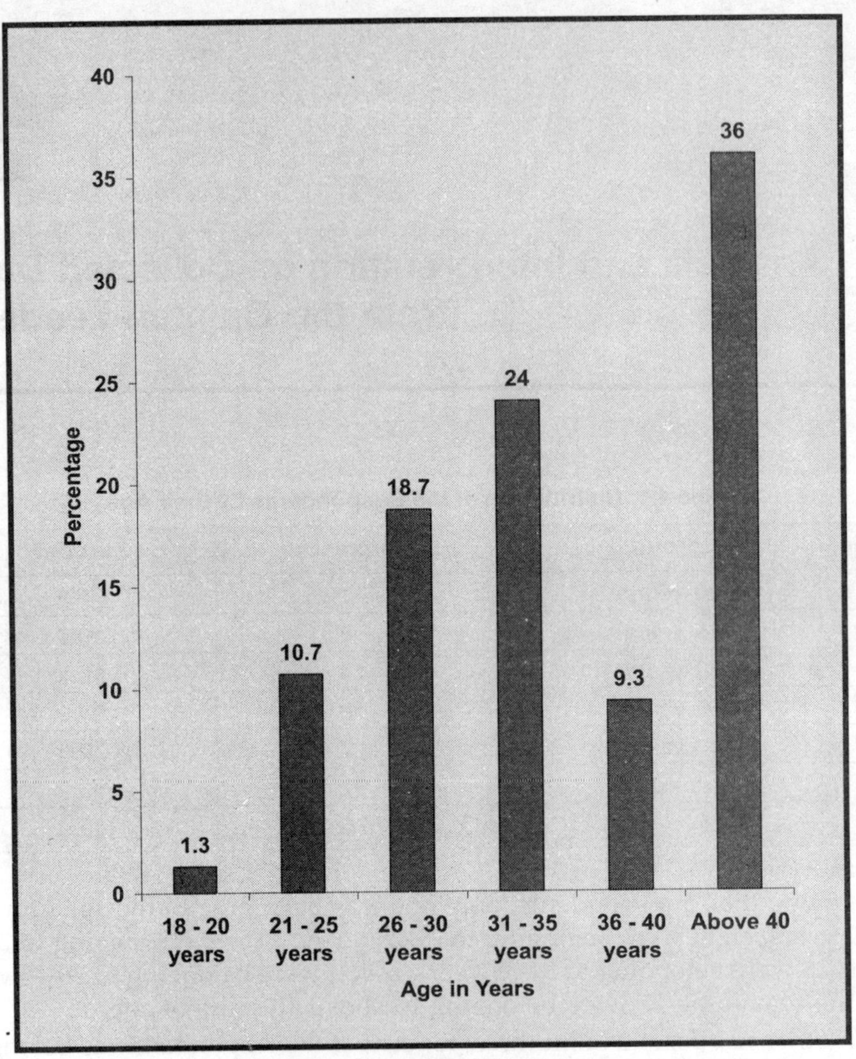

Chart 4.1 : Distribution of the respondents by their Age

were female. It is found out that majority (85.3 per cent) of the respondents were male.

Table 4.2: Distribution of the respondents by their Sex-wise

Sl.No.	Sex	Frequency	Percent
1.	Male	64	85.3
2.	Female	11	14.7
	Total	75	100.0

Source: Primary Data.

Table 4.3: Distribution of the Respondents by Occupation-wise

Sl.No.	Occupation	Frequency	Percent
1.	Acting	4	5.2
2.	Music Director	3	4.0
3.	Journalist	3	4.0
4.	Engineers	5	6.7
5.	Doctors	5	6.7
6.	Lawyers	5	6.7
7.	Principals	5	6.7
8.	Others	45	60.0
	Total	75	100.0

Source: Primary Data.

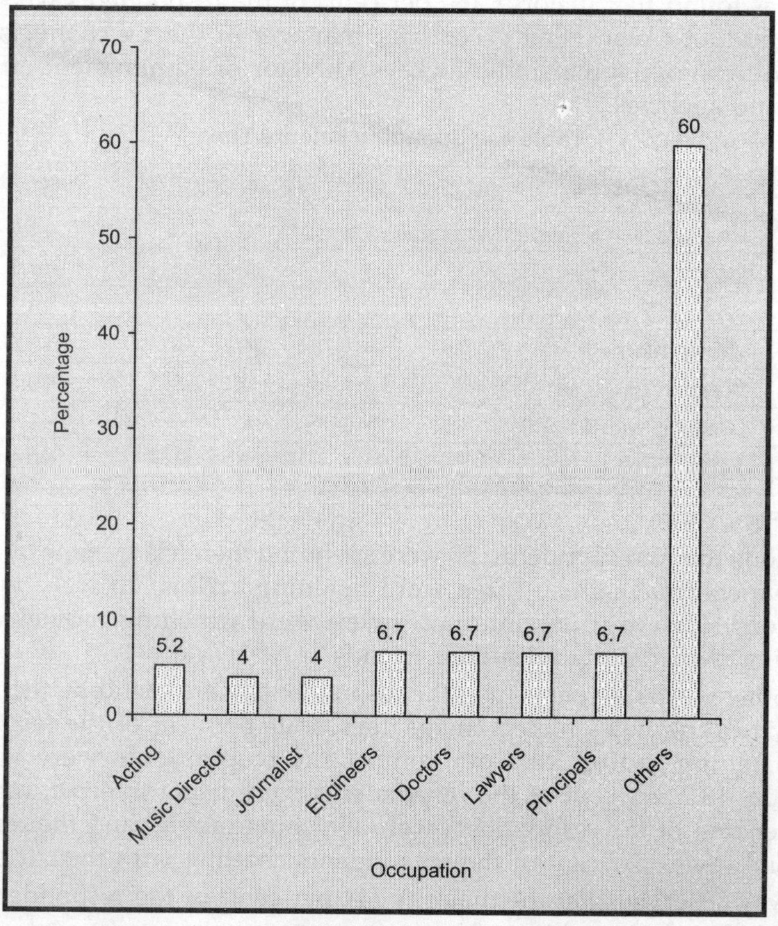

Chart 4.2 : Distribution of the respondents by their Occupation-wise

Among the total number of respondents four were actors, three were music directors, three were journalist, five were engineers, five were doctors, five were lawyers, five were college principals and the remaining 45 respondents were others namely auditors, marketing executives, manager of the TV channels, Radio station directors, popular radio jockeys, director of employment office and advertising agencies.

In other words, five point two per cent of the respondents were actors, four per cent of the respondents were music directors, another four per cent of the respondents were journalist, six point seven per cent were engineers, six point seven per cent were doctors, six point seven per cent were lawyers, six point seven per cent were college principals and the remaining 60 per cent of the respondents were others namely auditors, marketing executives, manager of the TV channels, Radio station directors, popular radio jockeys, director of employment office and advertising agencies.

It was found that majority (60 per cent) of the respondents were others namely auditors, marketing executives, manager of the TV channels, Radio station directors, popular radio jockeys, director of employment office and advertising agencies.

Table 4.4: Spending Leisure Time

Sl.No.	Leisure	Frequency	Percent
1.	Reading News paper/Magazine	33	44.0
2.	Listening to Radio	3	4.0
3.	Watching Television	20	26.7
4.	Using Internet	10	13.3
5.	Watching Movies	7	9.3
6.	Chatting with Friends	2	2.7
	Total	75	100.0

Source: Primary Data.

Among the 75 respondents, 33 were spending their leisure time by reading news papers/magazines, three were listening radios, 20 were watching television, 10 were using internet, seven were watching movies and the remaining two chatting with their friends.

In other words, 44 per cent of the respondents were spending their leisure time by reading news papers/magazines, four per cent of the respondents were listening radios, 26.7 per cent of the respondents were watching television, 13.3 per cent of the respondents were using internet, nine point three per cent of the respondents were watching movies and the remaining two point seven per cent of the respondents chatting with their friends.

It was observed that the majority (44 per cent) of the respondents were spending their by watching television.

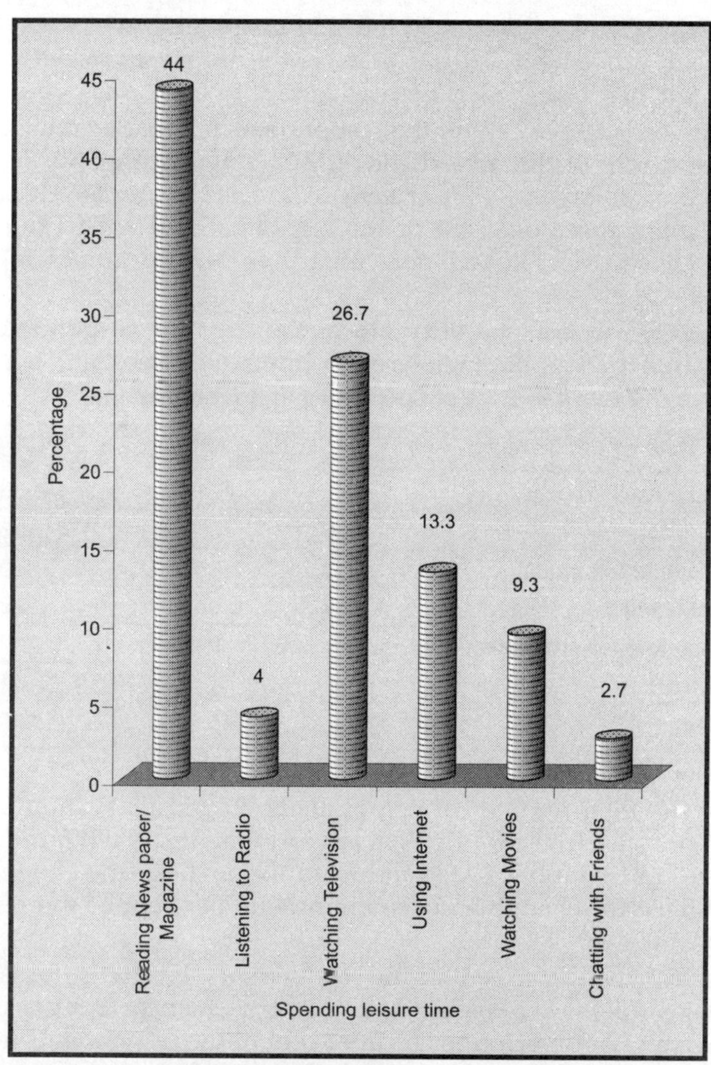

Chart 4.3 : Spending Leisure Time

Table 4.5: The Role of Advertisement

Sl.No.	Role of Advertisement	Frequency	Percent
1.	Create Awareness	36	48.0
2.	Create Lifestyle	10	13.3
3.	Create New wants	26	34.7
4.	Foundation of Civilisation	1	1.3
5.	Survive Democracy	2	2.7
	Total	75	100.0

Source: Primary Data

Among the 75 respondents, 36 felt that create awareness was the major role of the advertisement, 10 felt that create life style, 26 felt create new wants, one felt that foundation of civilization, two felt survive democracy.

In other words 48 per cent of the respondents felt that creating awareness was the major role of the advertisement, 13.3 per cent of the respondents felt that create life style, 34.7 per cent of the respondents felt create new wants, one point three per cent of the respondents felt that foundation of civilization, two point seven per cent of the respondents felt survive democracy.

It was observed that majority (48 percent) of the respondent felt that creating awareness was the major role of the advertisement.

Table 4.6: Role of Celebrities in Advertisements

Sl.No.	Role of Celebraties	Frequency	Percent
1.	Stimulate Interest	27	36.0
2.	Fair Description	10	13.3
3.	Truthful Information	8	10.7
4.	Inducted to purchase	20	26.7
5.	Suggest for change	9	12.0
6.	Others	1	1.3
	Total	75	100.0

Source: Primary Data.

Among the total number of respondents, 27 felt that stimulate interest was the major role of the celebrities in advertisements, 10 felt fair description, 8 felt truthful information, 20 felt inducted to purchase and the remaining 9 felt that suggest for change and remaining one per cent of the respondents felt that for improving the sales.

In other words, 36 per cent of the respondents felt that stimulate interest was the major role of the celebrities in advertisements, 13.3 per cent of the respondents felt fair description, 10.7 per cent of the respondents felt truthful information, 26.7 per cent of the respondents felt inducted to purchase and the remaining 12 per cent of the respondents felt that suggest for change and remaining one point seven per cent of the respondents felt that improving the sales.

It was found that majority (36 per cent) of the respondents felt that inducted to purchase was the major role of the celebrities in advertisements

Among the 75 respondents 12 respondents felt that they will use their celebrity influence to become popularize the cosmetics products, nine felt food, seven felt sports items, six felt that the automobile products, five felt that textile materials, 14 felt that medicine, 14 felt that electronic products and remaining eight felt that the other items such as jewelry and mobile phones.

Table 4.7: Using the Celebrities Influence for which Product to become Familiarize

Sl.No.	Products	Frequency	Percent
1.	Cosmetics	12	16.0
2.	Food	9	12.0
3.	Sports	7	9.3
4.	Automobiles	6	8.0
5.	Textile	5	6.7
6	Medicine	14	18.7
7.	Electronic Products	14	18.7
8.	Others	8	10.7
	Total	75	100.0

Source: Primary data.

In other words 16 per cent respondents felt that they will use their celebrity influence to become popularize the cosmetics products, twelve per cent felt food items, nine point three per cent felt sports items, eight per cent felt that the automobile products, six point seven per cent felt that textile materials, 18.7 per cent felt that medicine, 18.7 felt that electronic products and remaining 10.7 per cent felt that the other items such as jewelry and mobile phones

It was found out that the majority (18.7 per cent) felt that using their celebrities influence to become familiarize the medicine and electronic products.

Table 4.8: The Most Appealing Areas in Television Advertisement

Sl.No.	Attractive Parts	Frequency	Percent
1.	Lasting Impression	7	9.3
2.	Theme	11	14.7
3.	Sound Effect	4	5.3
4.	Celebrities	4	5.3
5.	Innovativeness	34	45.3
6.	Relevance	2	2.7
7.	Over All Effects	12	16.0
8.	Others	1	1.3
	Total	75	100.0

Source: Primary Data.

Among the total number of respondents, seven were consider that the lasting impression was the most appealing area in Television advertisement, 11 were consider the theme, four were consider the sound effect, four were consider the celebrities, 34 were consider the innovativeness, two were consider the relevance, 12 were consider the over all effects and the remaining one was consider the other factor like slogan.

In other words nine point three per cent of the respondents were consider that the lasting impression was the most appealing area in T.V. advertisement, 14.7 per cent of the respondents were consider the theme, five point three per cent of the respondents were consider the sound effect, five point three were consider the celebrities, 45.3 per cent of the respondents were consider the innovativeness, two point seven per cent of the respondents were consider the relevance, 16 per cent of the respondents were consider the over all effects and the remaining one point three per cent of the respondent was consider the other factor namely slogan.

It was observed that majority (45.3 per cent) of the respondents were consider the innovativeness was the most appealing area in Television advertisements.

Table 4.9: Opinion regarding the Features of the Advertisement

Sl.No.	Particulars		Strongly agree	Somewhat agree	Neither agree/ disagree	Strongly disagree	Somewhat disagree
			(n:75)	(n:75)	(n:75)	(n:75)	(n:75)
1.	The advertisement message is understandable	Frequency	33	34	3	3	2
		Percentage	44.0	45.3	4.0	4.0	2.7
2.	The advertisement is believable	Frequency	12	34	8	13	8
		Percentage	16.0	45.3	10.7	17.3	10.7
3.	The benefit described in the advertisement are believable to me	Frequency	7	38	15	12	3
		Percentage	9.3	50.7	20.0	16.0	4.0
4.	After acting/ watching this advertisement I would consider purchasing the product	Frequency	8	35	17	8	7
		Percentage	10.7	46.7	22.7	10.7	9.3
5.	This advertisement is much better than other advertisement for this product category	Frequency	14	38	12	6	5
		Percentage	18.7	50.7	16.0	8.0	6.7

Source: Primary data.

Among the total number of respondents 44.0 per cent had strongly agreed that the advertisement messages were understandable. 45.3 per cent had some what agreed, four point zero per cent was in neither agree/disagree position, four point zero had strongly disagreed and remaining two point seven per cent were somewhat disagree of this factor.

Among the total number of respondents 16.0 per cent had strongly agreed that the advertisement is believable. 45.3 per cent had some what agreed, 10.7 per cent were in neither agree/disagree position, 17.3 per cent had strongly disagreed and remaining 10.7 per cent were somewhat disagree of this factor.

Among the total number of respondents nine point three per cent had strongly agreed that the benefits described in the advertisement are believable. 50.7 per cent had some what agreed, 20.0 per cent was in neither agree/ disagree position, 16.0 had strongly disagreed and remaining four point zero per cent were somewhat disagree of this factor.

Table 4.10: Opinion regarding the Evaluation of the Product Advertisement

Sl.No.	Particulars		Strongly agree (n:75)	Somewhat agree (n:75)	Neither (n:75)	Strongly disagree (n:75)	Somewhat disagree (n:75)
1.	Advertisement is entertaining	Frequency	26	30	5	7	7
		Percentage	34.7	40.7	6.7	9.3	9.3
2.	Claims are accurate and justified	Frequency	13	29	9	17	7
		Percentage	17.3	38.7	12.0	22.7	9.3
3.	Undesirable influence on children and youth	Frequency	30	27	9	6	3
		Percentage	40.0	36.0	12.0	8.0	4.0
4.	Advertisement product is better quality	Frequency	11	34	11	14	5
		Percentage	14.7	45.3	14.7	18.7	6.7
5.	Advertisement is misleading	Frequency	9	27	17	18	4
		Percentage	12.0	36.0	22.7	24.0	5.3
6.	Advertisement is loud and vulgar	Frequency	6	13	13	28	15
		Percentage	8.0	17.3	17.3	37.3	20.0
7.	Advertisement is useful	Frequency	29	32	3	2	9
		Percentage	38.7	45.7	4.0	2.7	12.0
8.	Advertisement should not be banned	Frequency	22	24	10	7	12
		Percentage	29.3	32.0	13.3	9.3	16.0
9.	Advertisement promote wasteful consumption and anti saving	Frequency	11	42	10	8	4
		Percentage	14.7	56.0	13.3	10.7	5.3
10.	Advertisement is unproductive expenses and waste of resources	Frequency	6	26	14	15	14
		Percentage	8.0	34.7	18.7	20.0	18.7

Source: Primary data.

Among the total number of respondents 10.7 per cent had strongly agreed that after acting/watching this advertisement they would consider purchasing the product. 46.7 per cent had some what agreed, 22.7 per cent was in neither agree/disagree position, 10.7 had strongly disagreed and remaining nine point three per cent were somewhat disagree of this factor.

Among the total number of respondents 18.7 per cent had strongly agreed that this advertisement was much better than other advertisement for that product category. 50.7 per cent had some what agreed, 16.0 per cent was in neither agree/disagree position, eight point zero had strongly disagreed and remaining six point seven per cent were somewhat disagree of this factor.

The following were the responses of the respondents regarding evaluation of the product advertisement. Among the 75 respondents 34.7 per cent had strongly agreed that the advertisement is entertaining. 40.0 per cent were some what agree, six point seven per cent were in neither agree or disagree, nine point three per cent were strongly disagree and remaining nine point three per cent were some what disagree on this factor.

Among the 75 respondents 17.3 per cent had strongly agreed that the claims are accurate and justified in advertisement. 38.7 per cent were some what agree, 12.0 per cent were in neither agree or disagree, 22.7 per cent were strongly disagree and remaining nine point three per cent were some what disagree on this factor.

Among the 75 respondents 40.0 per cent had strongly agreed that the advertisement had undesirable influence on children and youth. 36.0 per cent were some what agree, 12.0 per cent were in neither agree or disagree, eight point zero per cent were strongly disagree and remaining four point zero percent were some what disagree on this factor.

Among the 75 respondents 14.7 per cent had strongly agreed that the advertised product is better quality. 45.3 per cent were some what agree, 14.7 per cent were in neither agree or disagree, 18.7 per cent were strongly disagree and remaining six point seven per cent were some what disagree on this factor.

Among the 75 respondents 12.0 per cent had strongly agreed that the advertisement is misleading. 36.0 per cent were some what agree, 22.7 per cent were in neither agree or disagree, 24.0 per cent were strongly disagree and remaining five point three per cent were some what disagree on this factor.

Among the 75 respondents eight point zero per cent had strongly agreed that the advertisement is loud and vulgar. 17.3 per cent were some what agree, 17.3 per cent were in neither agree nor disagree, 37.3 per cent were strongly disagree and remaining 20.0 per cent were some what disagree on this factor.

Among the 75 respondents 38.7 per cent had strongly agreed that the advertisement is useful. 45.7 per cent were some what agree, four point zero per cent were in neither agree or disagree, two point seven per cent were strongly disagree and remaining 12.0 per cent were some what disagree on this factor.

Among the 75 respondents 29.3 per cent had strongly agreed that the advertisement should not be banned. 32.0 per cent were some what agree, 13.3 per cent were in neither agree or disagree, nine point three per cent were strongly disagree and remaining 16.0 per cent were some what disagree on this factor.

Among the 75 respondents 14.7 per cent had strongly agreed that the advertisement promotes wasteful consumptions and anti-saving. 56.0 per cent were some what agree, 13.3 per cent were in neither agree or disagree, 10.7 per cent were strongly disagree and remaining five point three per cent were some what disagree on this factor.

Table 4.11: Opinion on the Attitude towards Advertising

Sl.No.	Particulars		Always (n:75)	Frequently (n:75)	Occasio-nally (n:75)	Never (n:75)	Can't say (n:75)
1.	Advertisement promotes competition	Frequency	40	25	10	0	0
		Percentage	53.3	33.3	13.3	-	-
2.	Promoting sales and reducing price	Frequency	13	26	29	4	3
		Percentage	17.3	34.7	38.7	5.3	4.0
3.	Promoting mass production	Frequency	28	17	22	4	4
		Percentage	37.3	22.7	29.3	5.3	5.3
4.	Results in high price	Frequency	17	19	30	4	5
		Percentage	22.7	25.3	40.0	5.3	6.7
5.	Fast Turnover	Frequency	29	27	12	0	7
		Percentage	38.7	36.0	16.0	-	9.3
6.	Advertised products are of better quality	Frequency	5	9	26	14	21
		Percentage	6.7	12.0	34.7	18.7	28.0
7.	Helps one manufacture at the expense of another without adding to growth	Frequency	11	18	26	8	12
		Percentage	14.7	24.0	34.7	10.7	16.0
8.	Helps larger manufacturer get a strangle hold	Frequency	27	22	9	3	14
		Percentage	36.0	29.3	12.0	4.0	18.7

Source: Primary data.

Among the 75 respondents 8.0 per cent had strongly agreed that the advertisement is unproductive expenses and waste of resources. 34.7 per cent were some what agree, 18.7 per cent were in neither agree or disagree, 20.0 per cent were strongly disagree and remaining 18.7 per cent were some what disagree on this factor.

Among the total number of respondents 53.3 per cent felt that advertisement always promotes competition. 33.3 per cent felt frequently, 13.3 per cent felt occasionally.

Among the total number of respondents 17.3 per cent felt that advertising always promoting sales and reducing price. 34.7 per cent felt frequently, 38.7 per cent felt occasionally, five point three per cent felt advertisement had never promote sales and reducing the price and the remaining four point zero per cent couldn't say any thing about this factor.

Among the total number of respondents 37.3 per cent felt that advertising always promoting mass production. 22.7 per cent felt frequently, 29.3 per cent felt occasionally, five point three per cent felt advertisement had never promote mass production and the remaining five point three per cent couldn't say any thing about this factor.

Among the total number of respondents 22.7 per cent felt that advertisement gave the results always in high price. 25.3 per cent felt frequently, 40.0 per cent felt occasionally, five point three per cent felt advertisement had never result in high price and the remaining five point three per cent couldn't say any thing about this factor.

Among the total number of respondents 38.7 per cent felt that advertisements always help to fast turnover. 36.0 per cent felt frequently, 16.0 per cent felt occasionally and the remaining nine point three per cent couldn't say any thing about this factor.

Among the total number of respondents six point seven per cent felt that advertised products were always better quality. 12.0 per cent felt frequently, 34.7 per cent felt occasionally, 18.7 per cent felt advertised products never has good quality and the remaining 28.0 per cent couldn't say any thing about this factor.

Among the total number of respondents 14.7 per cent felt that advertisement always helps one manufacturer at the expenses of another without adding to growth. 24.0 per cent felt frequently, 34.7 per cent felt occasionally, 10.7 per cent felt that never advertisement help one manufacturer at the expenses of another without adding to growth and the remaining 16.0 per cent couldn't say any thing about this factor.

Among the total number of respondents 36.0 per cent felt that advertisement always helps larger manufacturer get a strong hold. 29.3 per cent felt frequently, 12.0 per cent felt occasionally, four point zero per cent felt that never the advertisement help larger manufacturer get a strong hold and the remaining 18.7 per cent couldn't say any thing about this factor.

Table 4.12: Opinion on the Unethical Practices of Advertising

Sl.No.	Particulars		More in product/ consumer advertise-ment	More in service advertise-ment	Equal in both	Not in both
			(n:75)	(n:75)	(n:75)	(n:75)
1.	False and misleading presentation of facts	Frequency	42	8	18	7
		Percentage	56.0	10.7	24.0	9.3
2.	Deliberate omitting of required information	Frequency	28	20	23	4
		Percentage	37.3	26.7	30.7	5.3
3.	Implying a benefit that hardly exists	Frequency	36	17	16	6
		Percentage	48.0	22.7	21.3	8.0
4.	Trade puffing and exaggeration	Frequency	29	15	30	1
		Percentage	38.7	20.0	40.0	1.3
5.	Using un necessary, unwanted technical jargons	Frequency	28	15	25	7
		Percentage	37.3	20.0	33.3	9.3
6.	Creating cultural degenerations	Frequency	28	11	19	17
		Percentage	37.3	14.7	25.3	22.7
7.	Creating ambiguities in the minds of consumers	Frequency	30	5	28	12
		Percentage	40.0	6.7	37.3	16.0
8.	Creating fear in consumers	Frequency	12	17	16	30
		Percentage	16.0	22.7	21.3	40.0
9.	Open criticism of competitors	Frequency	44	6	15	10
		Percentage	58.7	8.0	20.0	13.3
10.	Sex in advertisement	Frequency	34	4	24	13
		Percentage	45.3	5.3	32.0	17.3
11.	Against the national and public interest	Frequency	17	6	20	32
		Percentage	22.7	8.0	26.7	42.7
12.	Affect life style of people	Frequency	32	6	21	16
		Percentage	42.7	8.0	28.0	21.3
13.	Creates monopoly	Frequency	36	8	14	17
		Percentage	48.0	10.7	18.7	22.7
14.	Unverifiable claims in a language	Frequency	16	14	25	20
		Percentage	21.3	18.7	33.3	26.7
15.	Subliminal message	Frequency	15	12	36	12.0
		Percentage	20.0	16.0	48.0	16.0

Source: Primary data.

The following were the responses of the respondents regarding unethical practices in advertisement. 56.0 per cent felt that the falls and misleading presentation of facts were more in product advertisement. 10.7 per cent felt more in service advertisement, 24.0 per cent equal in product and service advertisement and remaining nine point three per cent felt not in both advertisements.

Among the total number of respondents 37.3 per cent felt that the deliberate omitting of required information were in product advertisement. 26.7 per cent felt more in service advertisement, 30.7 per cent equal in product and service advertisement and remaining five point three per cent felt not in both advertisements.

Among the total number of respondents 48.0 per cent felt that the implying a benefit that hardly exists were in product advertisement. 22.7 per cent felt more in service advertisement, 21.3 per cent equal in product and service advertisement and remaining eight point zero per cent felt not in both advertisements.

Among the total number of respondents 38.7 per cent felt that the trade puffing and exaggeration were in product advertisement. 20.0 per cent felt more in service advertisement, 40.7 per cent equal in product and service advertisement and remaining one point three per cent felt not in both advertisements.

Among the total number of respondents 37.3 per cent felt that the using unnecessary, unwanted technical jargons were in product advertisement. 20.0 per cent felt more in service advertisement, 33.0 per cent equal in product and service advertisement and remaining nine point three per cent felt not in both advertisements.

Among the total number of respondents 37.3 per cent felt that creating cultural degeneration were in product advertisement. 14.7 per cent felt more in service advertisement, 25.3 per cent equal in product and service advertisement and remaining 22.7 per cent felt not in both advertisements.

Among the total number of respondents 40.0 per cent felt that creating ambiguities in the minds of consumers were in product advertisement. Six point seven per cent felt more in service advertisement, 37.3 per cent equal in product and service advertisement and remaining 16.0 per cent felt not in both advertisements.

Among the total number of respondents 16.0 per cent felt that creating fear in consumers were in product advertisement. 22.7 per cent felt more in service advertisement, 21.3 per cent equal in product and service advertisement and remaining 40.0 per cent felt not in both advertisements.

Among the total number of respondents 58.7 per cent felt that the open criticism of competitors were in product advertisement. Eight point zero per cent felt more in service advertisement, 20.0 per cent equal in product and service advertisement and remaining 13.3 per cent felt not in both advertisements.

Table 4.13: Respondents' Comments on Advertising

Sl.No.	Particulars		Always	Frequently	Occasionally	Never	Can't say
			(n:75)	(n:75)	(n:75)	(n:75)	(n:75)
1.	There is no ethical value in Advertising	Frequency	7	27	29	6	6
		Percentage	9.3	36.0	38.7	8.0	8.0
2.	Advertising is just an exaggeration, puffery and bluffing	Frequency	5	21	35	10	4
		Percentage	6.7	28.0	46.7	13.3	5.3
3.	Advertising degenerates our culture	Frequency	4	15	23	16	17
		Percentage	5.3	20.0	30.7	21.3	22.7
4.	Advertising degenerates the youth	Frequency	7	26	16	16	10
		Percentage	9.3	34.7	21.3	21.3	13.3
5.	Honesty in advertising is rare	Frequency	10	19	30	4	12
		Percentage	13.3	25.3	40.0	5.3	16.0
6.	Advertising causes false and misleading claims	Frequency	5	16	35	9	10
		Percentage	6.7	21.3	46.7	12.0	13.3
7.	Unfair advertisements are very common	Frequency	4	17	28	15	11
		Percentage	5.3	22.7	37.3	20.0	14.7
8.	It is not worth to go by advertising	Frequency	3	11	21	14	26
		Percentage	4.0	14.7	18.0	18.7	34.7
9.	Advertising boosting our self image	Frequency	20	22	17	8	8
		Percentage	26.7	29.3	22.7	10.7	10.7
10.	Advertising for harmful/prohibited products and services	Frequency	7	15	28	10	15
		Percentage	9.3	20.0	37.3	13.3	20.0
11.	Prepare young minds (children) for the product	Frequency	24	35	10	4	2
		Percentage	32.0	46.7	13.3	5.3	2.7
12.	Referring the product (or) incidents is not capable of being established	Frequency	8	23	28	8	8
		Percentage	10.7	30.7	37.3	10.7	10.7
13.	Give irrelevant statistical data and disproved scientific jargon	Frequency	8	22	30	6	9
		Percentage	107	29.3	40.0	8.0	12.0
14.	Containing disparaging reference to another product of service	Frequency	12	18	29	7	9
		Percentage	16.0	24.0	38.7	9.3	12.0
15.	Testimonials are misleading the viewers	Frequency	9	29	24	2	11
		Percentage	12.0	38.7	32.0	2.7	14.7

Source: Primary Data.

Among the total number of respondents 45.3 per cent felt that sex in advertisement were in product advertisement. Five point three per cent felt more in service advertisement, 32.0 per cent equal in product and service advertisement and remaining 17.3 per cent felt not in both advertisements.

Among the total number of respondents 22.7 per cent felt that against the national and public interest were in product advertisement. Eight point zero per cent felt more in service advertisement, 26.7 per cent equal in product and service advertisement and remaining 42.7 per cent felt not in both advertisements.

Among the total number of respondents 42.7 per cent felt that affects life style of people were in product advertisement. Eight point zero per cent felt more in service advertisement, 28.0 per cent equal in product and service advertisement and remaining 21.3 per cent felt not in both advertisements.

Among the total number of respondents 48.0 per cent felt that creates monopoly were in product advertisement. 10.7 per cent felt more in service advertisement, 18.7 per cent equal in product and service advertisement and remaining 22.7 per cent felt not in both advertisements.

Among the total number of respondents 21.3 per cent felt that unverifiable claims in a language were in product advertisement. 18.7 per cent felt more in service advertisement, 33.3 per cent equal in product and service advertisement and remaining 26.7 per cent felt not in both advertisements.

Among the total number of respondents 20.0 per cent felt that subliminal message were in product advertisement. 16.0 per cent felt more in service advertisement, 48.0 per cent equal in product and service advertisement and remaining 16.0 per cent felt not in both advertisements.

Among the 75 respondents 9.3 per cent felt that there is always no ethical value in advertising, 36.0 per cent felt that there is frequently, 38.7 per cent felt that there is occasionally, eight point zero per cent felt never and the remaining eight point zero per cent can't say anything about this factor.

Among the 75 respondents six point seven per cent felt that advertising is always just an exaggeration, puffery and bluffing, 28.0 per cent felt frequently, 46.7 per cent felt that occasionally, 13.3 per cent felt never and the remaining five point three per cent can't say anything about this factor.

Among the 75 respondents five point three per cent felt that advertising is always degenerates our culture, 20.0 per cent felt frequently, 30.7 per cent felt that occasionally, 21.3 per cent felt never and the remaining 22.7 per cent can't say anything about this factor.

Among the 75 respondents nine point three per cent felt that advertising is always degenerates the youth, 34.7 per cent felt frequently, 21.3 per cent felt that occasionally, 21.3 per cent felt never and the remaining 13.3 per cent can't say anything about this factor.

Among the 75 respondents 13.3 per cent felt that the honesty in advertising is always rare, 25.3 per cent felt frequently, 40.0 per cent felt that occasionally, five point three per cent felt never and the remaining 16.0per cent can't say anything about this factor.

Among the 75 respondents six point seven per cent felt that advertising is always for false and misleading claims, 21.3 per cent felt frequently, 46.7 per cent felt that occasionally, 12.0 per cent felt never and the remaining 13.3 per cent can't say anything about this factor.

Among the 75 respondents five point three per cent felt that always unfair advertising are very common, 22.7 per cent felt frequently, 37.3 per cent felt that occasionally, 20.0 per cent felt never and the remaining 14.7 per cent can't say anything about this factor.

Among the 75 respondents four point zero per cent felt that it is not worth to go by advertising always, 14.7 per cent felt frequently, 28.0 per cent felt that occasionally, 18.7 per cent felt never and the remaining 34.7 per cent can't say anything about this factor.

Among the 75 respondents 26.7 per cent felt that advertising is always boosting our self image, 29.3 per cent felt frequently, 22.7 per cent felt that occasionally, 10.7 per cent felt never and the remaining 10.7 per cent can't say anything about this factor.

Among the 75 respondents nine point three per cent felt that advertising is always for harmful/prohibited product and services, 20.0 per cent felt frequently, 37.3 per cent felt that occasionally, 13.3 per cent felt never and the remaining 20.0 per cent can't say anything about this factor.

Among the 75 respondents 32.0 per cent felt that advertising is always prepare young minds (children) for the product, 46.7 per cent felt frequently, 13.3 per cent felt that occasionally, five point three per cent felt never and the remaining two point seven per cent can't say anything about this factor.

Among the 75 respondents 10.7 per cent felt that referring the product/incidents in advertising is always not capable of being established, 30.7 per cent felt frequently, 37.3 per cent felt that occasionally, 10.7 per cent felt never and the remaining 10.7 per cent can't say anything about this factor.

Among the 75 respondents 10.7 per cent felt that advertising is always giving irrelevant statistical data and disproved scientific jargons, 29.3 per cent felt frequently, 40.0 per cent felt that occasionally, eight point three per cent felt never and the remaining 12.0 per cent can't say anything about this factor.

Among the 75 respondents 16.0 per cent felt that advertisement is always containing disparaging reference to another product of service, 24.0 per cent felt frequently, 38.7 per cent felt that occasionally, nine point three per cent felt never and the remaining 12.0 per cent can't say anything about this factor.

Among the 75 respondents 12.0 per cent felt that testimonials are always misleading the viewers, 38.7 per cent felt frequently, 32.0 per cent felt that occasionally, two point seven per cent felt never and the remaining 14.7 per cent can't say anything about this factor.

5

Analysis and Interpretation of Collected Data from the Students Respondents

Table 5.1: Distribution of the Respondents by their age

Sl.No.	Age (years)	Frequency	Percent
1.	20	12	4.6
2.	21	58	22.1
3.	22	84	31.9
4.	23	67	25.5
5.	24	24	9.1
6.	Above 24	18	6.8
	Total	263	100.0

Source: Primary Data.

Among the 263 respondents, 12 respondents were in the age group of 20 years, 58 respondents were belonging to the age group of 21 years, 84 respondents were belonging to the age group of 22 years, 67 respondents were at the age group of 23 years, 24 respondents at the age group 24 years and the remaining 18 respondents were above 24 years of age.

In other words four point six per cent respondents were in the age group of 20 years, 22.1 per cent of the respondents were belonging to the age group of 21 years, 31.9 per cent of the respondents were belonging to the age group of 22 years, 25.5 per cent of the respondents were at the age group of 23 years, nine point one per cent of the respondents were at the age group 24 years and the remaining six point eight per cent of the respondents were above 24 years of age.

It is found out that majority (31.9 per cent) of the respondents were belonging to the age group of 22 years.

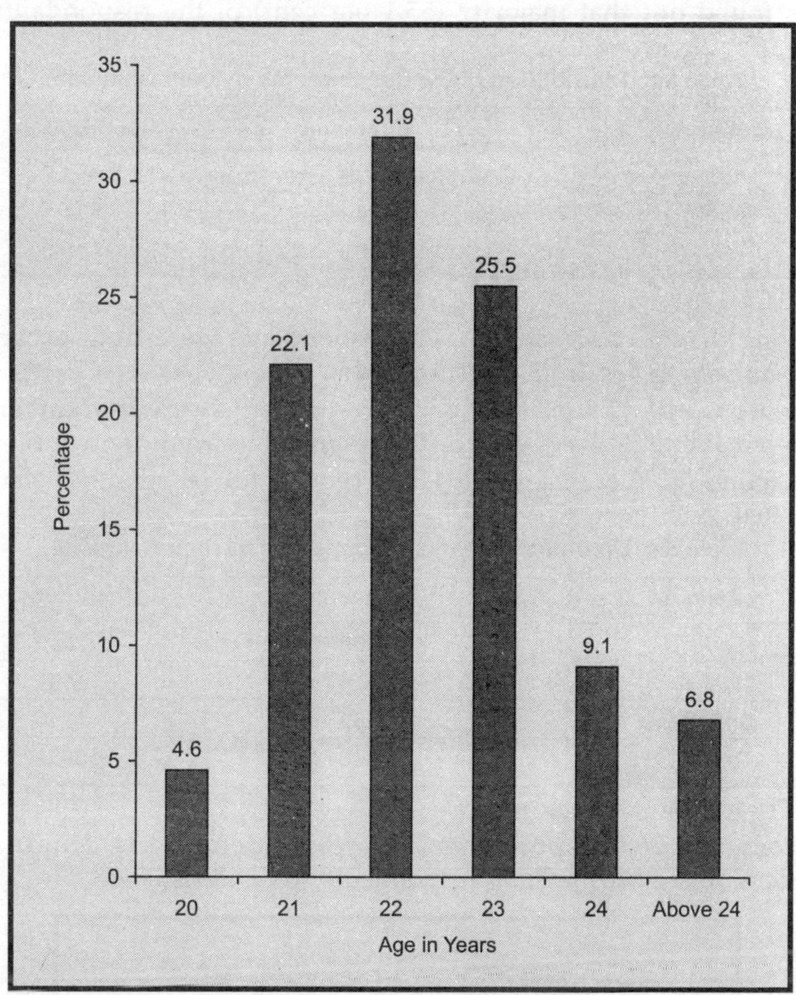

Chart 5.1: Distribution of the Respondents by their Age

Table 5.2: Distribution of the Respondents by Sex-wise

Sl.No.	Sex	Frequency	Percent
1.	Male	118	44.9
2.	Female	145	55.1
	Total	263	100

Source: Primary Data.

Among the total respondents, 118 respondents were male and the remaining 145 respondents were female.

In other words 44.9 per cent of the respondents were male and the remaining 55.1 per cent of the respondents were female.

It is found out that majority (55.1 per cent) of the respondents were female.

Table 5.3: Distribution of the Respondents by their Domicile

Sl.No.	Area	Frequency	Percent
1.	Urban	119	45.2
2.	Rural	144	54.8
	Total	263	100.0

Source: Primary Data

Among the 263 respondents, 119 respondents were from urban areas and the remaining 144 from the rural areas.

In other words 45.2 per cent of the respondents were from urban areas and the remaining 54.8 per cent of the respondents were from rural areas.

It is found out that majority (54.8 percent) of the respondents were from rural areas.

Table 5.4: Distribution of the Respondents by their Religions

Sl.No.	Religion	Frequency	Percent
1.	Hindu	200	76.1
2.	Muslim	4	1.5
3.	Christian	59	22.4
	Total	263	100.0

Source: Primary Data.

Among the 263 respondents, 200 respondents were Hindus, four respondents were Muslims, 59 respondents were Christians.

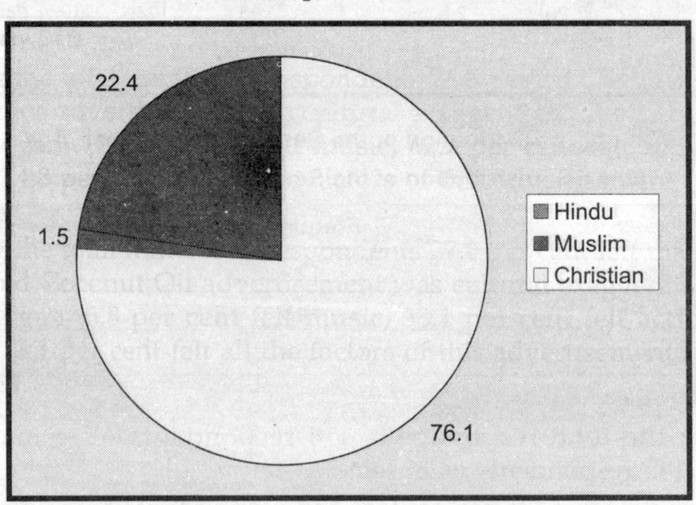

Chart 5.2 : Distribution of the Respondents by their Religions

In other words 76.1 per cent of the respondents were Hindus, one point five per cent of the respondents were belonging to Muslims, 22.4 per cent of the respondents were Christians.

It is found out that majority (76.1 per cent) were Hindus.

Table 5.5: Distribution of the Respondents by their Income

Sl.No.	Monthly Income	Frequency	Percent
1.	Rs. 17.917 & More pm	28	10.6
2.	Rs. 3,750 - 17,917 pm	103	39.2
3.	Rs. 1,833 - 3,750 pm	72	27.4
4.	Rs. 1,333 - 1,833 pm	36	13.7
5.	Below Rs. 1,333 pm	24	9.1
	Total	263	100.0

Source: Primary Data.

Among the 263 respondents, 28 respondents monthly income was above Rs. 17917 per month, 103 respondents monthly income was between Rs. 3,750 -17, 917, 72 respondents monthly income was between Rs. 1,833 – Rs. 3,750, 36 respondents monthly income was between Rs. 1,333 - Rs.1,833 and the remaining 24 respondents monthly income was below Rs. 1,333.

In other words, 10.06 per cent of the respondents monthly income was above Rs. 17917 per month, 39.2 per cent of the respondents monthly income was between Rs. 3,750 -17, 917, 27.4 per cent respondents monthly income was between Rs. 1,833 – Rs. 3,750, 13.7 per cent of the respondents monthly income was between Rs. 1,333 - Rs.1,833 and the remaining nine point one respondents monthly income was below Rs. 1,333. This income classification was made by National Applied Council for Economic Research India (NACER).

Table 5.6: Educational Qualification (Father)

Sl. No.	Educational Qualification	Frequency	Percent
1.	Illiterate	30	11.4
2.	Primary	29	11.0
3.	Middle	40	15.2
4.	High School	61	23.2
5.	Higher Secondary	38	14.4
6.	Graduation	41	15.6
7.	Post graduation	21	8.0
8.	Doctoral	1	.4
9.	Others	2	8
	Total	263	100.0

Source: Primary Data.

It is found out that majority (39.2 per cent) of the respondents monthly income was Rs. 3,750-Rs. 17,917.

Among the 263 respondents, the fathers of the 30 respondents were illiterate, 29 were upto primary (upto 5th std.) level, 40 were upto middle (upto 8th std.) level, 61 were upto high school (10th std.) level, 38 were upto higher secondary (+2) level, 41 were graduates, 21 were postgraduates, one respondent has doctoral degree and the remaining two respondents were diplomas namely electrical and mechanical.

In other words 11.4 per cent of the respondents were illiterate, 11.0 per cent of the respondents were upto primary (upto 5th std.) level, 15.2 per cent of the respondents were upto middle (upto 8th std.) level, 23.2 per cent of the respondents were upto high school (10th std.) level, 14.4 per cent of the respondents were upto higher secondary (+2) level, 15.6 per cent of the respondents were graduates, eight per cent of the respondents were postgraduates, zero point four per cent of the respondents respondent has doctoral degree and the remaining zero point eight per cent of the respondents were diplomas namely electrical and mechanical.

It is found out that majority (23.2 per cent) of the respondents were studied upto 10th standard. (High School Level).

Table 5.7: Educational Qualification (Mother)

Sl. No.	Educational Qualification	Frequency	Percent
1.	Illiterate	51	19.4
2.	Primary	41	15.6
3.	Middle	52	19.8
4.	High School	66	25.1
5.	Higher Secondary	34	12.9
6.	Graduation	14	5.3
7.	Post graduation	5	1.9
	Total	263	100.0

Source: Primary Data.

Among the 263 respondents, mothers of the 51 respondents were illiterate, 41 were upto primary (upto 5th std.) level, 52 were upto middle (upto 8th std.) level, 66 were upto high school (10th std.) level, 34 were upto higher secondary (+2) level, 14 were graduates, five were postgraduates.

In other words 19.4 per cent of the respondents were illiterate, 15.6 per cent of the respondents were upto primary (upto 5th std.) level, 19.8 per cent of the respondents were upto middle (upto 8th std.) level, 25.1 were upto high school (10th std.) level, 12.9 per cent of the respondents were upto higher secondary (+2) level, five point three per cent of the respondents were graduates, one point of nine were postgraduates.

It is found out that majority (25.1 per cent) of the respondents were studied upto 10th standard. (High School Level).

Table 5.8: Occupation of the Head of the Family

Sl.No.	Age	Frequency	Percent
1.	Agriculture	107	40.7
2.	Government	54	20.5
3.	Business	36	13.7
4.	Professional	7	2.7
5.	Private	49	18.6
6.	Others	10	3.8
	Total	263	100.0

Source: Primary Data

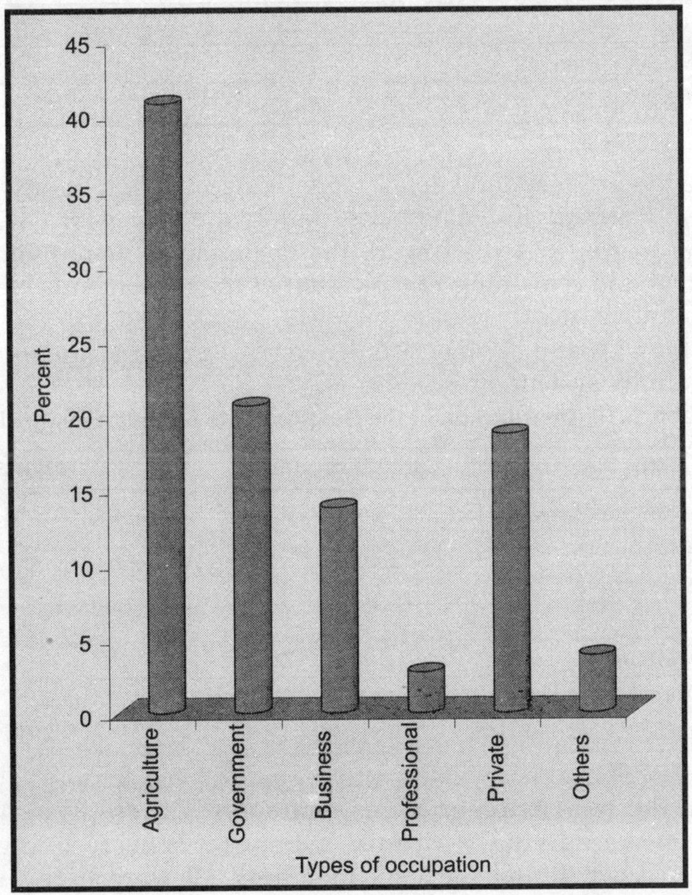

Chart 5.3: Occupation of the Head of the Family

Among the 263 respondents, 107 were involving in agricultural works, 54 were government employees, 36 were doing business, seven were professionals, 49 were working in private companies and the remaining 10 were labours.

In other words 40.7 per cent of the respondents were involving in agricultural works, 20.5 per cent of the respondents were government employees, 13.7 per cent of the respondents were doing business, two point seven per cent of the respondents were professionals, 18.6 per cent of the respondents were working in private companies and the remaining three point eight per cent of the respondents were labours.

It is found that majority (40.7 per cent) of the respondents were involved in agricultural works.

Table 5.9: Distribution of the Respondents by their Family Types

Sl.No.	Family Type	Frequency	Percent
1.	Joint Family	72	27.4
2.	Nuclear Family	191	72.6
	Total	263	100.0

Source: Primary Data

Among the 263 respondents, 72 were living in a joint family system and remaining 191 were living in a nuclear family system.

In other words, 27.4 per cent of the respondents were living in a joint family system and remaining 72.6 per cent of the respondents were living in a nuclear family system.

It was found that majority (72.6 per cent) of the respondents were living in nuclear family system.

Table 5.10: Distribution of the Respondents by their Family Size

Sl.No.	Family Size	Frequency	Percent
1.	3 Members	27	10.3
2.	4 Members	90	34.2
3.	5 Members	79	30.0
4.	6 Members	31	11.8
5.	7 Members	17	6.5
6.	Above 7 Members	19	7.2
	Total	263	100.0

Source: Primary Data.

Among the total number of respondents, 27 were living with three members, 90 were living with four members, 79 were living with five members, 31 were living with six members, 17 were living with seven members and the remaining 19 were living with above seven members in their families.

In other words 10.3 per cent of the respondents were living with three members, 34.2 per cent of the respondents were living with four members, 30.0 per cent of the respondents were living with five members, 11.8 per cent of the respondents were living with six members, six point five per cent of the respondents were living with seven members and the remaining seven point two per cent of the respondents were living with above seven members in their families.

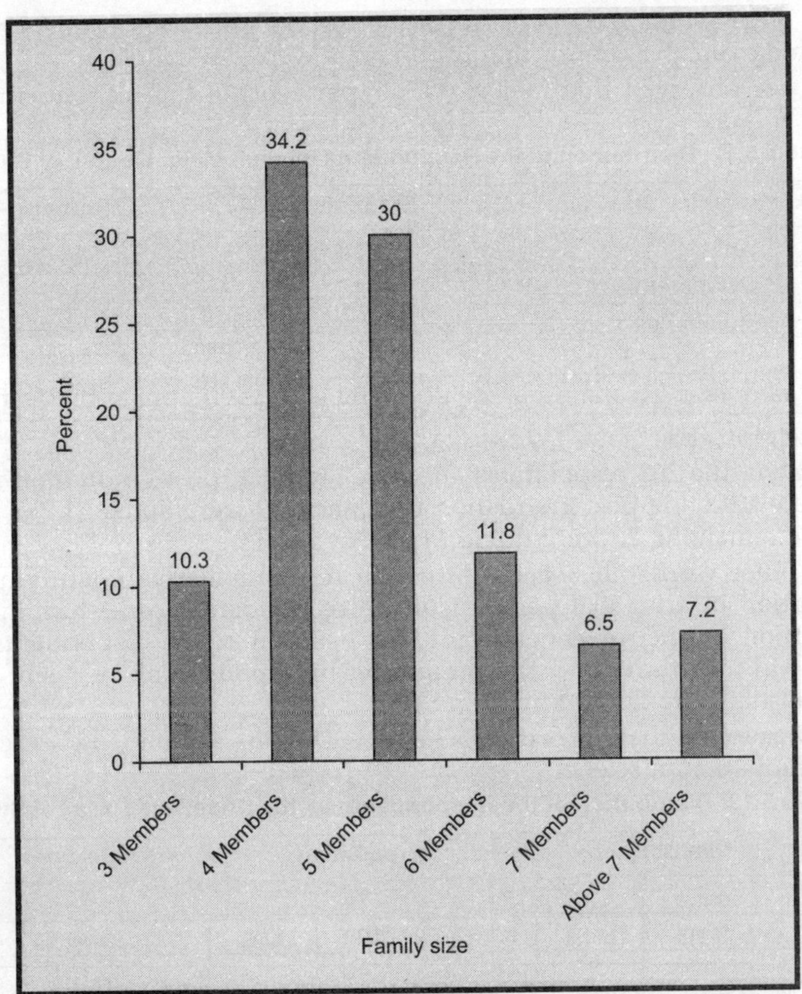

Chart 5.4: Distribution of the Respondents by the Family Size

It was observed that majority (34.2 per cent) were living with four members in their families.

Among the 263 respondents, 77 were hostellers and the remaining 186 were day-scholars.

Table 5.11: Distribution of the Respondents by their Residential Status

Sl.No.	Residential Status	Frequency	Percent
1.	Hostellers	77	29.3
2.	Day-Scholars	186	70.7
	Total	• 263	100.0

Source: Primary Data.

In other words, 29.3 per cent of the respondents were hostlers and the remaining 70.7 per cent of the respondents were day-scholars.

It was observed that majority (70.7 per cent) of the respondents were day-scholars.

Table 5.12: Distribution of the Respondents by their Major Course of Study

Sl.No.	Family Size	Frequency	Percent
1.	Arts-PG	70	26.6
2.	Science-PG	148	56.3
3.	Arts-M.Phil	19	7.2
4.	Science-M.Phil	26	9.9
	Total	263	100.0

Source: Primary Data.

Among the 263 respondents, 70 were studying post graduation in arts, 148 were studying post graduation in science, 19 were doing M.Phil in arts and the remaining 26 were doing M.Phil in Science.

In other words, 26.6 per cent of the respondents were studying post graduation in arts, 56.3 per cent of the respondents were studying post graduation in science, seven point two per cent of the respondents were doing M.Phil in arts and the remaining nine point nine per cent of the respondents were doing M.Phil in Science.

It was found that majority (56.3 per cent) of the respondents were doing post graduation in science.

Table 5.13: Distribution of the Respondents by their Academic Year of Study

Sl.No.	Year of Study	Frequency	Percent
1.	I Year	74	28.1
2.	II Years	104	39.5
3.	III Years	40	15.3
4.	M.Phil	45	17.1
	Total	263	100.0

Source: Primary Data

Among the total number of respondents 74 were I year students, 104 were II year students, 40 were III year students and the remaining 45 were M.Phil students.

In other words, 28.1 per cent of the respondents were I year students, 39.5 per cent of the respondents were II year students, 15.3 per cent of the respondents were III year students and the remaining 17.1 per cent of the respondents were M.Phil students.

It was found that majority (39.5 per cent) of the respondents were II year students. It is also observed that III year students belong to Master of Computer Applications.

Table 5.14: Mode of spending their Leisure time

Sl.No.	Leisure	Frequency	Percent
1.	Reading News paper/ Magazine	61	23.2
2.	Listening to Radio	42	16.0
3.	Watching Television	117	44.5
4.	Using Internet	43	16.3
	Total	263	100.0

Source: Primary Data

Among the total number of respondents, 61 were spending their leisure time in reading news papers/magazines, 42 were listening ratio, 117 were watching television and the remaining 43 were using internet.

In other words 23.3 per cent of the respondents were spending their leisure time in reading news papers/magazines, 16 percent of the respondents were listening ratio, 44.5 percent of the respondents were watching television and the remaining 16.3 percent of the respondents were using internet.

It was depicted that majority (44.5 per cent) of the respondents were spending their leisure by watching television.

Table 5.15: The most Appealing Areas in Television Advertisement

Sl.No.	Attractive Parts	Frequency	Percent
1.	Lasting Impression	14	5.3
2.	Theme	63	24.0
3.	Sound Effect	29	11.0
4.	Celebrities	26	9.9
5.	Innovativeness	61	23.2
6.	Relevance	6	2.3
7.	Over All Effects	63	24.0
8.	Others	1	.4
	Total	263	100.0

Source: Primary Data

Among the total number of respondents, 14 were consider that the lasting impression was the most appealing areas in Television advertisement, 63 were consider the theme, 29 were consider the sound effect, 26 were consider the celebrities, 61 were consider the innovativeness, six were consider the relevance, 63 were consider the over all effects and the remaining one was consider the other factor namely jingles.

In other words 5.3 per cent of the respondents were consider that the lasting impression was the most appealing areas in T.V. advertisement, 24 per cent per cent of the respondents were consider the theme, 11 per cent of the respondents were consider the sound effect, nine point nine were consider the celebrities, 23.2 per cent of the respondents were consider the innovativeness, two point three per cent of the respondents were consider the relevance, 24 per cent of the respondents were consider the over all effects and the remaining zero point four per cent of the respondent was consider the other factor namely jingles.

It was observed that majority (24 per cent) of the respondents were consider the theme was the most appealing areas in Television advertisements.

Table 5.16: Role of Advertisement

Sl.No.	Role of Advertisement	Frequency	Percent
1.	Create Awareness	107	40.7
2.	Create Lifestyle	61	23.2
3.	Create New wants	73	27.8
4.	Foundation of Civilisation	9	3.4
5.	Survive Democracy	12	4.6
6.	Others	1	.4
	Total	263	100.0

Source: Primary Data

The following were the responses of the respondents regarding the role of advertisement. Among the 263 respondents, 107 felt that create awareness was the major role of the advertisement, 61 felt that create life style, 73 felt create new wants, nine felt that foundation of civilization, 12 felt survive democracy and the remaining one respondent felt the other factor namely improve the business.

In other words 40.7 per cent of the respondents felt that creating awareness was the major role of the advertisement, 23.2 per cent of the respondents felt that create life style, 27.8 per cent of the respondents felt create new wants, three point four per cent of the respondents felt that foundation of civilization, four point six per cent of the respondents felt survive democracy and the remaining zero point four per cent of the respondents respondent felt the other factor namely improve the business.

It was observed that majority (40.7 percent) of the respondent felt that creating awareness was the major role of the advertisement.

Table 5.17: Role of Celebrities in Advertisements

Sl.No.	Role of Celebrities	Frequency	Percent
1.	Stimulate Interest	64	24.3
2.	Fair Description	21	8.0
3.	Truthful Information	65	24.7
4.	Inducted to purchase	80	30.4
5.	Suggest for change	33	12.5
	Total	263	100.0

Source: Primary Data

Among the total number of respondents, 64 felt that stimulate interest was the major role of the celebrities in advertisements, 21 felt fair description, 65 felt truthful information, 80 felt inducted to purchase and the remaining 33 felt that suggest for change.

In other words, 24.3 per cent of the respondents felt that stimulate interest was the major role of the celebrities in advertisements, eight per cent of the respondents felt fair description, 24.7 per cent of the respondents felt truthful information, 30.4 per cent of the respondents felt inducted to purchase and the remaining 12.5 per cent of the respondents felt that suggest for change.

It was found that majority (30.4 per cent) of the respondents felt that inducted to purchase was the major role of the celebrities in advertisements

Table 5.18: Celebrities Influence on the Purchase Decision

Sl.No.	Celebrities Part	Frequency	Percent
1.	Yes	105	39.9
2.	No	158	60.1
	Total	263	100

Source: Primary Data

Among the 263 respondents 105 considered the celebrities as an important factor for their purchase decisions and the remaining 158 won't consider the celebrities at the time of taking purchase decisions.

In other words 39.9 per cent of the respondents considered the celebrities as an important factor for their purchase decisions and the remaining 60.1 per cent of the respondents won't consider the celebrities at the time of taking purchase decisions.

It was observed that majority (60.1 per cent) respondents won't consider the celebrities at the time of taking purchase decisions.

Among the 105 respondents 16 were influenced by actor Vijay, 14 by Ajith, seven by Madhavan, six by Prakash Raj, 22 by Suriya, three by Amitabpachan, 11 by cricket player Sachin Tendelkur, two by actress Asin, three by Trisha, two by Sneka, four by Tamana, five by Ishwaray Roy, one by Sharuk Khan, eight by Cricket Player Dohni and the remaining one by other celebrity namely actor Kamalahasan.

Table 5.19: Influenced celebrities in Television Telecast

Sl.No.	Role of Advertisement	Frequency	Percent
1.	Vijay	16	6.1
2.	Ajith	14	5.3
3.	Madhavan	7	2.7
4.	Prakash Raj	6	2.3
5.	Suriya	22	8.4
6.	Amitabpachan	3	1.1
7.	Sachin Tendelkar	11	4.2
8.	Asin	2	.8
9.	Trisha	3	1.1
10.	Sneka	2	.8
11.	Tamana	4	1.5
12.	Ishwaray Roy	5	1.9
13.	Shark Khan	1	.4
14.	Dhoni	8	3.0
15.	Others	1	.4
16.	Not Important	158	60.1
	Total	263	100.0

Source: Primary Data

In other words six point one per cent of the respondents were influenced by actor Vijay, five point three per cent of the respondents by Ajith, two point seven per cent of the respondents by Madhavan, two point three per cent of the respondents by Prakash Raj, eight point four per cent of the respondents by Suriya, one point one per cent of the respondents by Amitabpachan, four point two per cent of the respondents by cricket player Sachin Tendelkur, zero point eight per cent of the respondents by actress Asin, one point one per cent of the respondents by Trisha, zero point eight per cent of the respondents by Sneka, one point five per cent of the respondents by Tamana, one point nine per cent of the respondents by Ishwaray Roy, zero point four per cent of the respondents by Sharuk Khan, three per cent of the respondents by Cricket Player Dohni and the remaining zero point four per cent of the respondent was influenced by other factor namely actor Kamalahasan.

It is found that majority (8.4 per cent) of the respondents were influenced by actor Suriya.

Table 5.20: Respondents Opinion about Unethical Practices in Advertisements

Sl.No.	Particulars		More in product/ consumer advertise-ments	More in service advertise-ment	Equal in both	Not in both
			(n:263)	(n:263)	(n:263)	(n:263)
1.	False and misleading presentation of facts	Frequency	118	28	104	13
		Percentage	44.9	10.6	39.5	4.9
2.	Deliberate omitting of required information	Frequency	131	59	68	5
		Percentage	49.8	22.4	25.9	1.9
3.	Implying a benefit that hardly exists	Frequency	106	53	95	9
		Percentage	40.3	20.2	36.1	3.4
4.	Trade puffing and exaggeration	Frequency	117	44	86	16
		Percentage	44.5	16.7	32.7	6.1
5.	Using un necessary, unwanted technical jargons	Frequency	147	46	54	16
		Percentage	55.9	17.5	20.5	6.1
6.	Creating cultural degenerations	Frequency	154	30	58	21
		Percentage	58.6	11.4	22.1	8.0
7.	Creating ambiguities in the minds of consumers	Frequency	111	37	12	13
		Percentage	42.2	14.1	38.8	4.9
8.	Creating fear in consumers	Frequency	88	59	94	22
		Percentage	33.5	22.4	35.7	8.4
9.	Open criticism of competitors	Frequency	142	38	72	11
		Percentage	54.0	14.4	27.4	4.2
10.	Sex in advertisement	Frequency	154	28	67	14
		Percentage	58.6	10.6	25.5	5.3
11.	Against the national and public interest	Frequency	81	59	68	55
		Percentage	30.8	22.4	25.9	20.9
12.	Affect life style of people	Frequency	127	39	72	25
		Percentage	48.3	14.8	27.4	9.5
13.	Creates monopoly	Frequency	156	44	55	8
		Percentage	59.3	16.7	20.9	3.0
14.	Unverifiable claims in a language	Frequency	105	56	80	22
		Percentage	39.9	21.3	30.4	8.4
15.	Subliminal message	Frequency	92	42	113	16
		Percentage	35.0	16.0	42.9	6.1

Source: Primary data

The above table described the unethical practices are existing whether in product advertisement, service advertisement, equal in both or not in both. Among the 263 respondents 44.9 per cent felt that false and misleading presentation of facts are existing in production advertisement, 10.6 per cent in service advertisement, 39.5 per cent felt that equal in both and the remaining four point nine per cent not in both.

Among the 263 respondents 49.8 per cent felt that deliberate omitting of required information are existing in product advertisement, 22.4 per cent in service advertisement, 25.9 per cent felt that it is equal in both and the remaining one point nine per cent not in both.

Among the 263 respondents 40.3 per cent felt that implying a benefit that hardly exist were in product advertisement, 20.2 per cent in service advertisement, 36.1 per cent felt that it is equal in both and the remaining three point four per cent not in both.

Among the 263 respondents 44.5 per cent felt that trade puffing and exaggeration were existing in product advertisement, 16.7 per cent in service advertisement, 32.7 per cent felt that it is equal in both and the remaining six point one per cent not in both.

Among the 263 respondents 55.9 per cent felt that using unnecessary and unwanted technical jargons were existing in product advertisement, 22.4 per cent in service advertisement, 25.9 per cent felt that it is equal in both and the remaining one point nine per cent not in both.

Among the 263 respondents 58.6 per cent felt that creating cultural degeneration were existing in product advertisement, 11.4 per cent in service advertisement, 22.1 per cent felt that it is equal in both and the remaining eight point zero per cent not in both.

Among the 263 respondents 42.2 per cent felt that creating ambiguities in the minds of consumer were existing in product advertisement, 14.1 per cent in service advertisement, 38.8 per cent felt that it is equal in both and the remaining four point nine per cent not in both.

Among the 263 respondents 33.5 per cent felt that creating fear in consumer were existing in product advertisement, 22.4 per cent in service advertisement, 35.7 per cent felt that it is equal in both and the remaining eight point four per cent not in both.

Among the 263 respondents 54.0 per cent felt that open criticism of competitors were existing in product advertisement, 14.4 per cent in service advertisement, 27.4 per cent felt that it is equal in both and the remaining four point two per cent not in both.

Among the 263 respondents 58.6 per cent felt that sex in advertisement were existing in product advertisement, 10.6 per cent in service advertisement, 25.5 per cent felt that it is equal in both and the remaining five point three per cent not in both.

Table 5.21: Respondents' Comments on Advertising

Sl.No.	Particulars		Always	Frequently	Occasionally	Never	Can't say
			(n:263)	(n:263)	(n:263)	(n:263)	(n:263)
1.	There is no ethical value in Advertising	Frequency	35	109	82	15	22
		Percentage	13.3	41.4	31.2	5.7	8.4
2.	Advertising is just an exaggeration, puffery and bluffing	Frequency	57	96	76	19	15
		Percentage	21.7	36.5	28.9	7.2	5.7
3.	Advertising degenerates our culture	Frequency	53	96	66	33	15
		Percentage	20.2	36.5	25.1	12.5	5.7
4.	Advertising degenerates the youth	Frequency	70	96	66	21	10
		Percentage	26.6	36.5	25.1	8.0	3.8
5.	Honesty in advertising is rare	Frequency	86	70	63	28	16
		Percentage	32.7	26.6	24.0	10.6	6.1
6.	Advertising causes false and misleading claims	Frequency	54	90	73	28	18
		Percentage	20.5	34.2	37.8	10.6	6.8
7.	Unfair advertisements are very common	Frequency	86	93	45	22	17
		Percentage	32.7	35.4	17.1	8.4	6.5
8.	It is not worth to go by advertising	Frequency	64	56	79	38	26
		Percentage	24.3	21.3	30.0	14.4	9.9
9.	Advertising boosting our self image	Frequency	50	64	74	56	19
		Percentage	19.0	24.3	28.1	21.3	7.2
10.	Advertising for harmful/ prohibited products and services	Frequency	66	60	84	30	23
		Percentage	25.1	22.8	31.9	11.4	8.7
11.	Prepare young minds (children) for the product	Frequency	100	86	39	24	14
		Percentage	38.0	32.7	14.8	9.1	5.3
12.	Referring the product (or) incidents is not capable of being established	Frequency	71	72	76	29	15
		Percentage	27.0	27.4	28.9	11.0	5.7
13.	Furnish irrelevant statistical data and disproved scientific jargon	Frequency	49	107	63	27	17
		Percentage	18.6	40.7	24.0	10.3	6.5
14.	Containing disparaging reference to another product of service	Frequency	17	82	74	18	19
		Percentage	26.6	31.2	28.1	6.8	7.2
15.	Testimonials are misleading the viewers	Frequency	101	77	51	17	17
		Percentage	38.4	29.3	19.4	6.5	6.5

Source: Primary Data

Among the 263 respondents 30.8 per cent felt that against the national and pubic interest were existing in product advertisement, 22.4 per cent in service advertisement, 25.9 per cent felt that it is equal in both and the remaining 20.9 per cent not in both.

Among the 263 respondents 48.3 per cent felt that affect life style of people were existing in product advertisement, 14.8 per cent in service advertisement, 27.4 per cent felt that it is equal in both and the remaining nine point five per cent not in both.

Among the 263 respondents 59.3 per cent felt that creates monopoly were existing in product advertisement, 16.7 per cent in service advertisement, 20.9 per cent felt that it is equal in both and the remaining three point zero per cent not in both.

Among the 263 respondents 39.9 per cent felt that unverifiable claims in a language were existing in product advertisement, 21.3 per cent in service advertisement, 30.4 per cent felt that it is equal in both and the remaining eight point four per cent not in both.

Among the 263 respondents 35.0 per cent felt that subliminal message were existing in product advertisement, 16.0 per cent in service advertisement, 42.9 per cent felt that it is equal in both and the remaining six point one per cent not in both.

Among the 263 respondents 13.3 per cent felt that there is always no ethical value in advertising, 41.4 per cent felt that there is frequently, 31.2 per cent felt that there is occasionally, five point seven per cent felt never and the remaining eight point four per cent can't say anything about this factor.

Among the 263 respondents 21.7 per cent felt that advertising is always just an exaggeration, puffery and bluffing, 36.5 per cent felt frequently, 28.9 per cent felt that occasionally, seven point two per cent felt never and the remaining five point seven per cent can't say anything about this factor.

Among the 263 respondents 20.2 per cent felt that advertising is always degenerates our culture, 36.5 per cent felt frequently, 25.1 per cent felt that occasionally, 12.5 per cent felt never and the remaining five point seven per cent can't say anything about this factor.

Among the 263 respondents 26.6 per cent felt that advertising is always degenerates the youth, 36.5 per cent felt frequently, 25.1 per cent felt that occasionally, eight point zero per cent felt never and the remaining three point eight per cent can't say anything about this factor.

Among the 263 respondents 32.7 per cent felt that the honesty in advertising is always rare, 26.6 per cent felt frequently, 24.0 per cent felt that occasionally, 10.6 per cent felt never and the remaining six point one per cent can't say anything about this factor.

Among the 263 respondents 20.5 per cent felt that advertising is always for false and misleading claims, 34.2 per cent felt frequently, 27.8 per cent felt that occasionally, 10.6 per cent felt never and the remaining six point eight per cent can't say anything about this factor.

Among the 263 respondents 32.7 per cent felt that always unfair advertising are very common, 35.4 per cent felt frequently, 17.1 per cent felt that occasionally, eight point four per cent felt never and the remaining six point five per cent can't say anything about this factor.

Among the 263 respondents 24.3 per cent felt that it is not worth to go by advertising always, 21.3 per cent felt frequently, 30.0 per cent felt that occasionally, 14.4 per cent felt never and the remaining nine point nine per cent can't say anything about this factor.

Among the 263 respondents 38.0 per cent felt that advertising is always prepare young minds (children) for the product, 32.7 per cent felt frequently, 14.8 per cent felt that occasionally, nine point one per cent felt never and the remaining five point three per cent can't say anything about this factor.

Among the 263 respondents 27.0 per cent felt that referring the product/incidents in advertising is always not capable of being established, 27.4 per cent felt frequently, 28.9 per cent felt that occasionally, 11.0 per cent felt never and the remaining five point seven per cent can't say anything about this factor.

Among the 263 respondents 18.6 per cent felt that advertising is always furnishing irrelevant statistical data and disproved scientific jargons, 40.7 per cent felt frequently, 24.0 per cent felt that occasionally, 10.3 per cent felt never and the remaining six point five per cent can't say anything about this factor.

Among the 263 respondents 26.7 per cent felt that advertisement is always containing disparaging reference to another product of service, 31.2 per cent felt frequently, 28.1 per cent felt that occasionally, six point eight per cent felt never and the remaining seven point two per cent can't say anything about this factor.

Among the 263 respondents 38.4 per cent felt that testimonials are always misleading the viewers, 29.3 per cent felt frequently, 19.4 per cent felt that occasionally, six point five per cent felt never and the remaining six point five per cent can't say anything about this factor.

Among the 263 respondents 19.0 per cent felt that advertising is always boosting our self image, 24.3 per cent felt frequently, 28.1 per cent felt that occasionally, 21.3 per cent felt never and the remaining seven point two per cent can't say anything about this factor.

Among the 263 respondents 25.1 per cent felt that advertising is always for harmful/prohibited product and services, 22.8 per cent felt frequently, 31.9 per cent felt that occasionally, 11.4 per cent felt never and the remaining eight point seven per cent can't say anything about this factor.

Table 5.22: Opinion regarding cultural exaggeration about the select advertisements

Sl.No.	Particulars		Theme	Slogan	Music	Action	All the factors
			(n:263)	(n:263)	(n:263)	(n:263)	(n:263)
1.	Binco Chips	Frequency	64	15	34	111	39
		Percentage	24.3	5.7	12.9	42.2	14.8
2.	VVD Gold Coconut oil	Frequency	71	52	18	87	35
		Percentage	27.0	19.8	6.8	33.1	13.3
3.	Horlicks	Frequency	76	59	22	63	43
		Percentage	28.9	22.4	8.4	24.0	16.3
4.	Nescafe Sunrise	Frequency	53	26	40	101	43
		Percentage	20.2	9.9	15.2	38.4	16.3
5.	KFC Chicken	Frequency	60	20	28	104	51
		Percentage	22.8	7.6	10.6	39.5	19.4
6.	Medimix Sandal Soap	Frequency	57	32	47	76	51
		Percentage	21.7	12.2	17.9	28.9	19.4
7.	Docomo	Frequency	34	28	83	65	53
		Percentage	12.9	10.6	31.6	24.7	20.2
8.	Yuva A810	Frequency	55	26	35	94	53
		Percentage	20.9	9.9	13.3	35.7	20.2
9.	Colgate Max Fresh	Frequency	62	26	39	90	46
		Percentage	23.6	9.9	14.8	34.2	17.5
10.	Spinz Deo	Frequency	47	15	62	84	55
		Percentage	17.9	5.7	23.6	31.9	20.9

Source: Primary Data

Among the total number of respondents 24.3 per cent felt that the theme of Binco Chips advertisement was cultural exaggerated, five point seven per cent felt slogan, 12.9 per cent felt music, 42.2 per cent felt action and the remaining 14.8 per cent felt all the factors of this advertisement are cultural exaggerated.

Among the total number of respondents 27.0 per cent felt that the theme of VVD Gold Coconut Oil advertisement was cultural exaggerated, 19.8 per cent felt slogan, 6.8 per cent felt music, 33.1 per cent felt action and the remaining 13.1 per cent felt all the factors of this advertisement are cultural exaggerated.

Among the total number of respondents 28.9 per cent felt that the theme of Horlicks advertisement was cultural exaggerated, 22.4 per cent felt slogan, 8.4 per cent felt music, 24.0 per cent felt action and the remaining 16.3 per cent felt all the factors of this advertisement are cultural exaggerated.

Among the total number of respondents 20.2 per cent felt that the theme of Nescafe Sunrise advertisement was cultural exaggerated, nine point nine per cent felt slogan, 15.2 per cent felt music, 38.4 per cent felt action and the remaining 16.3 per cent felt all the factors of this advertisement are cultural exaggerated.

Among the total number of respondents 22.8 per cent felt that the theme of KFC Chicken advertisement was cultural exaggerated, seven point six per cent felt slogan, 10.6 per cent felt music, 39.5 per cent felt action and the remaining 19.4 per cent felt all the factors of this advertisement are cultural exaggerated.

Among the total number of respondents 21.7 per cent felt that the theme of Medimix Sandal Soap advertisement was cultural exaggerated, 12.2 per cent felt slogan, 17.9 per cent felt music, 28.9 per cent felt action and the remaining 19.4 per cent felt all the factors of this advertisement are cultural exaggerated.

Among the total number of respondents 12.9 per cent felt that the theme of Docomo advertisement was cultural exaggerated, 10.6 per cent felt slogan, 31.6 per cent felt music, 24.7 per cent felt action and the remaining 20.2 per cent felt all the factors of this advertisement are cultural exaggerated.

Among the total number of respondents 20.9 per cent felt that the theme of Yuva A810 advertisement was cultural exaggerated, nine point nine per cent felt slogan, 13.3 per cent felt music, 35.7 per cent felt action and the remaining 20.2 per cent felt all the factors of this advertisement are cultural exaggerated.

Among the total number of respondents 23.6 per cent felt that the theme of Colgate Max Fresh advertisement was cultural exaggerated, nine point nine per cent felt slogan, 14.8 per cent felt music, 34.2 per cent felt action and the remaining 17.5 per cent felt all the factors of this advertisement are cultural exaggerated.

Among the total number of respondents 17.9 per cent felt that the theme of Spinz Deo advertisement was cultural exaggerated, five point seven per cent felt slogan, 23.6 per cent felt music, 31.9 per cent felt action and the remaining 20.9 per cent felt all the factors of this advertisement are cultural exaggerated.

The following were the responses of the respondents regarding opinion on ethical values about the selected advertisements. Sixteen point three per cent felt that the Binco Chips advertisement had ethical values; six point eight per cent felt it was highly ethical, 41.8 per cent felt unethical, 25.9 per cent felt highly unethical and the remaining nine point one per cent couldn't say any thing about this advertisement.

Among the total number of respondents 15.2 per cent felt that the VVD Gold Coconut Oil advertisement had ethical values, 13.7 per cent felt it was highly ethical, 41.8 per cent felt unethical, 19.0 per cent felt highly unethical and the remaining 10.3 per cent couldn't say any thing about this advertisement.

Table 5.23: Opinion Regarding Ethical values about the Select Advertisements

Sl.No.	Particulars		Ethical	Highly ethical	Unethical	Highly unethical	Can't say
			(n:263)	(n:263)	(n:263)	(n:263)	(n:263)
1.	Binco Chips	Frequency	43	18	110	68	24
		Percentage	16.3	6.8	41.8	25.9	9.1
2.	VVD Gold Coconut oil	Frequency	40	36	110	50	27
		Percentage	15.2	13.7	41.8	19.0	10.3
3.	Horlicks	Frequency	52	35	94	57	25
		Percentage	19.8	13.3	35.7	21.7	9.5
4.	Nescafe Sunrise	Frequency	73	39	81	43	27
		Percentage	27.8	14.8	30.8	16.3	10.3
5.	KFC Chicken	Frequency	18	20	96	105	24
		Percentage	6.8	7.6	36.5	39.9	9.1
6.	Medimix Sandal Soap	Frequency	44	30	77	86	26
		Percentage	16.7	11.4	29.3	32.7	9.9
7.	Docomo	Frequency	36	31	74	88	34
		Percentage	13.7	11.8	28.1	33.5	12.9
8.	Yuva A810	Frequency	27	31	83	77	45
		Percentage	10.3	11.8	31.6	29.3	17.1
9.	Colgate Max Fresh	Frequency	39	29	84	80	31
		Percentage	14.8	11.0	31.9	30.4	11.8
10.	Spinz Deo	Frequency	36	23	85	75	44
		Percentage	13.7	8.7	32.3	28.5	16.7

Source: Primary Data.

Among the total number of respondents 19.8 per cent felt that the Horlicks advertisement had ethical values, 13.3 per cent felt it was highly ethical, 35.7 per cent felt unethical, 21.7 per cent felt highly unethical and the remaining nine point five per cent couldn't say any thing about this advertisement.

Among the total number of respondents 27.8 per cent felt that the Nescafe Sunrise advertisement had ethical values, 14.8 per cent felt it was highly ethical, 30.8 per cent felt unethical, 16.3 per cent felt highly unethical and the remaining 10:3 per cent couldn't say any thing about this advertisement.

Among the total number of respondents six point eight per cent felt that the KFC Chicken advertisement had ethical values, seven point six per cent felt it was highly ethical, 36.5 per cent felt unethical, 39.9 per cent felt highly unethical and the remaining nine point one per cent couldn't say any thing about this advertisement.

Among the total number of respondents 16.7 per cent felt that the Medimix Sandal Soap advertisement had ethical values, 11.4 per cent felt it was highly ethical, 29.3 per cent felt unethical, 32.7 per cent felt highly unethical and the remaining nine point nine per cent couldn't say any thing about this advertisement.

Among the total number of respondents 13.7 per cent felt that the Docomo advertisement had ethical values, 11.8 per cent felt it was highly ethical, 28.1 per cent felt unethical, 33.5 per cent felt highly unethical and the remaining 12.9 per cent couldn't say any thing about this advertisement.

Among the total number of respondents 10.3 per cent felt that the Yuva A810 advertisement had ethical values, 11.8 per cent felt it was highly ethical, 31.6 per cent felt unethical, 29.3 per cent felt highly unethical and the remaining 17.1 per cent couldn't say any thing about this advertisement.

Among the total number of respondents 14.8 per cent felt that the Colgate Max Fresh advertisement had ethical values, 11.0 per cent felt it was highly ethical, 31.9 per cent felt unethical, 30.4 per cent felt highly unethical and the remaining 11.8 per cent couldn't say any thing about this advertisement.

Among the total number of respondents 13.7 per cent felt that the Spinz Deo advertisement had ethical values, eight point seven per cent felt it was highly ethical, 32.3 per cent felt unethical, 28.5 per cent felt highly unethical and the remaining 16.7 per cent couldn't say any thing about this advertisement.

Table 5.24: Recall value of Binco Chips Advertisement among different Age Groups

Sl. No.	Can you recall the adverti-sing	Age						
		20 years (n=12)	21 years (n=58)	22 years (n=84)	23 years (n=67)	24 years (n=24)	Above 24 years (n=18)	Statistical Inference
1.	Yes	8(4.6)	38(22.0)	60(34.7)	42(24.3)	15(8.7)	10(5.8)	$\chi2$ = 2.432 Sig=0.787 df = 5 P > 0.05 Not Significant
2.	No	4(4.4)	20(22.2)	24(26.7)	25(27.8)	9(10.0)	8(8.9)	

Source: Compiled from primary data

The above given table shows that there is no significant difference between the different age groups of respondents and their recall value of the advertisement. The $\chi2$ table shows that there is no statistically valid relation between different age group and their ability to recall the advertisement. The recall does not by itself measure a single underlying memory state. Rather memory is multi dimensional. Recall captures only a portion of memory. All the different age group of respondents have different recall value of this advertisement.

Table 5.25: Remembering the Content of Binco Chips advertisement among different Age Groups

Sl. No.	Can you remember the adverti-sing	Age						
		20 years (n=12)	21 years (n=58)	22 years (n=84)	23 years (n=67)	24 years (n=24)	Above 24 years (n=18)	Statistical Inference
1.	Yes	9(6.2)	36(24.7)	44(30.1)	33(22.6)	14(9.6)	10(6.8)	$\chi2$ = 4.329 Sig=0.503 df = 5 P > 0.05 Not Significant
2.	No	3(2.6)	22(18.8)	40(34.2)	34(29.1)	10(8.5)	8(6.8)	

Source: Compiled from primary data

The above table reveals that there is no significant difference between the different age groups of respondents and their remembering pattern of the content of the advertisement. The ÷2 table shows that there is no statistically valid relation between different age group and their ability to remember the content of the advertisement. All the different age groups of respondents have identical remembering skill about varied advertisements.

Table 5.26: Getting message from the Binco Chips Advertisement among different Age Groups

Sl. No.	Do you get mesage	Age						
		20 years (n=12)	21 years (n=58)	22 years (n=84)	23 years (n=67)	24 years (n=24)	Above 24 years (n=18)	Statistical Inference
1.	Yes	11(6.4)	37(21.6)	58(33.9)	37(21.6)	18(10.5)	10(5.8)	$\chi2$ = 8.971 Sig=0.110 df = 5 P > 0.05 Not Significant
2.	No	1(1.1)	21(22.8)	26(28.3)	30(32.6)	6(6.5)	8(8.7)	

Source: Compiled from primary data

The above table observes that there is no significant difference between the different age groups of respondents and getting message from the advertisement. The $\chi2$ table shows that there is no statistically valid relation between different age group and getting message from the advertisement. All the different age groups of respondents have got different message from different advertisement. This implies that the message received by the respondents on the basis of different age groups from the advertisement is not same and it is widely perceived and understood by entirely different manner.

The above table observes that there is no significant difference between the different age groups of respondents and received different kinds of

Table 5.27: Received different kinds of messages from Binco Chips Advertisement among different Age Groups

Sl. No.	Message	Age						
		20 years (n=11)	21 years (n=37)	22 years (n=58)	23 years (n=37)	24 years (n=18)	Above 24 years (n=10)	Statistical Inference
1.	Impact my life style	1(4.8)	7(33.7)	8(38.1)	2(9.5)	1(4.8)	2(9.5)	$\chi2$ = 36.332 Sig=0.067 df = 25 P > 0.05 Not Significant
2.	False technical jargon	2(6.7)	8(26.7)	10(33.3)	4(13.3)	6(20.0)	0(0.0)	
3.	Unethical value	3(6.7)	14(31.1)	14(31.1)	7(15.6)	5(11.1)	2(4.4)	
4.	Against the humanity	5(10.4)	7(14.6)	14(29.2)	14(29.2)	4(8.3)	4(8.3)	
5.	Dishonesty	0(0.0)	1(3.7)	12(44.4)	10(37.0)	2(7.4)	2(7.4)	

Source: Compiled from primary data

messages from the advertisement. The $\chi2$ table shows that there is no statistically valid relation between different age group and received different kinds of messages from the advertisement. All the different age groups of respondents have got different message from this advertisement. The messages relate to: (*i*) Impact my life style, (*ii*) False technical jargon (*iii*) Unethical value, (*iv*) Against the humanity, and (*v*) Dishonesty. The messages pertaining to the advertisement have not uniformly impacted the respondents. The respondents felt that the messages related to the above five mentioned aspects are not uniformly influence the respondents' behaviour.

Table 5.28: Acceptance of Binco Chips Advertisement among different Age Groups

Sl. No.	Do you accept	Age						
		20 years (n=12)	21 years (n=58)	22 years (n=84)	23 years (n=67)	24 years (n=24)	Above 24 years (n=18)	Statistical Inference
1.	Yes	2(6.1)	2(6.1)	12(36.4)	9(27.3)	5(15.2)	3(9.1)	$\chi2$ = 10.324 Sig=0.413 df = 10 P > 0.05 Not Significant
2.	No	8(4.1)	48(24.4)	59(29.9)	51(25.9)	16(8.1)	15(7.6)	
3.	Can't say	2(6.1)	8(24.2)	13(39.4)	7(21.2)	3(9.1)	0(0.0)	

Source: Compiled from primary data

The above given table depicts that there is no significant difference between the different age groups of respondents and their acceptance value of the advertisement. The χ2 table shows that there is no statistically valid relation between different age group and their acceptance value of the advertisement. All the different age groups of respondents have different opinion regarding acceptance of this advertisements. The respondents felt that the advertisements are really informative and educative only to some extent. The level of acceptance of the respondents has no bearing on the age composition of the respondents.

Table 5.29: Recall value of VVD Gold Coconut Oil Advertisement among different Age Groups

Sl. No.	Can you recall the advertising	Age						
		20 years (n=12)	21 years (n=58)	22 years (n=84)	23 years (n=67)	24 years (n=24)	Above 24 years (n=18)	Statistical Inference
1.	Yes	7(3.6)	38(19.7)	67(34.7)	49(25.4)	17(8.8)	15(7.8)	χ2 = 5.973 Sig=0.309 df = 5 P > 0.05 Not Significant
2.	No	5(7.1)	20(28.6)	17(24.3)	18(25.7)	7(10.0)	3(4.3)	

Source: Compiled from primary data

The above table depicts that there is no significant difference between the different age groups of respondents and their recall value of the advertisement. The χ2 table shows that there is no statistically valid relation between different age group and their ability to recall the advertisement. The recall does not by itself measure a single underlying memory state. Rather memory is multi dimensional. Recall captures only a portion of memory. All the different age group of respondents have different recall value of this advertisement.

Table 5.30: Remembering the content of VVD Gold Coconut Oil Advertisement among different age groups

Sl. No.	Can you remember the adverti-sing	Age						
		20 years (n=12)	21 years (n=58)	22 years (n=84)	23 years (n=67)	24 years (n=24)	Above 24 years (n=18)	Statistical Inference
1.	Yes	7(3.8)	41(22.0)	61(32.8)	47(25.3)	15(8.1)	15(8.1)	χ2 = 3.212 Sig=0.667 df = 5 P > 0.05 Not Significant
2.	No	5(6.5)	17(22.1)	23(29.9)	20(26.0)	9(11.7)	3(3.9)	

Source: Compiled from primary data.

The above table observes that there is no significant difference between the different age groups of respondents and their remembering pattern of the content of the advertisement. The $\chi 2$ table shows that there is no statistically valid relation between different age group and their ability to remember the content of the advertisement. All the different age groups of respondents have identical remembering skill about varied advertisements.

Table 5.31: Getting Message from VVD Gold Coconut Oil advertisement among different Age Groups

Sl. No.	Do you get message	Age						
		20 years (n=12)	21 years (n=58)	22 years (n=84)	23 years (n=67)	24 years (n=24)	Above 24 years (n=18)	Statistical Inference
1.	Yes	11(5.2)	49(23.0)	72(33.8)	49(23.0)	19(8.9)	13(6.1)	$\chi 2$ = 6.201 Sig=0.287 df = 5 P > 0.05 Not Significant
2.	No	1(2.0)	9(18.0)	12(24.0)	18(36.0)	5(10.0)	5(10.0)	

Source: Compiled from primary data

The above given table shows that there is no significant difference between the different age groups of respondents and getting message from the advertisement. The $\chi 2$ table shows that there is no statistically valid relation between different age group and getting message from the advertisement. All the different age groups of respondents have got different message from different advertisement. This implies that the message

Table 5.32: Received different kinds of Messages from VVD Gold Coconut Oil Advertisement among different Age Groups

Sl.No.	Message	Age						
		20 years (n=11)	21 years (n=49)	22 years (n=72)	23 years (n=49)	24 years (n=19)	Above 24 years (n=13)	Statistical Inference
1.	Impact my life style	2(7.4)	3(11.1)	10(37.0)	6(22.2)	4(14.8)	2(7.4)	$\chi 2$ = 19.509 Sig=0.772 df = 25 P > 0.05 Not Significant
2.	Affect my future purchase	1(2.9)	10(29.4)	12(35.3)	6(17.6)	3(8.8)	2(5.9)	
3.	Open criticism of competitors	4(5.1)	21(26.9)	25(32.1)	15(19.2)	6(7.7)	7(9.0)	
4.	Unfair comparison	3(6.1)	8(16.3)	16(32.7)	17(34.7)	3(6.1)	2(4.1)	
5.	Misleading presentation of fact	1(4.0)	7(28.0)	9(36.0)	5(20.0)	3(12.0)	0(0.0)	

Source: Compiled from primary data

received by the respondents on the basis of different age groups from the advertisement is not same and it is widely perceived and understood by entirely different manner.

The above table depicts that there is no significant difference between the different age groups of respondents and received different kinds of messages from the advertisement. The χ2 table shows that there is no statistically valid relation between different age group and received different kinds of messages from the advertisement. All the different age groups of respondents have got different message from this advertisement. The messages relates to: (*i*) Impact my life style, (*ii*) Affect my future purchase (*iii*) Open criticism of competitors, (*iv*) Unfair comparison and (*v*) Misleading presentation of facts. The messages pertaining to the advertisement have not uniformed impacted the respondents. The respondents felt that the messages related to the above mentioned aspects are not uniformly influence the respondents' behaviour.

Table 5.33: Acceptance of VVD Gold Coconut Oil Advertisement among different Age Groups

Sl. No.	Do you accept	Age						
		20 years (n=12)	21 years (n=58)	22 years (n=84)	23 years (n=67)	24 years (n=24)	Above 24 years (n=18)	Statistical Inference
1.	Yes	4(8.0)	4(8.0)	21(42.0)	12(24.0)	5(10.0)	4(8.0)	χ2 = 16.332 Sig=0.091 df = 10 P > 0.05 Not Significant
2.	No	8(4.6)	42(24.1)	53(30.5)	48(27.6)	14(8.0)	9(5.2)	
3.	Can't say	0(0.0)	12(30.8)	10(25.8)	7(17.9)	5.(12.8)	5(12.8)	

Source: Compiled from primary data

The above table reveals that there is no significant difference between the different age groups of respondents and their acceptance value of the advertisement. The χ2 table shows that there is no statistically valid relation

Table 5.34: Recall Value of Horlicks Advertisement among different Age Groups

Sl. No.	Can you recall the adverti-sing	Age						
		20 years (n=12)	21 years (n=58)	22 years (n=84)	23 years (n=67)	24 years (n=24)	Above 24 years (n=18)	Statistical Inference
1.	Yes	6(3.0)	45(22.2)	67(33.0)	53(26.1)	18(8.9)	14(6.9)	χ2 = 5.567 Sig=0.351 df = 5 P > 0.05 Not Significant
2.	No	6(10.0)	13(21.7)	17(28.3)	14(23.3)	6(10.0)	4(6.7)	

Source: Compiled from primary data.

between different age group and their acceptance value of the advertisement. All the different age groups of respondents have different opinion regarding acceptance of this advertisements. The respondents felt that the advertisements are really informative and educative only to some extent. The level of acceptance of the respondents has no bearing on the age composition of the respondents.

The above given table shows that there is no significant difference between the different age groups of respondents and their recall value of the advertisement. The $\chi2$ table shows that there is no statistically valid relation between different age group and their ability to recall the advertisement. The recall does not by itself measure a single underlying memory state. Rather memory is multi dimensional. Recall captures only a portion of memory. All the different age group of respondents have different recall value of this advertisement.

Table 5.35: Remembering the Content of Horlicks Advertisement among different Age Groups

Sl. No.	Can you remember the advertising	Age						
		20 years (n=12)	21 years (n=58)	22 years (n=84)	23 years (n=67)	24 years (n=24)	Above 24 years (n=18)	Statistical Inference
1	Yes	7(3.6)	47(24.4)	62(32.1)	46(23.8)	18(9.3)	13(6.7)	$\chi2$ = 3.949 Sig=0.557 df = 5 P > 0.05 Not Significant
2	No	5(7.1)	11(15.7)	22(31.4)	21(30.0)	6(8.6)	5.(7.1).	

Source: Compiled from primary data

The above table reveals that there is no significant difference between the different age groups of respondents and their remembering pattern of the content of the advertisement. The $\chi2$ table shows that there is no

Table 5.36: Getting Message from Horlicks Advertisement among different Age Groups

Sl. No.	Do you get mesage	Age						
		20 years (n=12)	21 years (n=58)	22 years (n=84)	23 years (n=67)	24 years (n=24)	Above 24 years (n=18)	Statistical Inference
1.	Yes	10(4.9)	47(22.8)	66(32.0)	50(24.3)	19(9.2)	14(6.8)	$\chi2$ = 0.984 Sig=0.964 df = 5 P > 0.05 Not Significant
2.	No	2(3.5)	11(19.3)	18(31.6)	17(29.8)	5(8.8)	4(7.0)	

Source: Compiled from primary data

statistically valid relation between different age group and their ability to remember the content of the advertisement. All the different age groups of respondents have identical remembering skill about varied advertisements.

The above table observes that there is no significant difference between the different age groups of respondents and getting message from the advertisement. The $\chi 2$ table shows that there is no statistically valid relation between different age group and getting message from the advertisement. All the different age groups of respondents have got different message from different advertisement. This implies that the message received by the respondents on the basis of different age groups from the advertisement is not same and it is widely perceived and understood by entirely different manner.

Table 5.37: Received different kinds of Messages from Horlicks Advertisement among different Age Groups

Sl. No.	Message	Age						
		20 years (n=10)	21 years (n=47)	22 years (n=66)	23 years (n=50)	24 years (n=19)	Above 24 years (n=14)	Statistical Inference
1.	Impact my life style	0(0.0)	5(18.5)	7(25.9)	9(33.3)	3(11.1)	3(11.1)	$\chi 2$ = 19.952 Sig=0.749 df = 25 P > 0.05 Not Significant
2.	Degenerates the youth	3(4.2)	14(19.4)	30(41.7)	18(25.0)	6(8.3)	1(1.4)	
3.	Affect my future purchase	1(5.3)	5(26.3)	7(36.8)	4(21.1)	2(10.5)	0(0.0)	
4.	Unethical value	4(9.8)	11(26.8)	11(26.8)	7(17.1)	3(7.3)	8(12.2)	
5.	Against public rules	2(4.3)	12(25.5)	11(23.4)	12(25.5)	5(10.6)	5(10.6)	

Source: Compiled from primary data.

The above table shows that there is no significant difference between the different age groups of respondents and received different kinds of messages from the advertisement. The $\chi 2$ table shows that there is no statistically valid relation between different age group and received different kinds of messages from the advertisement. All the different age groups of respondents have got different message from this advertisement. The messages relate to: (*i*) Degenerate the youth, (*ii*) Dishonesty, (*iii*) Against the humanity, (*iv*) Trade puffing and exaggeration and (*v*) Misleading information. The messages pertaining to the advertisement have not uniformed impacted the respondents. The respondents felt that the messages related to the above five mentioned aspects are not uniformly influenced the respondents' behaviour.

Table 5.38: Acceptance of Horlicks Advertisement among different Age Groups

Sl. No.	Do you accept	Age						
		20 years (n=12)	21 years (n=58)	22 years (n=84)	23 years (n=67)	24 years (n=24)	Above 24 years (n=18)	Statistical Inference
1.	Yes	2(4.5)	7(15.9)	15(34.1)	7(15.9)	7(15.9)	6(13.6)	$\chi2$ = 18.815 Sig=0.043 df = 10 P < 0.05 Significant
2.	No	5(2.9)	39(22.3)	54(30.9)	53(30.3)	15(8.6)	9(5.1)	
3.	Can't say	5(11.4)	12(27.3)	15(34.1)	7(15.9)	2(4.5)	3(6.8)	

Source: Compiled from primary data.

The above table reveals clearly there is a significant difference among different age groups and acceptance of Horlicks advertisement. The $\chi2$ table shows that there is statistically valid relationship between different age groups and acceptance of the Horlicks advertisement. The respondents felt that the advertisements are really informative and educative only to some extent. The level of acceptance of the respondents has no bearing on the age composition of the respondents.

Table 5.39: Recall value of Nescafe Sunrise advertisement among different Age Groups

Sl. No.	Can you recall the advertising	Age						
		20 years (n=12)	21 years (n=58)	22 years (n=84)	23 years (n=67)	24 years (n=24)	Above 24 years (n=18)	Statistical Inference
1.	Yes	7(3.3)	46(21.7)	69(32.5)	56(26.4)	19(9.0)	15(7.1)	$\chi2$ = 4.495 Sig=0.481 df = 5 P > 0.05 Not Significant
2.	No	5(9.8)	12(23.5)	15(29.4)	11(21.6)	5(9.8)	3(5.9)	

Source: Compiled from primary data.

The above given table shows that there is no significant difference between the different age groups of respondents and their recall value of the advertisement. The $\chi2$ table shows that there is no statistically valid relation between different age group and their ability to recall the advertisement. The recall does not by itself measure a single underlying memory state. Rather memory is multi dimensional. Recall captures only a portion of memory. All the different age group of respondents have different recall value of this advertisement.

Table 5.40: Remembering the content of Nescafe Sunrise advertisement among different Age Groups

Sl. No.	Can you remember the advertising	Age						
		20 years (n=12)	21 years (n=58)	22 years (n=84)	23 years (n=67)	24 years (n=24)	Above 24 years (n=18)	Statistical Inference
1.	Yes	10(5.0)	47(23.4)	61(30.3)	48(23.9)	20(10.0)	15(7.5)	$\chi2$ = 3.641 Sig=0.602 df = 5 P>0.05 Not Significant
2.	No	2(3.2)	11(17.7)	23(37.1)	19(30.6)	4(6.5)	3(4.8)	

Source: Compiled from primary data

The above table observes that there is no significant difference between the different age groups of respondents and their remembering pattern of the content of the advertisement. The $\chi2$ table shows that there is no statistically valid relation between different age group and their ability to remember the content of the advertisement. All the different age groups of respondents have identical remembering skill about varied advertisements.

Table 5.41: Getting message from the Nescafe Sunrise Advertisement among different Age Groups

Sl. No.	Do you get message	Age						
		20 years (n=12)	21 years (n=58)	22 years (n=84)	23 years (n=67)	24 years (n=24)	Above 24 years (n=18)	Statistical Inference
1.	Yes	11(5.2)	48(22.5)	65(30.5)	54(25.4)	21(9.9)	14(6.6)	$\chi2$ = 2.505 Sig=0.776 df = 5 P > 0.05 Not Significant
2.	No	1(2.0)	10(20.0)	19(38.0)	13(26.0)	3(6.0)	4(8.0)	

Source: Compiled from primary data

The above table depicts that there is no significant difference between the different age groups of respondents and getting message from the advertisement. The $\chi2$ table shows that there is no statistically valid relation between different age group and getting message from the advertisement. All the different age groups of respondents have got different message from different advertisement. This implies that the message received by the respondents on the basis of different age groups from the advertisement is not same and it is widely perceived and understood by entirely different manner.

Table 5.42: Received different kinds of messages from Nescafe Sunrise Advertisement among different Age Groups

Sl. No.	Message	Age						
		20 years (n=11)	21 years (n=48)	22 years (n=65)	23 years (n=54)	24 years (n=21)	Above 24 years (n=14)	Statistical Inference
1.	Impact my life style	6(7.6)	20(25.3)	19(24.1)	21(26.6)	9(11.4)	4(5.1)	$\chi2$ = 32.128 Sig=0.154 df = 25 P > 0.05 Not Significant
2.	Affect my future purchase	2(14.3)	2(14.3)	6(42.9)	3(21.4)	0(0.0)	1(7.1)	
3.	Trade Puffing and exagg-eration	0(0.0)	1(5.6)	9(50.0)	5(27.8)	1(5.6)	2(11.1)	
4.	Degenerate our culture	3(4.5)	21(31.3)	18(26.9)	12(17.9)	6(9.0)	7(10.4)	
5.	Unethical value	0(0.0)	4(11.4)	13(37.1)	13(37.1)	5(14.3)	0(0.0)	

Source: Compiled from primary data

The above table shows that there is no significant difference between the different age groups of respondents and received different kinds of messages from the advertisement. The $\chi2$ table shows that there is no statistically valid relation between different age group and received different kinds of messages from the advertisement. All the different age groups of respondents have got different message from this advertisement. The messages relates to (*i*) Impact my life style, (*ii*) Affect my future purchase, (*iii*) Trade puffing and exaggeration, (*iv*) Degenerates our culture and (*v*) Unethical value. The messages pertaining to the advertisement have not

Table 5.43: Acceptance of Nescafe Sunrise Advertisement among different Age Groups

Sl. No.	Do you accept	Age						
		20 years (n=12)	21 years (n=58)	22 years (n=84)	23 years (n=67)	24 years (n=24)	Above 24 years (n=18)	Statistical Inference
1	Yes	5(5.3)	19(20.0)	27(28.4)	26(27.4)	11(11.6)	7(7.4)	$\chi2$=14.317 Sig=0.159 df = 10 P > 0.05 Not Significant
2	No	6(4.4)	27(19.7)	46(33.6)	40(29.2)	9(6.6)	9(6.6)	
3	Can't say	1(3.2)	12(38.7)	11(35.5)	1(3.2)	4(12.9)	2(6.5)	

Source: Compiled from primary data

uniformed impacted the respondents. The respondents felt that the messages related to above five mentioned aspects are not uniformly influence the respondents' behaviour.

The above table reveals that there is no significant difference between the different age groups of respondents and getting message from the advertisement. The $\chi 2$ table shows that there is no statistically valid relation between different age group and getting message from the advertisement. All the different age groups of respondents have got different message from different advertisement. The respondents felt that the advertisements are really informative and educative only to some extent. The level of acceptance of the respondents has no bearing on the age composition of the respondents.

Table 5.44: Recall value of the KFC Chicken advertisement among different age groups

Sl. No.	Can you recall the advertising	Age						
		20 years (n=12)	21 years (n=58)	22 years (n=84)	23 years (n=67)	24 years (n=24)	Above 24 years (n=18)	Statistical Inference
1.	Yes	5(2.9)	42(24.1)	53(30.5)	46(26.4)	16(9.2)	12(6.9)	$\chi 2$ = 4.772 Sig=0.444 df = 5 P > 0.05 Not Significant
2.	No	7(7.9)	16(18.0)	31(34.8)	21(23.6)	8(9.0)	6(6.7)	

Source: Compiled from primary data

The above given table reveals that there is no significant difference between the different age groups of respondents and their recall value of the advertisement. The $\chi 2$ table shows that there is no statistically valid relation between different age group and their ability to recall the

Table 5.45: Remembering the content of the KFC Chicken advertisement among different Age Groups

Sl. No.	Can you remember the advertising	Age						
		20 years (n=12)	21 years (n=58)	22 years (n=84)	23 years (n=67)	24 years (n=24)	Above 24 years (n=18)	Statistical Inference
1.	Yes	6(3.9)	39(25.2)	49(31.6)	36(23.2)	15(9.7)	10(6.5)	$\chi 2$ = 3.023 Sig=0.697 df = 5 P > 0.05 Not Significant
2.	No	6(5.6)	19(17.6)	35(32.4)	31(28.7)	9(8.3)	8(7.4)	

Source: Compiled from primary data

advertisement. The recall does not by itself measure a single underlying memory state. Rather memory is multi dimensional. Recall captures only a portion of memory. All the different age group of respondents have different recall value of this advertisement.

The above table depicts that there is no significant difference between the different age groups of respondents and their remembering pattern of the content of the advertisement. The $\chi 2$ table shows that there is no statistically valid relation between different age group and their ability to remember the content of the advertisement. All the different age groups of respondents have identical remembering skill about varied advertisements.

Table 5.46: Getting Message from the KFC Chicken advertisement among different Age Groups

Sl. No.	Do you get message	Age						
		20 years (n=12)	21 years (n=58)	22 years (n=84)	23 years (n=67)	24 years (n=24)	Above 24 years (n=18)	Statistical Inference
1	Yes	9(4.6)	47(24.1)	62(31.8)	49(25.1)	17(8.7)	11(5.6)	$\chi 2$ = 3.214 Sig=0.667 df = 5 P > 0.05 Not Significant
2	No	3(4.4)	11(16.2)	22(32.2)	18(26.5)	7(10.3)	7(10.3)	

Source: Compiled from primary data

The above table observes that there is no significant difference between the different age groups of respondents and getting message from the advertisement. The $\chi 2$ table shows that there is no statistically valid relation

Table 5.47: Received different kinds of messages from KFC Chicken Advertisement among different Age Groups

Sl. No.	Message	Age						
		20 years (n=9)	21 years (n=47)	22 years (n=62)	23 years (n=49)	24 years (n=17)	Above 24 years (n=11)	Statistical Inference
1.	Impact my life style	1(6.3)	6(37.5)	3(18.8)	4(25.0)	2(12.5)	0(0.0)	$\chi 2$ = 22.367 Sig=0.614 df = 25 P > 0.05 Not Significant
2.	Degenerates the youth	2(6.3)	10(31.3)	10(31.3)	5(15.6)	3(9.4)	2(6.3)	
3.	Affect my future purchase	0(0.0)	5(35.7)	6(42.9)	1(7.1)	2(14.3)	0(0.0)	
4.	Unethical value	2(3.8)	6(11.5)	18(34.6)	18(34.6)	6(11.5)	2(3.8)	
5.	Against Public rules	4(4.9)	20(24.7)	25(30.9)	21(25.9)	4(4.9)	7(8.6)	

Source: Compiled from primary data

between different age group and getting message from the advertisement. All the different age groups of respondents have got different message from different advertisement. This implies that the message received by the respondents on the basis of different age groups from the advertisement is not same and it is widely perceived and understood by entirely different manner.

The above table reveals that there is no significant difference between the different age groups of respondents and received different kinds of messages from the advertisement. The $\chi 2$ table shows that there is no statistically valid relation between different age group and received different kinds of messages from the advertisement. All the different age groups of respondents have got different message from this advertisement. The messages related to (*i*) Impact my life style, (*ii*) Degenerates the youth, (*iii*) Affect my future purchase, (*iv*) Unethical value and (*v*) Against public rules. The messages pertaining to the advertisement have not uniformed impacted the respondents. The respondents felt that the messages related to above five mentioned aspects are not uniformly influence the respondents' behaviour.

Table 5.48: Acceptance of KFC Chicken Advertisement among different age groups

Sl. No.	Do you accept	Age						
		20 years (n=12)	21 years (n=58)	22 years (n=84)	23 years (n=67)	24 years (n=24)	Above 24 years (n=18)	Statistical Inference
1.	Yes	0(0.0)	4(17.4)	8(34.8)	4(17.4)	6(26.1)	1(4.3)	$\chi 2$ = 15.403 Sig=0.118 df = 10 P > 0.05 Not Significant
2.	No	8(4.0)	47(23.4)	67(33.3)	51(25.4)	14(7.0)	14(7.0)	
3.	Can't say	4(10.3)	7(17.9)	9(23.1)	12(30.8)	4(10.3)	3(7.7)	

Source: Compiled from primary data

The above table shows that there is no significant difference between the different age groups of respondents and getting message from the advertisement. The $\chi 2$ table shows that there is no statistically valid relation between different age group and getting message from the advertisement. All the different age groups of respondents have got different message from different advertisement. The respondents felt that the advertisements are really informative and educative only to some extent. The level of acceptance of the respondents has no bearing on the age composition of the respondents.

Table 5.49: Recall value of the Medimix Sandal Soap Advertisement among different Age Groups

Sl. No.	Can you recall the advertising	Age						
		20 years (n=12)	21 years (n=58)	22 years (n=84)	23 years (n=67)	24 years (n=24)	Above 24 years (n=18)	Statistical Inference
1.	Yes	9(4.7)	42(21.8)	62(32.1)	50(25.9)	19(9.8)	11(5.7)	$\chi2$ = 1.904 Sig=0.862 df = 7 P > 0.05 Not Significant
2.	No	3(4.3)	16(22.9)	22(31.4)	17(24.3)	5(7.1)	7(10.0)	

Source: Compiled from primary data

The above given table depicts that there is no significant difference between the different age groups of respondents and their recall value of the advertisement. The $\chi2$ table shows that there is no statistically valid relation between different age group and their ability to recall the advertisement. The recall does not by itself measure a single underlying memory state. Rather memory is multi dimensional. Recall captures only a portion of memory. All the different age group of respondents have different recall value of this advertisement.

Table 5.50: Remembering the content of Medimix Sandal Soap Advertisement among different Age Groups

Sl. No.	Can you remember the advertising	Age						
		20 years (n=12)	21 years (n=58)	22 years (n=84)	23 years (n=67)	24 years (n=24)	Above 24 years (n=18)	Statistical Inference
1.	Yes	9(5.2)	41(23.6)	54(31.0)	43(24.7)	17(9.8)	10(5.7)	$\chi2$ = 2.338 Sig=0.801 df = 5 P>0.05 Not Significant
2.	No	3(3.4)	17(19.1)	30(33.7)	24(27.0)	7(7.9)	8(9.0)	

Source: Compiled from primary data

The above table shows that there is no significant difference between the different age groups of respondents and their remembering pattern of the content of the advertisement. The $\chi2$ table shows that there is no statistically valid relation between different age group and their ability to remember the content of the advertisement. All the different age groups of respondents have identical remembering skill about varied advertisements.

Table 5.51: Getting Message from Medimix Sandal Soap advertisement among different Age Groups

Sl. No.	Do you get mesage	Age						
		20 years (n=12)	21 years (n=58)	22 years (n=84)	23 years (n=67)	24 years (n=24)	Above 24 years (n=18)	Statistical Inference
1	Yes	10(4.9)	46(22.3)	70(34.0)	51(24.8)	19(9.2)	10(4.9)	$\chi2$ = 7.151 Sig=0.210 df = 5 P > 0.05 Not Significant
2	No	2(3.5)	12(21.1)	14(24.6)	16(28.1)	5(8.8)	8(14.0)	

Source: Compiled from primary data

The above table reveals that there is no significant difference between the different age groups of respondents and getting message from the advertisement. The $\chi2$ table shows that there is no statistically valid relation between different age group and getting message from the advertisement. All the different age groups of respondents have got different message from different advertisement. This implies that the message received by the respondents on the basis of different age groups from the advertisement is not same and it is widely perceived and understood by entirely different manner.

Table 5.52: Received different kinds of messages from Medimix Sandal Soap Advertisement among different Age Groups

Sl. No.	Message	Age						
		20 years (n=10)	21 years (n=46)	22 years (n=70)	23 years (n=51)	24 years (n=19)	Above 24 years (n=10)	Statistical Inference
1.	Impact my life style	1(10.0)	6(13.1)	8(11.4)	4(7.8)	3(15.8)	0(0.0)	$\chi2$ = 22.367 Sig=0.614 df = 25 P > 0.05 Not Significant
2.	Deliberate omission of a needed information	2(20.0)	10(21.7)	10(14.3)	6(11.7)	3(15.8)	2(20.0)	
3.	Misleading presentation of facts	1(10.0)	4(8.6)	10(14.3)	6(11.7)	3(15.8)	0(0.0)	
4.	Unethical value	2(20.0)	6(13.1)	18(25.7)	14(27.6)	6(31.5)	2(20.0)	
5.	Degenerates our culture	4(40.0)	20(43.5)	24(34.3)	21(41.2)	4(21.1)	6(60.0)	

Source: Compiled from primary data

The above table reveals that there is no significant difference between the different age groups of respondents and received different kinds of messages from the advertisement. The $\chi 2$ table shows that there is no statistically valid relation between different age group and received different kinds of messages from the advertisement. All the different age groups of respondents have got different message from this advertisement. The messages relate to (*i*) Impact my life style, (*ii*) Deliberate omission of a needed information, (*iii*) Misleading presentation of facts, (*iv*) Unethical value and (*v*) Degenerates our culture. The messages pertaining to the advertisement have not uniformed impacted the respondents. The respondents felt that the messages related to above five mentioned aspects are not uniformly influence the respondents' behaviour.

Table 5.53: Acceptance of Medimix Sandal Soap advertisement among different Age Groups

Sl. No.	Do you accept	Age						
		20 years (n=12)	21 years (n=58)	22 years (n=84)	23 years (n=67)	24 years (n=24)	Above 24 years (n=18)	Statistical Inference
1.	Yes	2(4.9)	9(22.0)	12(29.3)	10(24.4)	6(14.6)	2(4.9)	$\chi 2$ = 9.790 Sig=0.459 df = 10 $P < 0.05$ Significant
2.	No	7(4.4)	36(22.6)	53(33.3)	41(25.8)	15(9.4)	7(4.4)	
3.	Can't say	3(4.8)	13(20.6)	19(30.2)	16(25.4)	3(4.8)	9(14.3)	

Source: Compiled from primary data

The above table observes clearly there is a significant difference among different age groups and acceptance of Medimix Sandal Soap advertisement. The $\chi 2$ table shows that there is statistically valid relationship between different age groups and acceptance of the Medimix Sandal Soap

Table 5.54: Recall value of the Docomo advertisement among different Age Groups

Sl. No.	Can you recall the adver-tising	Age						
		20 years (n=12)	21 years (n=58)	22 years (n=84)	23 years (n=67)	24 years (n=24)	Above 24 years (n=18)	Statistical Inference
1.	Yes	10(5.2)	44(22.7)	63(32.5)	49(25.3)	16(8.2)	12(6.2)	$\chi 2$ = 1.873 Sig=0.866 df = 5 $P > 0.05$ Not Significant
2.	No	2(2.9)	14(20.3)	21(30.4)	18(26.1)	8(11.6)	6(8.7)	

Source: Compiled from primary data

advertisement. The respondents felt that the advertisements are really informative and educative only to some extent. The level of acceptance of the respondents has no bearing on the age composition of the respondents.

The above given table revels that there is no significant difference between the different age groups of respondents and their recall value of the advertisement. The $\chi 2$ table shows that there is no statistically valid relation between different age group and their ability to recall the advertisement. The recall does not by itself measure a single underlying memory state. Rather memory is multi dimensional. Recall captures only a portion of memory. All the different age group of respondents have different recall value of this advertisement.

Table 5.55: Remembering the Content of Docomo Advertisement among different age groups

Sl. No.	Can you remember the adverti-sing	Age						
		20 years (n=12)	21 years (n=58)	22 years (n=84)	23 years (n=67)	24 years (n=24)	Above 24 years (n=18)	Statistical Inference
1.	Yes	10(5.8)	40(23.1)	59(34.1)	43(24.9)	13(7.5)	8(4.6)	$\chi 2$ = 7.800 Sig=0.168 df = 5 P > 0.05 Not Significant
2.	No	2(2.2)	18(20.0)	25(27.8)	24(26.7)	11(12.2)	10(11.1)	

Source: Compiled from primary data

The above table depicts that there is no significant difference between the different age groups of respondents and their remembering pattern of the content of the advertisement. The $\chi 2$ table shows that there is no statistically valid relation between different age group and their ability to remember the content of the advertisement. All the different age groups of respondents have identical remembering skill about varied advertisements.

Table 5.56: Getting Message from Docomo Advertisements among different Age Groups

Sl. No.	Do you get message	Age						
		20 years (n=12)	21 years (n=58)	22 years (n=84)	23 years (n=67)	24 years (n=24)	Above 24 years (n=18)	Statistical Inference
1.	Yes	6(3.2)	40(21.6)	64(34.6)	51(27.6)	17(9.2)	7(3.8)	$\chi 2$ = 13.421 Sig=0.020 df = 5 P < 0.05 Significant
2.	No	6(7.7)	18(23.1)	20(25.6)	16(20.5)	7(9.0)	11(14.1)	

Source: Compiled from primary data

The above table observes clearly there is a significant difference among different age groups and getting message from Docomo advertisement. The $\chi 2$ table shows that there is statistically valid relationship between different age groups and getting message from Docomo advertisement. This implies that the message received by the respondents on the basis of different age groups from the advertisement is not same and it is widely perceived and understood by entirely different manner.

Table 5.57: Received different kinds of messages from Docomo Advertisement among different Age Groups

Sl. No.	Message	Age						
		20 years (n=6)	21 years (n=40)	22 years (n=64)	23 years (n=51)	24 years (n=17)	Above 24 years (n=7)	Statistical Inference
1.	Impact my life style	2(6.7)	9(30.0)	8(26.7)	9(30.0)	2(6.7)	0(0.0)	$\chi 2$ = 29.33 Sig=0.263 df = 25 P > 0.05 Not Significant
2.	Misleading presentation of facts	0(0.0)	7(26.9)	8(30.8)	8(30.8)	2(7.7)	1(3.8)	
3.	Degenerates the youth	2(4.8)	11(26.8)	14(33.3)	8(19.0)	6(14.3)	1(2.4)	
4.	Degenerates our culture	1(2.9)	5(14.3)	13(37.1)	8(22.9)	4(11.4)	4(11.4)	
5.	Unethical value	1(1.9)	8(15.4)	21(40.4)	18(34.6)	3(5.8)	1(1.9)	

Source: Compiled from primary data

The above table depicts that there is no significant difference between the different age groups of respondents and received different kinds of messages from the advertisement. The $\chi 2$ table shows that there is no statistically valid relation between different age group and received different kinds of messages from the advertisement. All the different age groups of respondents have got different message from this advertisement. The messages relates to (*i*) Impact my life style, (*ii*) Misleading presentation of facts, (*iii*) Degenerates the youth, (*iv*) Degenerate our culture and (*v*) Unethical value. The messages pertaining to the advertisement have not uniformed impacted the respondents. The respondents felt that the messages related to above five mentioned aspects are not uniformly influence the respondents' behaviour.

Table 5.58: Acceptance of Docomo Advertisement among different Age Groups

Sl. No.	Do you accept	Age						
		20 years (n=12)	21 years (n=58)	22 years (n=84)	23 years (n=67)	24 years (n=24)	Above 24 years (n=18)	Statistical Inference
1.	Yes	3(7.0)	5(11.6)	18(41.9)	12(27.9)	4(9.3)	1(2.3)	$\chi2$ = 16.147 Sig=0.095 df = 10 P>0.05 Not Significant
2.	No	8(4.2)	47(24.5)	58(30.2)	50(26.0)	18(9.4)	11(5.7)	
3.	Can't say	1(3.6)	6(21.4)	8(28.6)	5(17.9)	2(7.1)	6(21.4)	

Source: Compiled from primary data

The above given table shows that there is no significant difference between the different age groups of respondents and their acceptance value of the advertisement. The $\chi2$ table shows that there is no statistically valid relation between different age group and their acceptance value of the advertisement. All the different age groups of respondents have different opinion regarding acceptance of this advertisements. The respondents felt that the advertisements are really informative and educative only to some extent. The level of acceptance of the respondents has no bearing on the age comparison of the respondents.

Table 5.59: Recall value of Yuva A810 advertisement among different Age Groups

Sl. No.	Can you recall the adverti-sing	Age						
		20 years (n=12)	21 years (n=58)	22 years (n=84)	23 years (n=67)	24 years (n=24)	Above 24 years (n=18)	Statistical Inference
1.	Yes	10(5.2)	42(21.8)	62(32.1)	52(26.9)	16(8.3)	11(5.7)	$\chi2$ = 3.200 Sig=0.669 df = 5 P > 0.05 Not Significant
2.	No	2(2.9)	16(22.9)	22(31.4)	15(21.4)	8(11.4)	7(10.0)	

Source: Compiled from primary data

The above given table shows that there is no significant difference between the different age groups of respondents and their recall value of the advertisement. The $\chi2$ table shows that there is no statistically valid relation between different age group and their ability to recall the advertisement. The recall does not by itself measure a single underlying memory state. Rather memory is multi dimensional. Recall captures only a portion of memory. All the different age group of respondents have different recall value of this advertisement.

Table 5.60: Remembering the content of Yuva A810 Advertisement among different Age Groups

Sl. No.	Can you remember the adverti-sing	Age						
		20 years (n=12)	21 years (n=58)	22 years (n=84)	23 years (n=67)	24 years (n=24)	Above 24 years (n=18)	Statistical Inference
1.	Yes	7(4.0)	42(24.0)	58(33.1)	45(25.7)	12(6.9)	11(6.3)	$\chi2$ = 4.698 Sig=0.454 df = 5 P > 0.05 Not Significant
2.	No	5(5.7)	16(18.2)	26(29.5)	22(25.0)	12(13.6)	7(8.0)	

Source: Compiled from primary data

The above table observes that there is no significant difference between the different age groups of respondents and their remembering pattern of the content of the advertisement. The $\chi2$ table shows that there is no statistically valid relation between different age group and their ability to remember the content of the advertisement. All the different age groups of respondents have identical remembering skill about varied advertisements.

Table 5.61: Getting message from Yuva A810 Advertisement among different Age Groups

Sl. No.	Do you get message	Age						
		20 years (n=12)	21 years (n=58)	22 years (n=84)	23 years (n=67)	24 years (n=24)	Above 24 years (n=18)	Statistical Inference
1.	Yes	9(4.6)	43(21.8)	63(32.0)	50(25.4)	20(10.2)	12(6.1)	$\chi2$ = 1.578 Sig=0.904 df = 5 P > 0.05 Not Significant
2.	No	3(4.5)	15(22.7)	21(31.8)	17(25.8)	4(6.1)	6(9.1)	

Source: Compiled from primary data

The above table depicts that there is no significant difference between the different age groups of respondents and getting message from the advertisement. The $\chi2$ table shows that there is no statistically valid relation between different age group and getting message from the advertisement. All the different age groups of respondents have got different message from different advertisement. This implies that the message received by the respondents on the basis of different age groups from the advertisement is not same and it is widely perceived entirely in a different manner.

Table 5.62: Received different kinds of messages from Yuva A810 Advertisement among different Age Groups

Sl. No.	Message	Age						
		20 years (n=9)	21 years (n=43)	23 years (n=63)	23 years (n=50)	24 years (n=20)	Above 24 years (n=12)	Statistical Inference
1.	Impact my life style	2(11.1)	4(22.5)	8(44.4)	3(16.7)	1(5.6)	0(0.0)	χ2 = 25.929 Sig=0.411 df = 25 P>0.05 Not Significant
2.	Degenerates the youth	2(3.8)	12(23.1)	12(23.1)	19(36.5)	4(7.7)	3.(5.8)	
3.	Misleading presentation of facts	0(0.0)	3(14.3)	9(42.9)	3(14.3)	3(14.3)	3(14.3)	
4.	Encourage immoral thins	5(7.2)	17(24.6)	25(35.6)	13(18.8)	6(8.7)	3(4.3)	
5.	Unethical value	0(0.0)	6(17.1)	9(25.7)	12(34.23)	6(17.1)	2(5.7)	

Source: Compiled from primary data

The above table shows that there is no significant difference between the different age groups of respondents and received different kinds of messages from the advertisement. The $\chi 2$ table shows that there is no statistically valid relation between different age group and received different kinds of messages from the advertisement. All the different age groups of respondents have got different message from this advertisement. The messages relate to (*i*) Impact my life style, (*ii*) Degenerates the youth, (*iii*) Misleading presentation of facts, (*iv*) Encourage immoral things and

Table 5.63: Acceptance of Yuva A810 advertisement among different Age Groups

Sl. No.	Do you accept	Age						
		20 years (n=12)	21 years (n=58)	22 years (n=84)	23 years (n=67)	24 years (n=24)	Above 24 years (n=18)	Statistical Inference
1.	Yes	5(12.2)	7(17.1)	16(39.0)	9(22.0)	2(4.9)	2(4.9)	χ2 = 11.452 Sig=0.323 df = 10 P>0.05 Not Significant
2.	No	5(2.7)	42(22.5)	56(29.9)	52(27.8)	18(9.6)	14(7.5)	
3.	Can't say	2(5.7)	9(25.7)	12(34.3)	6(17.1)	4(11.4)	2(5.7)	

Source: Compiled from primary data.

(*v*) Unethical value. The messages pertaining to the advertisement have not uniformed impacted the respondents. The respondents felt that the messages related to above five mentioned aspects do not uniformly influence the respondents' behaviour.

The above given table reveals that there is no significant difference between the different age groups of respondents and their acceptance value of the advertisement. The $\chi 2$ table shows that there is no statistically valid relation between different age group and their acceptance value of the advertisement. All the different age groups of respondents have different opinion regarding acceptance of this advertisements. The respondents felt that the advertisements are really informative and educative only to some extent. The level of acceptance of the respondents has no bearing on the age comparision of the respondents.

Table 5.64: Recall value of the Colgate Max Fresh advertisement among different Age Groups

Sl. No.	Can you recall the advertising	Age						
		20 years (n=12)	21 years (n=58)	22 years (n=84)	23 years (n=67)	24 years (n=24)	Above 24 years (n=18)	Statistical Inference
1.	Yes	9(4.2)	48(22.5)	70(32.9)	52(22.4)	20(9.4)	14(6.6)	$\chi 2$ = 1.400 Sig=0.924 df = 5 P>0.05 Not Significant
2.	No	3(6.0)	10(20.0)	14(28.0)	15(30.0	4(8.0)	4(8.0)	

Source: Compiled from primary data

The above given table depicts that there is no significant difference between the different age groups of respondents and their recall value of the advertisement. The $\chi 2$ table shows that there is no statistically valid

Table 5.65: Remembering the content of Colgate Max Fresh Advertisement among different Age Groups

Sl. No.	Can you remember the adverti-sing	Age						
		20 years (n=12)	21 years (n=58)	22 years (n=84)	23 years (n=67)	24 years (n=24)	Above 24 years (n=18)	Statistical Inference
1.	Yes	9(4.8)	44(23.3)	62(32.8)	43(22.8)	19(10.1)	12(6.3)	$\chi 2$ = 3.504 Sig=0.623 df = 5 P>0.05 Not Significant
2.	No	3(4.1)	14.(18.9)	22(29.7)	24(32.4)	5(6.8)	6(8.1)	

Source: Compiled from primary data

relation between different age group and their ability to recall the advertisement. The recall does not by itself measure a single underlying memory state. Rather memory is multi dimensional. Recall captures only a portion of memory. All the different age group of respondents have different recall value of this advertisement.

The above table shows that there is no significant difference between the different age groups of respondents and their remembering pattern of the content of the advertisement. The $\chi 2$ table shows that there is no statistically valid relation between different age group and their ability to remember the content of the advertisement. All the different age groups of respondents have identical remembering skill about varied advertisements.

Table 5.66: Getting Message from Colgate Max Fresh Advertisement among different Age Group

Sl. No.	Do you get message	Age						
		20 years (n=12)	21 years (n=58)	22 years (n=84)	23 years (n=67)	24 years (n=24)	Above 24 years (n=18)	Statistical Inference
1.	Yes	9(4.3)	46(21.9)	68(32.4)	54(25.7)	21(10.0)	12(5.7)	$\chi 2$ = 3.090 Sig=0.686 df = 5 P>0.05 Not Significant
2.	No	3(5.7)	12(22.6)	16(30.2)	13(24.5)	3(5.7)	6(11.3)	

Source: Compiled from primary data.

The above table reveals that there is no significant difference between the different age groups of respondents and getting message from the advertisement. The $\chi 2$ table shows that there is no statistically valid relation between different age group and getting message from the advertisement. All the different age groups of respondents have got different message from different advertisement. This implies that the message received by the respondents on the basis of different age groups from the advertisement is not same and it is widely perceived entirely in a different manner.

The below table shows that there is no significant difference between the different age groups of respondents and received different kinds of messages from the advertisement. The $\chi 2$ table shows that there is no statistically valid relation between different age group and received different kinds of messages from the advertisement. All the different age groups of respondents have got different message from this advertisement. The messages relate to (*i*) Misleading presentation of facts, (*ii*) Against public rules, (*iii*) Degenerate our culture, (*iv*) Degenerate the youth and (*v*) Unethical value. The messages pertaining to the advertisement have not uniformed

Table 5.67: Received different kinds of messages from Colgate Max Fresh Advertisement among different Age Groups

Sl. No.	Message	Age						
		20 years (n=9)	21 years (n=46)	22 years (n=68)	23 years (n=54)	24 years (n=21)	Above 24 years (n=12)	Statistical Inference
1	Misleading presentation of facts	1(11.1)	5(10.9)	9(13.2)	6(11.1)	4(19.0)	0(0.0)	$\chi2$ = 25.929 Sig=0.411 df = 25 P>0.05 Not Significant
2.	Against public rules	2(22.2)	10(21.7)	10(14.7)	5(9.3)	3(14.3)	3(25.0)	
3.	Degenerates our culture	0(0.0)	5(10.9)	6(8.8)	4(7.4)	4(19.0)	0(0.0)	
4.	Degenerates the youth	2(22.2)	6(13.0)	18(26.5)	18(33.3)	6(28.6)	2(16.7)	
5.	Unethical value	4(44.5)	20(43.5)	25(36.8)	21(38.9)	4(19.0)	7(58.3)	

Source: Compiled from primary data

impacted the respondents. The respondents felt that the messages related to above five mentioned aspects do not uniformly influence the respondents' behaviour.

The above table shows that there is no significant difference between the different age groups of respondents and received different kinds of messages from the advertisement. The $\chi2$ table shows that there is no statistically valid relation between different age group and received different kinds of messages from the advertisement. All the different age groups of

Table 5.68: Acceptance of Colgate Max Fresh advertisement among different Age Groups

Sl. No.	Do you accept	Age						
		20 years (n=12)	21 years (n=58)	22 years (n=84)	23 years (n=67)	24 years (n=24)	Above 24 years (n=18)	Statistical Inference
1.	Yes	2(4.0)	12(24.0)	18(36.0)	5(10.0)	7(14.0)	6(12.0)	$\chi2$ = 19.794 Sig=0.031 df = 10 P<0.05 Significant
2.	No	4(2.5)	36(22.4)	53(32.9)	44(27.3)	14(8.7)	10(6.2)	
3.	Can't say	6(11.5)	10(19.2)	13(25.0)	18(34.6)	3(5.8)	2(3.8)	

Source: Compiled from primary data

respondents have got different message from this advertisement. The messages relate to (*i*) Misleading presentation of facts, (*ii*) Against public rules, (*iii*) Degenerate our culture, (*iv*) Degenerate the youth and (*v*) Unethical value. The messages pertaining to the advertisement have not uniformed impacted the respondents. The respondents felt that the messages related to above five mentioned aspects do not uniformly influence the respondents' behaviour.

The above table observes clearly there is a significant difference among different age groups and acceptance of Colgate Max Fresh advertisement. The $\chi 2$ table shows that there is statistically valid relationship between different age groups and acceptance of the Colgate Max Fresh advertisement. The respondents felt that the advertisements are really informative and educative only to some extent. The level of acceptance of the respondents has no bearing on the age comparison of the respondents.

Table 5.69: Recall value of Spinz Deo advertisement among different Age Groups

Sl. No.	Can you recall the adverti-sing	Age						
		20 years (n=12)	21 years (n=58)	22 years (n=84)	23 years (n=67)	24 years (n=24)	Above 24 years (n=18)	Statistical Inference
1.	Yes	9(4.6)	44(22.6)	59(30.3)	51(26.2)	19(9.7)	13(6.7)	$\chi 2$ = 1.249 Sig=0.940 df = 5 P>0.05 Not Significant
2.	No	3(4.4)	14(20.6)	25(36.8)	16(23.5)	5(7.4)	5(7.4)	

Source: Compiled from primary data

The above given table evident that there is no significant difference between the different age groups of respondents and their recall value of the advertisement. The $\chi 2$ table shows that there is no statistically valid

Table 5.70: Remembering the content of Spinz Deo Advertisement among different Age Groups

Sl. No.	Can you remember the adverti-sing	Age						
		20 years (n=12)	21 years (n=58)	22 years (n=84)	23 years (n=67)	24 years (n=24)	Above 24 years (n=18)	Statistical Inference
1.	Yes	8(4.7)	38(22.1)	56(32.6)	41(23.8)	16(9.3)	13(7.6)	$\chi 2$ = 0.979 Sig=0.964 df = 5 P>0.05 Not Significant
2.	No	4(4.4)	20(22.0)	28(30.8)	26(28.6)	8(8.8)	5(5.5)	

Source: Compiled from Primary Data.

relation between different age group and their ability to recall the advertisement. The recall does not by itself measure a single underlying memory state. Rather memory is multi dimensional. Recall captures only a portion of memory. All the different age group of respondents have different recall value of this advertisement.

The above table explains that there is no significant difference between the different age groups of respondents and their remembering pattern of the content of the advertisement. The $\chi 2$ table shows that there is no statistically valid relation between different age group and their ability to remember the content of the advertisement. All the different age groups of respondents have identical remembering skill about varied advertisements.

Table 5.71: Getting message from Spinz Deo Advertisement among different age group

Sl. No.	Do you get message	Age						
		20 years (n=12)	21 years (n=58)	22 years (n=84)	23 years (n=67)	24 years (n=24)	Above 24 years (n=18)	Statistical Inference
1.	Yes	10(4.7)	47(22.2)	69(32.5)	51(24.1)	21(9.9)	14(6.6)	$\chi 2$ = 1.875 Sig=0.866 df = 5 P>0.05 Not Significant
2.	No	2(3.9)	11(21.6)	15(29.4)	16(31.4)	3(5.9)	4(7.8)	

Source: Compiled from primary data

The above table depicts that there is no significant difference between the different age groups of respondents and getting message from the advertisement. The $\chi 2$ table shows that there is no statistically valid relation between different age group and getting message from the advertisement. All the different age groups of respondents have got different message from different advertisement. This implies that the message received by the respondents on the basis of different age groups from the advertisement is not same and it is widely perceived entirely in a different manner.

The below table observes that there is no significant difference between the different age groups of respondents and received different kinds of messages from the advertisement. The $\chi 2$ table shows that there is no statistically valid relation between different age group and received different kinds of messages from the advertisement. All the different age groups of respondents have got different message from this advertisement. The messages relate to (*i*) Impact my life style, (*ii*) Degenerate the youth, (*iii*) Misleading presentation of fact, (*iv*) Against general rules and (*v*) Unethical value. The messages pertaining to the advertisement have not uniformed impacted the respondents. The respondents felt that the messages related to

Table 5.72: Received different kinds of messages from Spinz Deo Advertisement among different Age Groups

Sl. No.	Message	Age						
		20 years (n=10)	21 years (n=47)	22 years (n=69)	23 years (n=51)	24 years (n=21)	Above 24 years (n=14)	Statistical Inference
1.	Impact my life style	1(6.7)	5(33.3)	5(33.3)	2(13.3)	1(6.7)	1(6.7)	$\chi2$ = 13.751 Sig=0.966 df = 25 P > 0.05 Not Significant
2.	Degenerate the youth	3(3.8)	17(21.5)	29(36.7)	19(24.1)	7(8.9)	4(5.1)	
3.	Misleading the presentation of the fact	2(5.9)	11(32.4)	8(23.4)	7(20.6)	4(11.8)	2(5.9)	
4.	Against general rule	0(0.0)	6(20.7)	9(31.0)	10(34.5)	2(6.9)	2(6.9)	
5.	Unethical value	4(7.3)	8(14.5)	18(32.7)	13(23.6)	7(12.7)	5(9.1)	

Source: Compiled from primary data

above five mentioned aspects do not uniformly influence the respondents' behaviour.

Table 5.73: Acceptance of Spinz Deo advertisement among different Age Groups

Sl. No.	Do you accept	Age						
		20 years (n=12)	21 years (n=58)	22 years (n=84)	23 years (n=67)	24 years (n=24)	Above 24 years (n=18)	Statistical Inference
1.	Yes	1(3.6)	4(14.3)	10(35.7)	5(17.9)	4(14.3)	4(14.3)	$\chi2$ = 9.231 Sig=0.510 df = 10 P >0.05 Not Significant
2.	No	10(5.0)	48(23.8)	59(29.2)	56(27.7)	17(8.4)	12(5.9)	
3.	Can't say	1(3.0)	6(18.2)	15(45.5)	6(18.2)	3(9.1)	2(6.1)	

Source: Compiled from primary data

The above given table reveals that there is no significant difference between the different age groups of respondents and their acceptance value of the advertisement. The $\chi2$ table shows that there is no statistically valid relation between different age group and their acceptance value of the advertisement. All the different age groups of respondents have different opinion regarding acceptance of this advertisements.

Table 5.74: Personal Life Score

Sl.No.		Opinion about their personal Life	Low	High	Statistical Inference
1.	Sex	Male (n=118)	63(46.7)	55(43.0)	$\chi^2 = 0.363$ P=0.547 df = 1 $P > 0.05$ Not Significant
2.		Female (n=145)	72(53.3)	73(57.0)	
3.	Age (Years)	20 (n=12)	5(3.7)	7(5.5)	$\chi^2 = 12.34$ P=0.030 df = 5 $P < 0.05$ Significant
4.		21(n=58)	40(29.6)	18(14.1)	
5.		22(n=84)	39(28.9)	45(35.2)	
6.		23(n=67)	27(20.0)	40(31.3)	
7.		24(n=24	14(10.4)	10(7.8)	
8.		Above 24 (n=18)	10(7.4)	8(6.3)	
9.	Area	Urban (n=119)	65(48.1)	54(42.2)	$\chi^2 = 0.942$ P=0.332 df = 1 $P < 0.05$ Not Significant
10.		Rural (n=144)	70(51.9)	74(57.8)	
11.	Major	Arts PG n=(68)	36(26.7)	32(25.0)	$\chi^2 = 2.998$ P=0.392 df = 3 $P > 0.05$ Not Significant
12.		Science PG n=(26)	16(11.9)	10(7.8)	
13.		Arts M.Phil N=(145)	74(54.8)	71(55.5)	
14.		Science M.Phil (n=24)	9(6.7)	15(11.7)	

Source: Compiled from primary data

The opinion about their personal life (Q.No. 20, personal life score) is analysed with demographic data, like, sex, age, area and major subject of the respondents.

The personal life score for the female respondents is high (57 per cent) compared to their male counter parts (53.3 per cent). The higher personal life score secured by female respondents is due to their perception that they are grossly exploited by the society on various counts. They feel bad that the advertisements are exploiting their sex appeal to promote the sales of the product. They have a very strong opinion about various issues confronting the women folk, including advertisement. The sensitivity of gender bias is one of the factors for female outscoring men in the personal life scoring index.

Based on the opinion survey scoring as indicated by Table, the personal life score is very high for the age groups of 22 years. It is low at 3.7 per cent for the age groups of 20 years. It reaches the maximum of 29.6 per cent for the age groups of 21 years and then it starts sliding to 28.9 per cent for 22 years and reaches the lowest level of 7.4 per cent for the age group of 24 years and above. It is a sensitive index which broadly explains the vibrancy of the age group about the factors influencing the human life. Advertisement is one of the key factors influencing human life. From the personal life scoring index, it is evident that the most sensitive age group is 22 years. It implies advertisement has telling impact on the age group of 22 years but its impact drops significantly after that and it reaches the lowest level for the age group of 24 years and above.

The personal life scoring index is relatively high in the rural areas compared to urban areas. In the urban area it stood at 42.2 per cent and in the rural areas it is as high as 57.8 per cent. It shows clearly personal life scoring is high for rural people due to the vexing issues confronting the rural economy viz., low income, unemployment, poverty and apathy of Government initiatives. Its score on the area wise classification of respondents indicates that rural people are more prone to the impact of advertisement than urban people. The sensitivity and complexity of rural life contribute to the high scoring.

The personal life scoring index of the respondents from Arts major is higher than the respondents of science major. The arts students are having the personal life score of 55.5 per cent compare to that of science students 11.7 percent. The personal life score of Arts student is high due to proximity and insight about social life. The arts major are teaching the practical and current issues haunting the economy. So the students of Arts are exposed to the current upheavals of the society. The exposure of science students to the current problem is some what less and this account for lower score secured by them.

Many female respondents felt that the unethical practices in advertisements are high (56.5 per cent) compare to their male respondents (43.5 per cent). The female respondents felt that unethical practices in advertisements is higher than the male respondents, because of their perception of the advertisements. The advertising companies are using female model in vulnerable manner and irrelevant to the product and expose only their sex appeal to the customers in their product advertisements. Female respondents are more sensitive to express their view highly regarding unethical practices in advertisements.

Table 5.75: Dimensions of Unethical Practices in Advertisement

Sl.No.		Unethical Practices in Advertisements	Low	High	Statistical Inference
1.	Sex	Male (n=118)	61(46.2)	71(53.8)	χ2 = 0.194 P=0.660 df = 1 P >0.05 Not Significant
2.		Female (n=145)	57(43.5)	74(56.5)	
3.	Age (Years)	20 (n=12)	5(3.7)	7(5.5)	χ2 = 5.409 P=0.369 df = 5 P>0.05 Not Significant
4.		21(n=58)	40(29.6)	18(14.1)	
5.		22(n=84)	39(28.9)	45(35.2)	
6.		23(n=67)	27(20.0)	40(31.3)	
7.		24(n=24	14(10.4)	10(7.8)	
8.		Above 24 (n=18)	10(7.4)	8(6.3)	
9.	Area	Urban (n=119)	47(35.6)	72(55.0)	χ2 = 9.943 P=0.002 df = 1 P<0.05 Significant
10.		Rural (n=144)	85(64.4)	59(45.0)	
11.	Major	Arts PG n=(68)	26(19.7)	42(32.1)	χ2 = 7.416 P=0.060 df = 3 P <0.05 Significant
12.		Science PG n=(26)	12(9.1)	14(10.7)	
13.		Arts M.Phil N=(145)	78(59.1)	67(51.1)	
14.		Science M.Phil (n=24)	16(12.1)	8(6.1)	

Source: Compiled from primary data

The age group of 22 years felt that the unethical practices in advertisement is very high (35.2 per cent). It is low at 3.7 per cent for the age group of 20 years. It reaches the maximum 29.6 per cent for the age group 21 years and then it starts sliding to 28.9 per cent for the age group of 22 years. It reaches the lowest level of 7.4 per cent for the age group of 24 years and above. This table clearly shows that the age group of 22 years are more informative, matured and they have good analyzing capacity. When the company gives advertisement for their product simply they give false information, deliberately omitting required information, imply a benefit that hardly exist, trade puffing, using unnecessary technical jargons, create cultural degeneration, creating ambiguities in the minds of consumers, creating fear, open criticism of competitors, sex in advertisement, against the national and public interest, affects the life style of the people, creates monopoly, unverifiable claims in a language and subliminal message. The age group 22 years felt that the above mentioned important factors are highly unethical. It implied that the advertisement has telling impact on the age group of 22 years.

Table 5.76: Comments on Advertising

Sl.No.		Comment on Advertising	Low	High	Statistical Inference
1.	Sex	Male (n=118)	62(43.4)	56(46.7)	$\chi2$ = 0.289 P=0.591 df = 1 P >0.05 Not Significant
2.		Female (n=145)	81(56.6)	64(53.3)	
3.	Age (Years)	20 (n=12)	5(3.5)	7(5.8)	$\chi2$ = 7.579 P=0.181 df = 5 P>0.05 Not Significant
4.		21(n=58)	37(25.6)	21(17.5)	
5.		22(n=84)	39(27.3)	45(37.5)	
6.		23(n=67)	35(24.5)	32(26.7)	
7.		24(n=24	14(9.8)	10(8.3)	
8.		Above 24 (n=18)	13(9.1)	5(4.2)	
9.	Area	Urban (n=119)	64(44.8)	55(45.8)	$\chi2$ = 0.031 P=0.861 df = 1 P > 0.05 Not Significant
10.		Rural (n=144)	79(55.2)	65(54.2)	
11.	Major	Arts PG n=(68)	36(25.2)	32(26.7)	$\chi2$ = 1.703 P=0.636 df = 3 P >0.05 Not Significant
12.		Science PG n=(26)	17(11.9)	9(7.5)	
13.		Arts M.Phil N=(145)	76(53.1)	69(57.5)	
14.		Science M.Phil (n=24)	14(9.8)	10(8.3)	

Source: Compiled from primary data

The unethical practices in advertisement is relatively high in urban areas compared to rural areas. In the rural area it stood at 45.0 per cent and in the urban area it is as high as 55.0 per cent. It reveals clearly the urban people are informative, educative and have a capability of differentiating the thing between right and wrong, suitable and unsuitable, useful and useless. So they can easily judge whether this advertisement is ethical or unethical. But in rural areas, due to their ignorance, poor awareness of the product, addiction of celebrities and hero worship they could be easily impressed by the advertisement. And also they could not classify the advertisements in terms of ethical and unethical.

The unethical practices in advertisement is higher from the respondents of arts major than the respondents of science major. The arts students (P.G and M.Phil) are having the high opinion about the unethical practices in advertisement 32.1 per cent and 51.1 per cent respectively compare to 10.7 per cent and 6.1 per cent of science students (P.G and M.Phil) respectively.

The above table depicts that the female respondents gives high level of comment on advertising (53.3 per cent) compare to male respondents (46.7 per cent). Female respondents felt that they are directly affected by advertisements. The advertisers are concentrating the female of the society especially their beauty consciousness, motherlyhood sentiments and their prominent role of house hold activities. The female respondents easily engulfed the advertisements and buy the products. When they find differences in the products from the advertisements, they feel they are cheated by them. Obviously they exude high level of commenting on advertisements compared to male respondents on this aspects.

The above table shows that the age group of 22 years give high level of comment on advertising (37.5 per cent). It is low at 3.5 per cent for the age group of 20 years. It reaches the maximum 27.3per cent for the age group of 22 years and then it starts sliding to 24.5 per cent for 33 years and reaches the lowest level 9.1 per cent for the age group of 24 years and above. This table clearly explains that the matured age group of 22 years is giving high level of comment on advertising. At this stage only the respondents are in a position to take a buying decision independently.

The above table shows that rural respondents give high level of comment on advertising (54.2 per cent) compared to urban respondents (45.8 per cent). It stood low in urban at 44.8 per cent and at 55.2 per cent in rural areas. The television is the only media for the entertainment of rural people in comparison to urban people. They spend more time on watching television. They will consider the advertisement as the important source of getting first hand information about their product. So they can give comment on advertisement.

There is no relationship between major (arts and science) and comment on advertisements.

From the table it is clear that female respondents felt that the cultural exaggeration in select advertisement is higher (54.2 per cent) than male respondents (45.8 per cent). It stood as low as 44.2 per cent in male respondents and 55.8 per cent in female respondents. The female respondents are spending more time for watching television than male respondents. They have normally more attachment with family members and believe and follow our culture by traditionally. They can easily react for the advertisement which is in cultural exaggeration nature.

Table 5.77: Cultural exaggeration in Select Advertisements

Sl.No.		Cultural exaggeration	Low	High	Statistical Inference
1.	Sex	Male (n=118)	69(44.2)	49(45.8)	$\chi 2 = 0.063$ P=0.802 df = 1 P >0.05 Not Significant
2.		Female (n=145)	87(55.8)	58(54.2)	
3.	Age (Years)	20 (n=12)	6(3.8)	6(5.6)	$\chi 2 = 7.415$ P=0.192 df = 5 P>0.05 Not Significant
4.		21(n=58)	31(19.9)	27(25.2)	
5.		22(n=84)	46(29.5)	38(35.5)	
6.		23(n=67)	44(28.2)	23(21.5)	
7.		24(n=24	14(19.0)	10(9.3)	
8.		Above 24 (n=18)	15(9.6)	3(2.8)	
9.	Area	Urban (n=119)	68(43.6)	51(47.7)	$\chi 2 = 0.425$ P=0.514 df = 1 P > 0.05 Not Significant
10.		Rural (n=144)	88(56.4)	56(52.3)	
11.	Major	Arts PG n=(68)	41(26.3)	27(25.2)	$\chi 2 = 1.420$ P=0.701 df = 3 P >0.05 Not Significant
12.		Science PG n=(26)	17(10.9)	9(8.4)	
13.		Arts M.Phil N=(145)	82(52.6)	63(58.9)	
14.		Science M.Phil (n=24)	16(10.3)	8(7.5)	

Source: Compiled from primary data

Based on cultural exaggeration in select advertisement as indicated by the table, the age group of 22 years felt that the cultural exaggeration in select advertisement is higher (35.5 per cent). It is low at 3.8 per cent for the age group 20 years. It reaches the maximum 29.5 per cent for the age group 22 years and then it starts sliding to 28.2 per cent for 23 years and reaches the lowest level of 9.0 per cent for the age group of 24 years. It reveals clearly that the age group of 22 years are matured, having analyzing capacity and having knowledge of identifying the advertisements which are degenerates our culture and youth. The age groups of 22 years are more sensitive in terms of our culture and values of the society.

From the above table it is clear that the cultural exaggeration in select advertisement is high in rural area (52.3 per cent) compared to urban area (47.7 per cent). The rural people are mostly belonging to orthodox group, have family sentiments and more attached to our culture. If an advertisement exaggerates our culture the rural people will react highly towards it.

The above table reveals that the cultural exaggeration in select advertisement is higher in arts major respondents. 25.2 per cent of PG and 58.9 per cent of M.Phil than science major respondents. 8.4 per cent of PG and 7.5 per cent of M.Phil. The arts major respondents are learning more about the culture, customs and values of our society than science major respondents. Based on their assimilated knowledge the arts major respondents can easily identify and react highly towards cultural exaggeration in select advertisements.

Table 5.78: Ethical values in select advertisements

Sl.No.		Ethical Values	Low	High	Statistical Inference
1.	Sex	Male (n=118)	65(47.1)	53(42.4)	$\chi2$ = 0.586 P = 0.444 df = 1 P>0.05 Not Significant
2.		Female (n=145)	73(52.9)	72(57.6)	
3.	Age (Years)	20 (n=12)	7(5.1)	5(4.0)	$\chi2$ = 2.109 P=0.834 df = 5 P>0.05 Not Significant
4.		21(n=58)	33(23.9)	25(20.0)	
5.		22(n=84)	43(31.2)	41(32.8)	
6.		23(n=67)	36(26.1)	31(24.8)	
7.		24(n=24	12(8.7)	12(9.6)	
8.		Above 24 (n=18)	7(5.1)	11(8.8)	
9.	Area	Urban (n=119)	64(46.4)	55(44.0)	$\chi2$ = 0.150 P = 0.699 df = 1 P>0.05 Not Significant
10.		Rural (n=144)	74(53.6)	70(56.0)	
11.	Major	Arts PG n=(68)	40(29.0)	28(22.4)	$\chi2$ = 2.771 P = 0.428 df = 3 P>0.05 Not Significant
12.		Science PG n=(26)	11(8.0)	15(12.0)	
13.		Arts M.Phil N=(145)	73(52.9)	72(57.6)	
14.		Science M.Phil (n=24)	14(10.1)	10(8.0)	

Source: Compiled from primary data

The ethical values in select advertisements are measured by five point scale. The female respondents felt that the ethical value is select advertisement is high (57.6 per cent) compared to male respondents (42.4 per cent). Female respondents are more orthodox, closely associated with our culture and value system of our society. They can easily judge the advertisements based on their ethical perspective.

Based on the ethical values in select advertisement as indicated by the table, the ethical values in select advertisements is high for the age group of 22 years. It is low at 5.1 per cent for the age group of 20 years and above 24 years. It reaches the maximum 31.2 per cent for the age group of 22 years and than it starts decline, 26.1 per cent for the age group of 23 years and reaches the lowest level of 8.7 per cent for the age group of 24 years. It is a sensitive index which clearly explains that the age group of 22 years are matured and well informed and aware of consumer acts and rights clearly. They can easily determine that the advertisements are ethical or unethical.

The above table depicts that the ethical values in select advertisement is high in rural area 56.0 per cent compared to urban area 44.0 per cent. It is low at 53.6 per cent in rural area and 46.4 per cent in urban area. Rural people are living with our own prestigious culture follow the customs of society in a very strict manner and they will maintain the some important values of human being. If any advertisement comes with the nature of the degenerate the youth and culture, they will highly react towards of it.

The above table observes that the ethical values in select advertisements are higher in arts major respondents than science major respondents. In arts major respondents are having ethical value in select advertisement of 22.4 per cent of PG and 57.6 per cent of M.Phil respondents compared to science major respondents of 12.0 per cent of PG and 8.0 per cent of M.Phil respondents. Because of their subjects Arts major respondents are doing any activity under the humanitarian ground and also well aware of the business ethics compared to science major respondents. These Arts major respondents can easily react to unethical nature of advertisements.

Hypothesis Testing-1

There is a significant variation among the respondents about the remembering the content of the advertisement. The foregoing analysis proved beyond doubt that, there is no significant variances among the respondents about the remembering the content of the advertisement. The Chi-square test applied to prove the relationships between group of respondents classified on the basis of age and their remembering pattern shows that there is no significant relation between the age of the respondents and their remembering capability of select advertisements.

So the first hypothesis states that there is a significant variation among the respondents and their remembering the content of the select advertisements, is disproved.

Table 5.79: One way Analysis of Variance among different Age Group with Effectiveness of Select Advertisements

Sl. No.	Source	Df	SS	MS	$\bar{X}$	Statistical Inference
1.	**Opinion about their Personal life style** Between Groups Within Groups	5 257	174.493 7375.134	34.899 28.697	G1=41.0000 G2=39.2931 G3=40.8810 G4=40.2985 G5=38.4167 G6=39.5556	F=1.216 P>0.05 Not Significant
2.	**Unethical Practices** Between Groups Within Groups	5 257	132.032 8383.961	26.406 32.622	G1=44.6667 G2=44.3448 G3=46.2381 G4=45.4776 G5=45.2083 G6=45.6111	F=0.809 P > 0.05 Not Significant
3.	**Comments on advertising** Between Groups Within Groups	5 257	548.327 17896.152	109.665 69.635	G1=56.0000 G2=52.3276 G3=55.1786 G4=54.0149 G5=54.6250 G6=50.5556	F=1.575 P > 0.05 Not Significant
4.	**Advertisements regarding Cultural exaggeration** Between Groups Within Groups	5 257	451.971 10862.143	90.394 42.265	G1=32.5000 G2=28.5345 G3=29.5833 G4=27.8209 G5=28.1667 G6=25.7778	F=2.139 P > 0.05 Not Significant
5.	**Advertisement regarding in ethical values** Between Groups Within Groups	5 257	91.801 12053.218		G1=30.0000 G2=28.2241 G3=29.5595 G4=29.0149 G5=28.7500 G6=30.0556	F=0.391 P > 0.05 Not Significant

G_1=20 Years G_2= 21 Years G_3=22 Years G_4=23 Years
G_5=24 Years G_6= Above 24 Years

From the above table, it is revealed that there is no significant difference between different age groups of respondents and their opinion about personal life. The F test clearly shows that the advertisements have not altered the opinion of the respondents dramatically. There is a similarity of opinion among different age groups and the different age groups view advertisements with identical mindset and perception.

There is no significant difference between different age groups of respondent and unethical practices in advertisements. The F test clearly shows that the advertisements are viewed uniformly in terms of unethical practices by the different age groups of respondents.

There is no significant difference between different age groups of respondent and comments on advertisements. The F test clearly shows that the advertisements are getting the same type of comments from various age groups of respondents.

There is no significant difference between different age groups of respondents and cultural exaggeration in select advertisements. The F test clearly shows that the opinion about cultural exaggerations in select advertisements is not closely associated with the different age groups of respondents.

There is no significant difference between different age groups of respondent and ethical values in select advertisements. The F test clearly shows that the opinion about ethical values in select advertisements is not closely associated with the different age groups of respondents.

Table 5.80: One way analysis of variance among different religions with Effectiveness of Select Advertisement

Sl. No.	Source	Df	SS	MS	$\bar{X}$	Statistical Inference
1.	**Opinion about their Personal life style** Between Groups Within Groups	3 259	87.423 7462.204	29.141 28.812	G1=40.3668 G2=40.5000 G3=39.0169 G4=42.0000	F=1.011 P>0.05 Not Significant
2.	**Unethical Practices** Between Groups Within Groups	3 259	206.918 8309.075	68.973 32.081	G1=45.1608 G2=41.5000 G3=46.6610 G4=39.0000	F=2.150 P > 0.05 Not Significant
3.	**Comments on advertising** Between Groups Within Groups	3 259	87.892 18356.587	29.297 70.875	G1=53.7688 G2=57.0000 G3=54.3390 G4=48.0000	F=0.413 P > 0.05 Not Significant
4.	**Advertisements regarding Cultural exaggeration** Between Groups Within Groups	3 259	173.065 11141.049	57.688 43.016	G1=28.8543 G2=25.2500 G3=28.3559 G4=18.0000	F=0.341 P > 0.05 Not Significant
5.	**Advertisements regarding ethical values** Between Groups Within Groups	3 259	121.360 12023.659	40.453 46.423	G1=29.1910 G2=31.0000 G3=28.8644 G4=19.0000	F=0.871 P > 0.05 Not Significant

G1=Hindu G2=Muslim G3=Christian G4= Other (Specify)

From the above table, it is depicts that there is no significant difference between different religion of respondents and their opinion about personal life. The F test clearly shows that the different religions are not closely associated with opinion about the personal life of the respondents.

There is no significant difference between different religion of respondents and unethical practices in advertisements. The F test clearly shows the different groups of religion are not closely associated with unethical practices of advertisements.

There is no significant difference between different religion of respondents and their comments on advertisements. The F test clearly shows that the different respondents of different religions are having the same type of comments to offer about the advertisement. The comments are uniform from the respondents irrespective of their religion.

There is no significant difference between different religion of respondents and cultural exaggeration in select advertisements. The F test clearly shows that cultural exaggerations in select advertisements are not closely associated with the different religion of respondents.

There is no significant difference between different religion of respondents and ethical values in select advertisements. The F test clearly shows that the ethical values in select advertisements are not closely associated with the different religion of respondents.

Table 5.81: One way analysis of variance among different income group with Effectiveness of select advertisements

Sl. No.	Source	Df	SS	MS	$\bar{X}$	Statistical Inference
1.	**Opinion about their Personal life style** Between Groups Within Groups	4 258	75.771 7473.857	18.943 28.968	G1=40.0357 G2=40.0777 G3=39.8750 G4=41.1944 G5=39.0000	F=0.654 P > 0.05 Not Significant
2.	**Unethical Practices** Between Groups Within Groups	4 258	348.555 8167.438	87.139 31.657	G1=48.0000 G2=45.8252 G3=45.0000 G4=44.4167 G5=43.4167	F=2.753 P < 0.05 Significant
3.	**Comments on advertising** Between Groups Within Groups	4 258	479.212 17965.267	119.803 69.633	G1=53.0000 G2=52.7767 G3=55.8472 G4=53.2500 G5=55.1667	F=1.720 P > 0.05 Not Significant
4.	**Advertisements regarding Cultural exaggeration** Between Groups Within Groups	4 258	52.450 11261.664	13.113 43.650	G1=29.5357 G2=28.2330 G3=28.7778 G4=28.4444 G5=29.2917	F=0.300 P > 0.05 Not Significant
5.	**Advertisements regarding ethical values** Between Groups Within Groups	4 258	255.566 11889.453	63.892 46.083	G1=31.1071 G2=28.7961 G3=29.2917 G4=27.3889 G5=30.1250	F=1.386 P > 0.05 Not Significant

G_1= Rs 17,917 & More pm G_2= Rs. 3,750-17,917 pm G_3= Rs. 1,833 - 3,750pm
G_4= Rs. 1,333 - 1,833 pm G_5= Below Rs. 1,333 pm

From the above table, it is observed that there is no significant difference between different income groups of respondents and their opinion about personal life. The F test clearly shows that the personal opinions about the life are not closely associated with different income groups of respondents.

The above table reveals clearly that there is a significant difference among different income groups on the effectiveness of advertisement on unethical practices. The different income groups ranging from poor to affluent have vastly varied and altogether dramatically different opinion about unethical practices pursued in advertisements.

There is no significant difference between different income groups of respondent and comments on advertisements. The F test clearly shows that the advertisements are getting the same type of comments from various income groups of respondents.

There is no significant difference between different income groups of respondents and cultural exaggeration in select advertisements. The F test clearly shows that Cultural exaggerations in select advertisements are not closely associated with the different income groups of respondents.

Table 5.82: One way Analysis of Variance among different Major (Arts & Science) Group with Effectiveness of Select Advertisements

Sl. No.	Source	Df	SS	MS	$\bar{X}$	Statistical Inference
1.	**Opinion about their Personal life style** Between Groups Within Groups	3 259	73.307 7476.321	24.436 28.866	G1=40.1765 G2=38.8077 G3=40.0621 G4=41.2083	F = 0.847 P > 0.05 Not Significant
2.	**Unethical Practices** Between Groups Within Groups	3 259	224.776 8291.216	74.925 32.012	G1=46.5735 G2=46.7308 G3=44.8690 G4=44.0417	F=2.341 P < 0.05 Significant
3.	**Comments on advertising** Between Groups Within Groups	3 259	163.649 18280.830	54.550 70.582	G1=55.2353 G2=53.3462 G3=53.5586 G4=53.0417	F=0.773 P > 0.05 Not Significant
4.	**Advertisements regarding Cultural exaggeration** Between Groups Within Groups	3 259	81.007 11233.107	27.002 43.371	G1=28.3235 G2=27.3462 G3=29.0828 G4=28.3333	F=0.623 P > 0.05 Not Significant
5.	**Advertisements regarding ethical values** Between Groups Within Groups	3 259	91.349 12053.670	30.450 46.539	G1=28.1471 G2=29.1154 G3=29.5517 G4=29.1250	F=0.654 P > 0.05 Not Significant

G_1= Arts-PG G_2= Science PG G_3= Arts M.Phil G_4= Science M.Phil

There is no significant difference between different income groups of respondent and ethical values in select advertisements. The F test clearly shows that the ethical values in select advertisements are not closely associated with the different income groups of respondents.

From the above table, it is observed that there is no significant difference between different major (Arts and Science) of respondents and their opinion about personal life. The F test clearly shows that the personal opinions about the life are not closely associated with different major of respondents.

The above table reveals clearly that there is a significant difference among different major on the effectiveness of advertisement on unethical practices. The F test clearly shows that the unethical practices in advertisement is closely associated with different major group of respondents. The opinion of the Arts students about unethical practices of advertisement is vocal and highly pronounced as indicated in the Table (5.75) But the respondents belonging to the Science major are not able to gauge the unethical dimensions of advertisement since their focus area is science and humanity.

There is no significant difference between different major of respondent and comments on advertisements. The F test clearly shows that the advertisements are getting similar comments from the respondents studying different major.

There is no significant difference between different major of respondents and cultural exaggeration in select advertisements. The F test clearly shows that Cultural exaggerations in select advertisements are not closely associated with the different major of respondents.

There is no significant difference between different major of respondent and ethical values in select advertisements. The F test clearly shows that the ethical values in select advertisements are not closely associated with the different major of respondents.

Hypothesis Testing-2

The second hypothesis which states that the effectiveness of advertisement diverges differs widely among the respondents on the basis on their age, religion, income and major subjects perceived for their studies. This hypothesis the forgoing analysis proves that the effectiveness of the advertisement has not differed vastly among respondents on the basis of their age, religion, income and major subjects perceived by the students. The effectiveness of advertisements is viewed from five different criteria namely, opinion about the personal life style, unethical practices in advertisements, comment on advertising, cultural exaggeration in select advertisements and ethical values in select advertisements. Judged from above five criteria the effectiveness of advertisement has a same impact on respondents irrespective of their age, religion, income and major subjects perceived by them.

The notable exception is there is differences in the different income categories of respondents on their view on unethical practices advertisement. The same result is found for unethical practices for the students perusing different major.

Barring all these exceptions the over all result is the effectiveness of advertisements is not significantly differ among respondents mainly on the basis of age, religion, income and major areas of studies.

Table 5.83: 't' test for Comparing sex and Effectiveness of Advertisement

Sex	N	Mean	Std. Deviation	Std. Error Mean	t	df	
Sex Vs opinion about personal life							
Male	118	1.4661	0.50098	0.04612	0.601	261	Sig. Val=0.548 P>0.05 Not Significant
Female	145	1.5034	0.50172	0.04167	0.601	250.400	
Sex Vs Unethical practices in advertisements							
Male	118	1.4831	0.50184	0.04620	0.439	261	Sig. Val=0. 661 P>0.05 Not Significant
Female	145	1.5103	0.50163	0.04166	0.439	250.211	
Sex Vs Comment on advertising							
Male	118	1.4746	0.50148	0.4617	0.536	261	Sig. Val=0. 593 P>0.05 Not Significant
Female	145	1.4414	0.49827	0.04138	0.535	249.611	
Sex Vs Cultural exaggeration in Select Advertisements							
Male	118	1.4153	0.49487	0.04556	0.250	261	Sig. Val=0. 803 P>0.05 Not Significant
Female	145	1.4000	0.49160	0.04082	0.249	249.590	
Sex Vs ethical values in select advertisements							
Male	118	1.4492	0.49953	0.4599	0.763	261	Sig. Val=0. 446 P>0.05 Not Significant
Female	145	1.4966	0.50172	0.04167	0.764	250.683	

The above table shows that there is no significant difference between sex of the respondents and their opinion about their personal life. The 't' test clearly shows that the sex of the respondents are not closely associated with the opinion of their personal life.

There is no significant difference between the different sex of the respondents and unethical practices in advertisement. The 't' test clearly shows that advertisements are viewed uniformly in terms of unethical practices by different sex of the respondents.

There is no significant difference between the different sex of respondents and comment on advertisement. 't' test depicts that the advertisements are getting comments from different sex of respondents.

There is no significant difference between different sex of respondents and cultural exaggeration in select advertisements. The 't' test observes that the opinions about cultural exaggerations in select advertisement are not closely associated with different sex of respondents.

Table 5.84: 't' test for Comparing Area and Effectiveness of Advertisement

Sex	N	Mean	Std. Deviation	Std. Error Mean	t	df	
Area Vs opinion about personal life							
Urban	119	1.4538	0.049996	0.04583	0.969	261	Sig. Val=0.334 P>0.05 Not Significant
Rural	144	1.5139	0.50155	0.4180	0.969	252.038	
Area Vs Unethical practices in advertisements							
Urban	119	1.6050	0.49091	0.04500	3.202	261	Sig. Val=0. 002 P<0.05 Significant
Rural	144	1.4097	0.49350	0.04112	3.204	259.229	
Area Vs Comment on advertising							
Urban	119	1.4622	0.50068	0.04590	0.174	261	Sig. Val=0. 862 P>0.05 Not Significant
Rural	144	1.4514	0.49937	0.04161	0.174	251.502	
Area Vs Cultural exaggeration in Select Advertisements							
Urban	119	1.4286	0.49696	0.04556	0.650	261	Sig. Val=0. 517 P>0.05 Not Significant
Rural	144	1.3889	0.48920	0.04077	0.649	250.238	
Area Vs ethical values in Select Advertisements							
Urban	119	1.4622	0.50068	0.045090	0.385	261	Sig. Val=0. 700 P>0.05 Not Significant
Rural	144	1.4861	0.50155	0.04180	0.385	251.908	

Table 5.85: Opinion of Respondents and opinion-leaders about Unethical Practices in Advertisements

Sl.No.	Particulars		More in product/ consumer adverti-sement	More in service adverti-sement	Equal in both	Not in both
1.	False and misleading presentation of facts	Respondents	118(44.9)	28(10.6)	104(39.5)	13(4.9)
		Opinion-leaders	42(56.0)	8(10.7)	18(24.0)	7(9.3)
2.	Deliberate omitting of required information	Respondents	131.(49.8)	59(22.4)	68(25.9)	5(1.9)
		Opinion-leaders	28(37.3)	20(26.7)	23(30.7)	4(5.3)
3.	Implying a benefit that hardly exists	Respondents	106(40.3)	53(20.2)	95(36.1)	9(3.4)
		Opinion-leaders	36(48.0)	17(22.7)	16(21.3)	6(8.0)
4.	Trade puffing and exaggeration	Respondents	117(44.5)	44(16.7)	86(32.7)	16(6.1)
		Opinion-leaders	29(38.7)	15(20.0)	30(40.0)	1(1.3)
5.	Using unnecessary unwanted technical jargons	Respondents	147(55.9)	46(17.5)	54(20.5)	16(6.1)
		Opinion-leaders	28(37.3)	15(20.0)	25(33.3)	7(9.3)
6.	Creating cultural degenerations	Respondents	154(58.6)	30(11.4)	58(22.1)	21(8.0)
		Opinion-leaders	28(37.3)	11(14.7)	19(25.3)	17(22.7)
7.	Creating ambiguities in the minds of consumer	Respondents	111(42.2)	37(14.1)	12(38.8)	13(4.9)
		Opinion-leaders	30(40.0)	5(6.7)	28(37.3)	12(16.0)
8.	Creating fear in consumers	Respondents	88(33.5)	59(22.4)	94(35.7)	22(8.4)
		Opinion-leaders	12(16.0)	17(22.7)	16(21..3)	30(40.0)
9.	Open criticisms of competitors	Respondents	142(54.0)	38(14.4)	72(27.4)	11(4.2)
		Opinion-leaders	44(58.7)	6(8.0)	15(20.0)	10(13.3)
10.	Sex in advertisement	Respondents	154(58.6)	28(10.6)	67(25.5)	14(5.3)
		Opinion-leaders	34(45.3)	4(5.3)	24(32.0)	13(17.3)
11.	Against the national and public interest	Respondents	81(30.8)	59(22.4)	68(25.9)	55(20.9)
		Opinion-leaders	17(22.7)	6(8.0)	20(26.7)	32(42.7)
12.	Affect life style of people	Respondents	127(48.3)	39(14.8)	72(27.4)	25(9.5)
		Opinion-leaders	32(42.7)	6(8.0)	21(28.0)	16(21.3)
13.	Creates monopoly	Respondents	156(59.3)	44(16.7)	55(20.9)	8(3.0)
		Opinion-leaders	36(48.0)	8(10.7)	14(18.7)	17(22.7)
14.	Unverifiable claims in a language	Respondents	105(39.9)	56(21.3)	80(30.4)	22(8.4)
		Opinion-leaders	16(21.3)	14(18.7)	25(33.3)	20(26.7)
15.	Subliminal message	Respondents	92(35.0)	42(16.0)	113(42.9)	16(6.1)
		Opinion-leaders	15(20.0)	12(16.0)	36(48.0)	12(16.0)

Source: Primary data

There is no significant difference between different sex of respondents and ethical values in select advertisements. The 't' test depicts that the opinion about the ethical values in select advertisements are not closely associated with different sex of respondents.

The above table shows that there is no significant difference between area of the respondents and their opinion about their personal life. The 't' test clearly observes that the area of the respondents are not closely associated with the opinion of their personal life.

There is a significant difference between the different area of the respondents and unethical practices in advertisement. The 't' test reveals that advertisements are viewed uniformly in terms of unethical practices by different area of the respondents.

There is no significant difference between the different area of respondents and comment on advertisement. 't' test evident that the advertisements are getting comments from different area of respondents.

There is no significant difference between different area of respondents and cultural exaggeration in select advertisements. The 't' test depicts that the opinions about cultural exaggerations in select advertisement are not closely associated with different area of respondents.

There is no significant difference between different area of respondents and ethical values in select advertisements. The 't' test clearly shows that the opinion about the ethical values in select advertisements are not closely associated with different area of respondents.

The unethical practices are viewed from the following four criteria. (*i*) More in produc consumer advertisement, (*ii*) more in service advertisement, (*iii*) equal in both, (*iv*) not in both. The table clearly shows that in all the 15 important facts of unethical practices in advertisements, the opinion-leaders as well as student respondents have identical views and opinions. There is no marked difference between these two important stake holders of advertisements.

Hypothesis Testing-3

The third hypothesis states that there is a perfect uncertainty of views about unethical dimensions of advertisements among opinion-leaders and students respondents. The hypothesis is proved correct. The above table shows that in all the fifteen critical unethical practices in advertisements they have similar views. The following is the opinion of both opinion-leaders and students respondents about the unethical practices in advertisements. Majority of the respondents felt that the unethical practices are featuring more in product and consumer advertisement for the sizable section of the opinion-leaders and the students respondents feel that the unethical practices in advertisements are found in equal measures in product and service. Another section of respondents comprising opinion-leaders and student respondents feel that the unethical practices are more pronounced in services. A very small section felt that the unethical practices are not present in product and service. The above analysis clearly shows that both opinion-leaders and students have identical opinions about the occurrence of unethical practices. The third hypothesis which states that there is certainty among opinion-leaders and student respondents is proved correct.

Table 5.86: Respondents and opinion-leaders' Comments on Advertising

Sl.No.	Particulars		Always	Frequently	Occasionally	Never	Can't say
1	2	3	4	5	6	7	8
1.	There is no ethical value in advertising	Respondents	35(13.3)	109(41.4)	82(31.2)	15(5.7)	22(8.7)
		Opinion –leaders	7(9.3)	27(36.0)	29(38.7)	6(8.0)	6(8.0)
2.	Advertising is just an exaggeration, puffery and bluffing	Respondents	57921.7)	96(36.5)	76(28.9)	19(7.2)	15(5.7)
		Opinion –leaders	5(6.7)	21(28.0)	35(46.7)	10(13.3)	4(5.3)
3.	Advertising degenerates our culture	Respondents	53(20.2)	96(36.5)	66(25.1)	33(12.5)	15(5.7)
		Opinion –leaders	4(5.3)	15(20.0)	23(30.7)	16(21.3)	17(22.7)
4.	Advertising degenerates the youth	Respondents	70(26.6)	96(36.5)	66(25.1)	21(8.0)	10(3.8)
		Opinion–leaders	7(9.3)	26(34.7)	16(21.3)	16(21.3)	10(13.3)
5.	Honesty in advertising is rare	Respondents	86(32.7)	70(26.6)	63(24.0)	28(10.6)	16(6.1)
		Opinion –leaders	10(13.3)	19(25.3)	30()40.0)	4(5.3)	12(16.0)
6.	Advertising causes false and misleading claims	Respondents	54(20.5)	90(34.2)	73(37.8)	28(10.6)	18(6.8)
		Opinion –leaders	5(6.7)	16(21.3)	35(46.7)	9(12.0)	10(13.3)
7.	Unfair advertising are very common	Respondents	86(32.7)	93(35.4)	45(17.1)	22(8.4)	17(6.5)
		Opinion –leaders	4(5.3)	17(22.7)	28(37.3)	15(20.0)	11(14.7)
8.	It is not worth to go by advertising	Respondents	64924.3)	56(21.3)	79(30.0)	38(14.4)	26(9.9)
		Opinion-leaders	3(4.0)	11(14.7)	21(18.0)	14(18.7)	26(34.7)
9.	Advertising boosting our self image	Respondents	50(19.0)	64(24.3)	74(28.1)	56(21.3)	19(7.2)
		Opinion–leaders	20(26.7)	22(29.3)	17(22.7)	8(10.7)	8(10.7)
10.	Advertising for harmful/prohibited products and service	Respondents	66(25.1)	60(22.8)	84(31.9)	30(11.4)	23(8.7)
		Opinion –leaders	7(9.3)	15(20.0)	28(37.3)	10(13.3)	15(20.0)
11.	Prepare young minds (children) for the product	Respondents	100(38.0)	86(32.7)	39(14.8)	24(9.1)	14(5.3)
		Opinion –leaders	24(32.0)	35(46.7)	10(13.3)	4(5.3)	2(2.7)

1	2	3	4	5	6	7	8
12.	Referring the product (or) incidents is not capable of being established	Respondents	71(27.0)	72(27.4)	76(28.9)	29(11.0)	15(5.7)
		Opinion- leaders	8(10.7)	23(30.7)	28(37.3)	8(10.7)	8(10.7)
13.	Give irrelevant statistical data and disproved scientific jargon	Respondents	49(18.6)	107(40.7)	63(24.0)	27(10.3)	17(6.5)
		Opinion –leaders	8(10.7)	22(29.3)	30(40.0)	6(8.0)	9(12.0)
14.	Containing disparaging reference to another product of service	Respondents	17(26.6)	82(31.2)	74(28.1)	18(6.8)	19(7.0)
		Opinion –leaders	12(16.0)	18(24.0)	29(38.7)	7(9.3)	9(12.0)
15.	Testimonials are misleading the viewers	Respondents	101(38.4)	77(29.3)	51(19.4)	17(6.5)	17(6.5)
		Opinion- leaders	9(12.0)	29(38.7)	24(32.0)	2(2.7)	11(14.7)

Source: Primary data

The above table shows that, the respondents and opinion-leaders comment on advertising. The comments are measured on a five point scale, namely, (*i*) always, (*ii*) frequently, (*iii*) occasionally, (*iv*) never, (*v*) can't say. The table unambiguously reveals that, the comments of the opinion-leaders and respondents are same. The comments of the respondents and the opinion are on the following things. (*i*) There is no ethical values in advertising, (*ii*) Advertising is just an exaggeration, puffery and bluffing, (*iii*) Advertising degenerates our culture, (*iv*) Advertising degenerates the youth, (*v*) Honesty in advertising is rare, (*vi*) Advertising causes false and misleading claims, (*vii*) Unfair advertisements are very common, (*viii*) It is not worth to go by advertising, (*ix*) Advertising boosting our self image, (*x*) Advertising for harmful are prohibited products and service, (*xi*) Prepare young minds (children) for the product, (*xii*) Referring the product or incidence is not capable of being established, (*xiii*) Give irrelevant statistical data and disproved scientific jargons, (*xiv*) Containing disparaging reference to another product of service and (*xv*) Testimonials are misleading the viewers. The comments are more or less uniform. There is no considerable difference between the opinion-leaders and the student respondents. The student respondents are toeing the line of the opinion-leaders.

6

Findings, Suggestions and Conclusion

In this chapter the researcher is going to present the finings of this research work. This part is classified in two parts. They are findings from the opinion-leaders and findings from the student respondents.

The Nature of Respondents: Opinion-leaders

- It was observed that majority (36 per cent) of the respondents were above 40 years of age and it implies that they are having vast experience in their own fields of knowledge.
- Among the total respondents, 64 respondents were male and the remaining 11 respondents were female. In other words 85.3 per cent of the respondents were male and the remaining 14.7 per cent of the respondents were female. It is found out that majority (85.3 per cent) of the respondents were male.
- Among the total number of respondents four were actors, three were music directors, three were journalists, five were engineers, five were doctors, five were lawyers, five were college principals and the remaining 45 respondents were other occupations namely auditors, marketing executives, manager of the TV channels like Clock TV, Ten TV and STV, Radio station directors, like Suriyan FM and All India Radio, popular radio jockeys like Sakthi and J.E. Sagar, director of employment office and advertising agencies like Mudra, Lintas, JWT, Leevi, Archana and Ray.
- Among the 75 respondents, it was found that 33 were spending their leisure time by reading news papers / magazines, three were listening radios, 20 were watching televisions, 10 were using internets, seven were watching movies and the remaining two chatting with their friends. It was observed that the majority (44 per cent) of the respondents were spending their leisure time by reading news papers or magazines.

- Among the 75 respondents, it was observed that 36 respondents considered the create awareness was the major role of the advertisement, 10 felt that create life style, 26 felt create new wants, one felt that foundation of civilization, two felt survive democracy. It was observed that majority (48 percent) of the respondent felt that creating awareness was the major role of the advertisement.
- Among the total number of respondents, 27 persons were the opinion that stimulate interest was the major role of the celebrities in advertisements, 10 felt fair description, eight felt truthful information, 20 felt inducted to purchase and the remaining nine felt that suggest for change and remaining one per cent of the respondents felt that for improving the sales. It was found out that majority (36 per cent) of the respondents felt that they were induced to purchase, was the major role of the celebrities in advertisements
- Among the 75 respondents it was reckoned that 12 respondents considered that they would use their celebrity influence to become popularize the cosmetics products, nine inclined towards advertisements of food, seven towards sports items, six towards the automobile products, five towards textile materials, 14 towards medicine, 14 towards electronic products and remaining eight felt that the other items such as jewelry and mobile phones. It was found out that the majority (18.7 per cent) felt that using their celebrities influence to become familiarize the medicines and electronic products.
- Among the total number of respondents, seven considered that the lasting impression was most attractive part in Television advertisement, 11 considered the theme, four considered the sound effect, four considered the celebrities, 34 were consider the innovativeness, two were consider the relevance, 12 considered the over all effects and the remaining one considered the other factor like slogan. It was observed that majority (45.3 per cent) of the respondents considered the innovativeness was most attractive part in Television advertisements.
- Among the total number of respondents 44.0 per cent had strongly agreed that the advertisement messages were understandable. 45.3 per cent some what agreed, four per cent was in neither agreed nor disagreed of the advertisement message is understandable, four had strongly disagreed and remaining two point seven per cent of the respondents were somewhat negative of this factor.
- Among the total number of respondents 16.0 per cent had strongly agreed that the advertisement is believable. 45.3 per cent some what agreed that the advertisement is believable.

- Among the total number of respondents nine point three per cent had strongly agreed that the benefits described in the advertisement are believable. 50.7 per cent had somewhat agreed, 20.0 per cent was in neither agreed nor disagreed of the benefits described in the advertisement are believable, 16.0 had strongly disagreed and remaining four point zero per cent were somewhat disagreed with this factor of advertisements are believable.
- Among the total number of respondents 10.7 per cent had strongly agreed that after acting/watching this advertisement they would consider purchasing the product. 46.7 per cent some what agreed with this views.
- Among the total number of respondents 18.7 per cent had strongly agreed that this advertisement was much better than other advertisement for that product category. 50.7 per cent had somewhat agreed with the views.
- Among the 75 respondents 34.7 per cent had strongly agreed that the advertisement is entertaining. 40 per cent were somewhat agreed that the advertising is entertaining.
- Among the 75 respondents 17.3 per cent had strongly agreed that the claims are accurate and justified in advertisement. 38.7 per cent were somewhat agreed with the views.
- Among the 75 respondents 40.0 per cent had strongly agreed that the advertisement had undesirable influence on children and youth. 36.0 per cent were somewhat agreed with the views.
- Among the 75 respondents 14.7 per cent had strongly agreed that the advertised product is better quality. 45.3 per cent were somewhat agreed, 14.7 per cent were in neither agreed nor disagreed for the advertisement product is better quality or disagreed this statement.
- Among the 75 respondents 12.0 per cent had strongly agreed that the advertisement is misleading. 36.0 per cent were somewhat agreed with the views.
- Among the 75 respondents eight per cent had strongly agreed that the advertisements are loud and vulgar. 17.3 per cent were somewhat agreed with the views.
- Among the 75 respondents 38.7 per cent strongly agreed that the advertisement is useful. 45.7 per cent were somewhat agreed with the views.
- Among the 75 respondents 29.3 per cent had strongly agreed that the advertisement should not be banned. 32.0 per cent were somewhat agreed with the views.

- Among the 75 respondents 14.7 per cent had strongly agreed that the advertisements promote wasteful consumptions and anti-saving. 56.0 per cent were somewhat agreed with the views.
- Among the 75 respondents eight per cent had strongly agreed that the advertisement is unproductive expenses and waste of resources. 34.7 per cent were somewhat agreed with the views.
- Among the total number of respondents 53.3 per cent considered that advertisement always promotes competition and 33.3 per cent felt that frequently, 13.3 per cent felt that occasionally.
- Among the total number of respondents 17.3 per cent felt that advertising always promoting sales and reducing prices. 34.7 per cent felt that frequently, 38.7 per cent felt that occasionally.
- Among the total number of respondents 37.3 per cent were of the opinion that advertising always promoting mass production. 22.7 per cent felt that frequently, 29.3 per cent felt occasionally.
- Among the total number of respondents 38.7 per cent felt that advertisements always help to fast turnover. 36.0 per cent felt that frequently, 16.0 per cent felt that occasionally and the remaining nine point three per cent couldn't say any thing about this factor.
- Among the total number of respondents six point seven per cent felt that advertised products were always of better quality. 12.0 per cent felt that frequently, 34.7 per cent felt that occasionally, 18.7 per cent felt that advertised products never had good quality and the remaining 28.0 per cent couldn't say any thing about this factor.
- Among the total number of respondents 14.7 per cent considered that advertisement always helps a manufacturer at the expenses of another without adding to growth. 24.0 per cent felt that frequently, 34.7 per cent felt that occasionally, 10.7 per cent felt that advertisement did not help a manufacturer at the expenses of another without adding to growth and the remaining 16.0 per cent couldn't say any thing about this factor.
- Among the total number of respondents 36.0 per cent considered that advertisement always helped larger manufacturers to get a strangle hold in the market. 29.3 per cent felt that frequently, 12.0 per cent felt that occasionally, four point zero per cent felt that never the advertisement did not help larger manufacturers to get a strong hold in the market and the remaining 18.7 per cent couldn't say any thing about this factor.

- 56.0 per cent felt that the false and misleading presentation of facts were more in product advertisements. Among the total number of respondents 37.3 per cent felt that the deliberate omitting of required information were in product advertisement.
- Among the total number of respondents 48.0 per cent felt that the implying a benefit that hardly exists were in product advertisement.
- Among the total number of respondents it was noticed that 38.7 per cent considered that the trade puffing and exaggeration were in product advertisement. 20.0 per cent felt that more in service advertisement, 40.7 per cent equal in product and service advertisement and remaining one point three per cent felt that not in both advertisements.
- Among the total number of respondents 37.3 per cent felt that unnecessary, unwanted technical jargons were used in product advertisement. 20 per cent felt that more in service advertisement, 33 per cent equal in product and service advertisement and remaining nine point three per cent felt that not in both advertisements.
- Among the total number of respondents 37.3 per cent felt that creating cultural degeneration were in product advertisement. 14.7 per cent felt more in service advertisement, 25.3 per cent equal in product and service advertisement and remaining 22.7 per cent felt that not in both advertisements.
- Among the total number of respondents 40 per cent felt that creating ambiguities in the minds of consumers were in product advertisement. Six point seven per cent felt more in service advertisement, 37.3 per cent equal in product and service advertisement and remaining 16 per cent felt that not in both advertisements.
- Among the total number of respondents 16 per cent felt that creating fear in the minds of consumers were in product advertisement. 22.7 per cent felt more in service advertisement, 21.3 per cent equal in product and service advertisement and remaining 40 per cent felt not in both advertisements.
- Among the total number of respondents 58.7 per cent felt that the open criticism of competitors were in product advertisement. Eight per cent felt more in service advertisement, 20 per cent equal in product and service advertisement and remaining 13.3 per cent felt not in both advertisements.
- Among the total number of respondents 45.3 per cent felt that sex in advertisements were in product advertisement. Five point three

per cent felt that more in service advertisement, 32 per cent equal in product and service advertisement where as remaining 17.3 per cent felt that not in both advertisements.

- Among the total number of respondents 22.7 per cent felt that most advertisements were against the national and public interest in product advertisement. Eight per cent felt that more in service advertisement, 26.7 per cent equal in product and service advertisement and remaining 42.7 per cent felt that not in both advertisements.
- Among the total number of respondents 48 per cent felt that advertisements create monopoly in product advertisement.
- Among the total number of respondents 21.3 per cent felt that unverifiable claims in a language were in product advertisement. 18.7 per cent felt more in service advertisement, 33.3 per cent equal in product and service advertisement and remaining 26.7 per cent felt not in both advertisements.
- Among the 75 respondents nine point three per cent felt that there is always no ethical value in advertising, 36 per cent felt that there is frequently, 38.7 per cent felt that there is occasionally, eight point zero per cent felt never and the remaining eight point zero per cent couldn't say anything about this factor.
- Among the 75 respondents six point seven per cent felt that advertising is always just an exaggeration, puffery and bluffing, 28 per cent felt frequently, 46.7 per cent felt that occasionally, 13.3 per cent felt never and the remaining five point three per cent can't say anything about this factor.
- Among the 75 respondents five point three per cent felt that advertising is always degenerates our culture, 20 per cent felt frequently, 30.7 per cent felt that occasionally, 21.3 per cent felt never and the remaining 22.7 per cent couldn't say anything about this factor.
- Among the 75 respondents nine point three per cent felt that advertising is always degenerates the youth, 34.7 per cent felt frequently, 21.3 per cent felt that occasionally, 21.3 per cent felt never and the remaining 13.3 per cent couldn't say anything about this factor.
- Among the 75 respondents 13.3 per cent felt that the honesty in advertising is always rare, 25.3 per cent felt frequently, 40 per cent felt that occasionally, five point three per cent felt never and the remaining 16 per cent couldn't say anything about this factor.

- Among the 75 respondents 26.7 per cent felt that advertising is always boosting our self image, 29.3 per cent felt frequently, 22.7 per cent felt that occasionally, 10.7 per cent felt never and the remaining 10.7 per cent couldn't say anything about this factor.
- Among the 75 respondents 32 per cent felt that advertising is always prepare young minds (children) for the product, 46.7 per cent felt frequently, 13.3 per cent felt that occasionally, five point three per cent felt never and the remaining two point seven per cent couldn't say anything about this factor.
- Among the 75 respondents 10.7 per cent felt that advertising is always giving irrelevant statistical data and disproved scientific jargons, 29.3 per cent felt frequently, 40 per cent felt that occasionally, eight point three per cent felt never and the remaining 12 per cent couldn't say anything about this factor.

The Nature of Respondents : Students

- Among the 263 respondents, 12 respondents were in the age group of 20 years, 58 respondents were belonging to the age group of 21 years, 84 respondents were belonging to the age group of 22 years, 67 respondents were at the age group of 23 years, 24 respondents at the age group 24 years and the remaining 18 respondents were above 24 years of age. It was found out that majority (31.9 per cent) of the respondents were belonging to the age group of 22 years.
- Among the total respondents, 118 respondents were male and the remaining 145 respondents were female.
- Among the 263 respondents, 119 respondents were from urban areas and the remaining 144 from the rural areas. It was found out that majority (54.8 percent) of the respondents were from rural areas.
- Among the 263 respondents, 200 respondents were Hindus, four respondents were Muslims and 59 respondents were Christians.
- Among the 263 respondents, 28 respondents monthly income was above Rs. 17917 per month, 103 respondents monthly income was between Rs. 3,750 -17, 917, 72 respondents monthly income was between Rs. 1,833 – Rs. 3,750, 36 respondents monthly income was between Rs. 1,333 - Rs.1,833 and the remaining 24 respondents monthly income was below Rs. 1,333.
- Among the 263 respondents, the fathers of the 30 respondents were illiterate, 29 were upto primary (upto 5th std.) level, 40 were upto middle (upto 8th std.) level, 61 were upto high school (10th

std.) level, 38 were upto higher secondary (+2) level, 41 were graduates, 21 were postgraduates, one respondent has doctoral degree and the remaining two respondents were diplomas namely electrical and mechanical. It is found out that majority (23.2 per cent) of the respondents were studied upto 10th standard. (High School Level).

- Among the 263 respondents, the mothers of the 51 respondents were illiterate, 41 were upto primary (upto 5th std.) level, 52 were upto middle (upto 8th std.) level, 66 were upto high school (10th std.) level, 34 were upto higher secondary (+2) level, 14 were graduates, five were postgraduates.
- Among the 263 respondents, 107 were involving in agricultural works, 54 were government employees, 36 were doing business, seven were professionals, 49 were working in private companies and the remaining 10 were labourers. Among the 263 respondents, 72 were living in a joint family system and remaining 191 were living in a nuclear family system. It was found out that majority (72.6 per cent) of the respondents were living in nuclear family system.
- Among the 263 respondents, 77 were hostellers and the remaining 186 were day-scholars.
- Among the 263 respondents, 70 were studying post graduation in arts, 148 were studying post graduation in science, 19 were doing M.Phil in arts and the remaining 26 were doing M.Phil in Science.
- Among the total number of post graduate respondents 74 were I year students, 104 were II year students, 40 were III year students and the remaining 45 were M.Phil students. It was found out that majority (39.5 per cent) of the respondents were II year students. It was also observed that Post Graduate III year students belong to Master of Computer Applications.
- Among the total number of respondents, 61 spend their leisure time in reading news papers/magazines, 42 listen ratio, 117 watch television and the remaining 43 use internet.
- Among the total number of respondents, 14 were considering that the lasting impression was most attractive part in Television advertisement, 63 were considering the theme, 29 were considering the sound effect, 26 were considering the celebrities, 61 were considering the innovativeness, six were considering the relevance, 63 were considering the over all effects and the remaining one was considering the other factor namely jingles.

- Among the 263 respondents, 107 felt that creating awareness was the major role of the advertisement, 61 felt that create life style, 73 felt create new wants, nine felt that foundation of civilization, 12 felt survive democracy and the remaining one respondent felt the other factor namely improvement of business.
- It was found out that majority (30.4 per cent) of the respondents felt that inducted to purchase was the major role of the celebrities in advertisements
- Among the 263 respondents 105 considered that the celebrities as an important factor for their purchase decisions and the remaining 158 do not consider the celebrities at the time of purchase decisions.
- Among the 105 respondents 16 were influenced by actor Vijay, 14 by Ajith, seven by Madhavan, six by Prakash Raj, 22 by Suriya, three by Amitabpachan, 11 by cricket player Sachin Tendelkur, two by actress Asin, three by Trisha, two by Sneka, four by Tamana, five by Ishwaraya Roy, one by Sharuk Khan, eight by Cricket Player Dohni and the remaining one by other celebrity namely the actor Kamalahasan.
- Among the 263 respondents 44.9 per cent felt that false and misleading presentation of facts are existing in production advertisement, 10.6 per cent in service advertisement, 39.5 per cent felt that equal in both and the remaining four point nine per cent not in both cases.
- Among the 263 respondents 49.8 per cent felt that deliberate omitting of required information are existing in product advertisement, 22.4 per cent in service advertisement, 25.9 per cent felt that it is equal in both and the remaining one point nine per cent not in both cases.
- Among the 263 respondents 44.5 per cent felt that trade puffing and exaggeration were existing in product advertisement, 16.7 per cent in service advertisement, 32.7 per cent felt that it is equal in both and the remaining six point one per cent not in both cases.
- Among the 263 respondents 55.9 per cent felt that using unnecessary and unwanted technical jargons were existing in product advertisement, 22.4 per cent in service advertisement, 25.9 per cent felt that it is equal in both and the remaining one point nine per cent not in both cases.
- Among the 263 respondents 58.6 per cent felt that creating cultural degeneration were existing in product advertisement, 11.4 per cent in service advertisement, 22.1 per cent felt that it is equal in both and the remaining eight point zero per cent not in both cases.

- Among the 263 respondents 42.2 per cent felt that creating ambiguities in the minds of consumer were existing in product advertisement, 14.1 per cent in service advertisement, 38.8 per cent felt that it is equal in both and the remaining four point nine per cent not in both cases.
- Among the 263 respondents 54.0 per cent felt that open criticism of competitors were existing in product advertisement, 14.4 per cent in service advertisement, 27.4 per cent felt that it is equal in both and the remaining four point two per cent not in both cases.
- Among the 263 respondents 58.6 per cent felt that sex in advertisement were existing in product advertisement, 10.6 per cent in service advertisement, 25.5 per cent felt that it is equal in both and the remaining five point three per cent not in both cases.
- Among the 263 respondents 30.8 per cent felt that against the national and pubic interest were existing in product advertisement, 22.4 per cent in service advertisement, 25.9 per cent felt that it is equal in both and the remaining 20.9 per cent not in both cases.
- Among the 263 respondents 48.3 per cent felt that affect life style of people were existing in product advertisement, 14.8 per cent in service advertisement, 27.4 per cent felt that it is equal in both and the remaining nine point five per cent not in both cases.
- Among the 263 respondents 59.3 per cent felt that creates monopoly were existing in product advertisement.
- Among the 263 respondents 39.9 per cent felt that unverifiable claims in a language were existing in product advertisement, 21.3 per cent in service advertisement, 30.4 per cent felt that it is equal in both and the remaining eight point four per cent not in both cases.
- Among the 263 respondents 35.0 per cent felt that subliminal message were existing in product advertisement, 16.0 per cent in service advertisement, 42.9 per cent felt that it is equal in both and the remaining six point one per cent not in both cases.
- Among the 263 respondents 13.3 per cent felt that there is always no ethical value in advertising, 41.4 per cent felt that there is frequently, 31.2 per cent felt that there is occasionally, five point seven per cent felt never and the remaining eight point four per cent couldn't say anything about this factor.
- Among the 263 respondents 21.7 per cent felt that advertising is always just an exaggeration, puffery and bluffing, 36.5 per cent felt frequently, 28.9 per cent felt that occasionally, seven point two per cent felt never and the remaining five point seven per cent couldn't say anything about this factor.

- Among the 263 respondents 20.2 per cent felt that advertising is always degenerates our culture, 36.5 per cent felt frequently, 25.1 per cent felt that occasionally, 12.5 per cent felt never and the remaining five point seven per cent couldn't say anything about this factor.
- Among the 263 respondents 26.6 per cent felt that advertising is always degenerates the youth, 36.5 per cent felt frequently, 25.1 per cent felt that occasionally, eight point zero per cent felt never and the remaining three point eight per cent couldn't say anything about this factor.
- Among the 263 respondents 32.7 per cent felt that the honesty in advertising is always rare, 26.6 per cent felt frequently, 24.0 per cent felt that occasionally, 10.6 per cent felt never and the remaining six point one per cent can't say anything about this factor.
- Among the 263 respondents 18.6 per cent felt that advertising is always giving irrelevant statistical data and disproved scientific jargons, 40.7 per cent felt frequently, 24.0 per cent felt that occasionally, 10.3 per cent felt never and the remaining six point five per cent couldn't say anything about this factor.
- Among the 263 respondents 25.1 per cent felt that advertising is always for harmful/prohibited product and services, 22.8 per cent felt frequently, 31.9 per cent felt that occasionally, 11.4 per cent felt never and the remaining eight point seven per cent couldn't say anything about this factor.
- Cultural exaggeration in select advertisement of the products is found in theme, slogan, music in all the factors. In all the 10 products viz., Binco Chips, VVD Gold Coconut Oil, Horlicks, Nescafe Sunrise, KFC Chicken, Medimix sandal soap, Docomo, Motoyuva Y810, Colgate Max Fresh and Spinz Deo, cultural exaggeration is more in action followed by theme and music. Cultural exaggeration is very low in the slogans of the advertisements.
- According to the respondents unethical under pinning are found in the select advertisement of all the 10 product viz., Binco Chips, VVD Gold Coconut Oil, Horlicks, Nescafe Sunrise, KFC Chicken, Medimix sandal soap, Docomo, Motoyuva Y810, Colgate Max Fresh and Spinz Deo. Majority of the respondents ranging from 28.1 per cent to 41.8 per cent felt that advertisement have unethical values. Another section of the respondents ranging from 16.3 per cent to 39.9 per cent felt that the advertisements have highly unethical values. Only a small section of the respondents felt that the advertisements are having ethical moorings.

- There are no significant differences between different age group of respondents and their recall value, remembering pattern of the content in an advertisement, getting message from the advertisement, receiving different kinds of message and acceptance value of the Binco chip advertisement.
- There is no significant difference between different age group of respondents and their recall value, remembering pattern of the content, getting message from the advertisement, receiving different kinds of message and acceptance value of the VVD gold coconut oil advertisement.
- There is no significant difference between different age group of respondents and their recall value, remember pattern of the content, getting message from the advertisement and receiving different kinds of message. There is a significant difference between different age group of respondents and their acceptance value of Horlicks advertisement.
- There is no significant difference between different age group of respondents and their recall value, remembering pattern of the content, getting message from the advertisement, receiving different kinds of message and acceptance value of the Nescafe Surriserise advertisement.
- There is no significant difference between different age group of respondents and their recall value, remembering pattern of the content, getting message from the advertisement, receiving different kinds of message and acceptance value of the KFC Chicken advertisement.
- There is no significant difference between different age group of respondents and their recall value, remember pattern of the content, getting message from the advertisement and receiving different kinds of message. There is a significant difference between different age group of respondents and their acceptance value of Medimix sandal soap advertisement.
- There is no significant difference between difference age group of respondents and their recall value, remembering pattern of the content, receiving different kinds of message and acceptance value of Docomo advertisement. But there is a significant difference between different age group of respondents and getting message from this advertisement.
- There is no significant difference between different age group of respondents and their recall value, remembering pattern of the content, getting message from the advertisement, receiving

different kinds of message and acceptance value of the Motoyuva Y810 advertisement.

- There is no significant difference between different age group of respondents and their recall value, remember pattern of the content, getting message from the advertisement and receiving different kinds of message. There is a significant difference between different age group of respondents and their acceptance value of Colgate Max Fresh advertisement.
- There is no significant relationship between different age group of respondents and their recall value, remembering pattern of the content, getting message from the advertisement, receiving different kinds of message and acceptance value of the Spinz Deo advertisement.
- The Personal Life Score index is relatively high for the female respondents, the age group of 22 years, rural area respondents and Arts major (PG, M.Phil) respondents compare to male respondents, the age group of 20 years, 21 years, 23 years, 24 years and above 24 years, urban area respondents and science major (PG and M.Phil) respondents respectively.
- The female respondents, the age group of 22 years, rural area respondents and Arts major (PG, M.Phil) respondents are felt that the unethical practices in advertisements are high in comparison to male respondents, the age group of 20 years, 21 years, 23 years, 24 years and above 24 years, urban area respondents and Major Science students (PG and M.Phil) respondents respectively.
- The female respondents, the age group of 22 years, rural area respondents and Arts major (PG, M.Phil) respondents gave high level of comment on advertising compare to male respondents, the age group of 20 years, 21 years, 23 years, 24 years and above 24 years, urban area respondents and Major Science (PG and Mphil) students respondents respectively.
- The female respondents, the age group of 22 years, rural area respondents and Arts major (PG, M.Phil) respondents felt that the cultural exaggeration in select advertisement is high compare to male respondents, the age group of 20 years, 21 years, 23 years, 24 years and above 24 years, urban area respondents and Major Science students (PG and Mphil) respondents respectively.
- There is no significant difference between different age group of respondents and their opinion about personal life, unethical practices in advertisements, comment on advertising, cultural exaggeration in select advertisement and ethical value in select advertisement.

- There is no significant relationship between different religious group of respondents and opinion about their personal life, unethical practices in advertisements, comment on advertising, cultural exaggeration in select advertisement and ethical value in select advertisement.
- There is no significant relationship between different income group of respondents and opinion about their personal life, comment on advertising, cultural exaggeration in select advertisements and ethical value in select advertisements. But there is a significant difference between different income group of respondents and unethical practices in advertisements.
- There are no significant differences between different major Arts students as well as Science students of respondents and opinion about their personal life, comment on advertising, cultural exaggeration in select advertisements and ethical value in select advertisements. But there is a significant difference between different major of respondents and unethical practices in advertisements.
- There is no significant relationship between the respondents different sex groups and opinion about their personal life, unethical practices in advertisements, comment on advertising, cultural exaggeration in select advertisement and ethical value in select advertisement.
- There is no significant relationship between difference different area of respondents and opinion about their personal life, comment on advertising, cultural exaggeration in select advertisement and ethical value in select advertisement. But there is a significant difference between different area of respondents and unethical practices in advertisement.

Suggestions and Policy Implications

- With regard to product advertisement, it was found out that both the opinion-leaders and the respondents expressed that there was a fear of puffing, exaggeration. unnecessary and unwanted technical jargons, disproved scientific jargon, cultural degeneration, creating ambiguity in the minds of consumers, creating fear, criticizing the competitors, use of sex in advertisement, subliminal message and irrelevant statistical data. As a consequence, there is a fear of degenerating the youth is clear and despite the powerful lobby of the makers of these products should not be allowed to dictate attraction to the youth which leads to Narcissism. In India, as in several advanced economies there is only one body for self regulation in advertisement. The Advertising Standards Council of India (1985) which is interested in safe guarding the interest of consumers whilst monitoring or guiding the commercial communications of practitioners in advertising on behalf of advertisers, for advertisements carried by the media, in their endeavours to influence buying decisions of the consuming public. It is suggested that the young youth can file any complaints against such advertisements by providing the background information like a copy of the advertisement name and date of publications (or) the channel name, date and timing of hearing and brief description of TV Commercial or Radio Spot. A specimen copy of the complaint to Advertising Standards Council of India regarding the advertisements is enclosed in the annexure. The complaint can be send to the secretary general, the Advertisement Standards Council of India, 205, Bombay Market, Post Box No: 7939, Tardeo Road, Mumbai-400034. Their e-mail id is asci@dnl.com.

- It is understood from the study that the recall memory of the science students is low when compared to arts students. The students service organizations in universities and colleges, such as N.S.S. N.C.C. Nature Club and Placement Cell should create awareness about the misleading advertisements. For this purpose the above mentioned service organizations can organize seminars, symposium, workshop, rally for creating awareness about the wilful and misleading, degenerating the youth advertisement to the students as well as the public and file a combined complaint to the Advertising Standards Council of India, Mumbai. This will ensure and enhance that the advertisement confirms to its code for self regulations, to the members and competitors as a control mechanism.
- The universities and colleges must start a consumer club and make the students to joint in the consumer club. Through this consumer club as a moment to the students and opinion leaders can register and raise their voice against such willful advertisements. These consumers club in the colleges should have a link with a consumer forum in each district. In turn the consumer forum in each district can have a link with the Advertising Standard Council of India in Mumbai. These three tire structure will help to represent and file complaint against misleading, defective and degenerate our culture through advertisement.
- The media moguls like O & M, McCann-Erickson, Lowe Lintas, Leo Burnett, JWT, Mudra, Grey World Wide, Rediffusion DYR,

Contract, FCB Ulka, RK Swamy, Saatchi and Saatchi, Bates enterprise, Euro RSCG and Ambiene Publics are advised to have a control and check over misleading, degenerating culture and other bad consequences to the society. The Advertising Standard Council of India should have a control over the above advertising agencies. Their media-mix should be edited and censored by the Advertising Standards Council of India, Mumbai.

- In post-test, recall memory is very effective to findout the effectiveness of advertisement. The marketer, advertising agencies should consider these points for their effectiveness of the advertisements inorder to find a suitable place in mind of the youth. The viewers of the advertisement can easily attract and arrest their mind by using music, slogan and action in the advertisement jingles. In future the advertiser may use this formula as a technique to find suitable place in the minds of the consumers.
- According to 2001 census 45 per cent of the Indian population was less than 19 years old. The fear of degenerating the youth is real and the powerful lobby of the makers of these products should not be allowed to dictate terms to the concern use of puffery, exaggeration regarding product function and benefit claims must be shunned at all the cultures, viewers, marketers, users and society. At this point the role of social responsibility is very much felt. The celebrities of advertisements and opinion leaders should take a lead to be gained the youth of our country. Most celebrities', endorsement comes mostly from the entertainment world. (Suriya, Vijay) Close Sports World (Tendulkar, Dhoni) appear in the advertisements. These celebrities should check, verify and satisfy themselves whether the advertisements in which they act has moral, ethical, social values. Similarly opinion leaders inturn should also inculcate the students about puffery, exaggeration, unnecessary and unwanted technical jargons, disproved scientific jargons, cultural degenerations, creating ambiguities in the minds of the consumers, creating fear, criticizing the competitors, use of sex in advertisement, subliminal message and irrelevant statistical data. (e.g., Binco chips advertisement V.V.D. Gold Coconut Oil, Horlicks, Nescafe Sunrise, KFC Chicken, Medimix Sandal Soap, Docomo, Motoyuva Y810, Colgate max fresh and Spinz Deo).
- The opinion leaders and student respondents spend their leisure time primarily on two things viz., Watching Television channel and reading news papers. They fond of channels beaming comedy, songs and sports. It is suggested that advertising agencies could telecast their advertisements in these popular channels inorder to get more effectiveness of their advertisements.

- As this study clearly reveals that, both opinion leaders and student respondents view 'create awareness' as the main role of advertisement. The Advertising agencies should concentrate on disseminating information about the products, place, price, promotion, quality content and son on. This will ensure the maximum effectiveness of the advertisement.
- This study is clearly depicts that both student respondents and opinion leaders have expressed different opinions on most attractive part in television advertisement. For student respondents, the most appealing areas of television advertisement is 'the theme' and for the opinion leaders, 'innovation' seems to attract more than other areas of advertisement. It is suggested that, any advertisement targeting the students, should give relevant, concise and clear message in the advertisement. Any advertisement targeting the opinion leaders should pay attention in innovation and unique ways of preparing and presenting the advertisements so as to increase its effectiveness.
- It is clearly observed from the study that, the student respondents and opinion leaders have different opinion about the role of celebrities in advertisement. It is suggested that any advertisement focusing students could include one or two celebrities which can greatly induce them to purchase the product, thereby increasing the overall effectiveness of advertisement. As the opinion leaders felt that, 'stimulation of interest' is the major role of celebrities in advertisements, hence to achieve maximum effectiveness advertising agencies should pay attention in stimulating interest in the product.
- It is understood from the study that, more than one third of the students' respondents consider advertisement as something unethical, giving disproved a scientific jargons, dishonesty, and presenting testimonials that are misleading the viewers (e.g., Spinz Deo) and hence inorder to achieve the maximum effectiveness of advertisement, true, honesty, ethical and scientifically proven data could be presented in the advertisement. The opinion leaders felt that, advertisement indirectly coerce the children (e.g., Horlicks) and youngsters (e.g., Motoyuva Y810) into buying the product by including children and children related stuff in the advertisements. As this is seen as a negative method by the opinion-leaders, this kind of coercion could be avoided as to increase the effectiveness of the advertisement.
- The opinions about the personal life of the respondents had no bearing on their age composition, religion, income and the major

disciplines. They had been perusing. The opinion about personal life covers their mode of dressing, mingling with women and relatives, approach towards marital life, respecting elders, dining, shopping, joint family system, fatalism, hospitality and buying behaviour. The 'ANNOVA' test shows clearly that the age religion, income and major subjects perused by the students had no significant relations with the opinion expressed by the respondents about the personal life. It is suggested that the advertising agencies when design advertisement strategies for their product, should consider these above mentioned factors. They can use their own creativity, innovativeness and follow different strategies to attract the different group of respondents through their advertisement.

- With regard to unethical practices in advertisement, it is found out that, there is no close association between age, religion and unethical practices in advertisement. But there is a significant relationship between different income group, different major student and unethical practices in advertisement. As India is a secular country, it has different religion, community and language. They have their own traditional culture, customs and values. It is suggested that, the makers of the advertisement need not bring in any religious sentiments and practices for popularizing their product through their advertisements. Since income and subjects pursued by the students have strong linkage with unethical practices of the advertisement, the advertisement plan has to incorporate these two factors into their advertisement. The advertisements should be tailor made to suit the different income groups. It should also be distinct and different with regard to the students studying different major disciplines. The advertisement should be designed to suit the interests of different income groups and the students of different disciplines.
- It is clearly observed from this study that, there is no statistical relationship (ANNOVA) between comment on advertising and respondents of different age group, religion, income and major studies. The respondents have different opinion about various advertisements. It is suggested that, the advertisement featuring unfair comparison (e.g., VVD Gold Coconut oil) and undermining the products of competitors should be avoided. Cheating the consumer about the utility of the product with help of testimonials should be carefully monitored. The advertisements should contain all the specific details of the product required by the consumers and it should encourage social harmony and national integration. So that the effectiveness of their advertisement will be felt.

- It is found out that there is no close associate cultural exaggeration in select advertisements and different group of age, religion, income and major. The nature of cultural exaggeration in select advertisement are falling on the following any one of the criteria such as theme, slogan, music, action and all the factors. What-ever the respondents observe in advertisements, they will try to imitate in their real life. It is suggested that, the advertising agencies should avoid misleading and fancied advertisements (e.g., Docomo) which creates false opinions about the product and services and pay more attention on slogan and theme of the advertisement. So that the effectiveness of advertisement will improve.
- With regard to ethical values in select advertisements, it is found out that, there is no statistical relationship between ethical values in select advertisements and respondents' age structure, religion, income and major subjects. Ethical values in select advertisements are determined on the basis of the following criteria such as ethical, highly ethical, unethical, highly unethical and can't say. It is suggested that, advertising agency should avoid creating a defective mind set of the consumer devoid of facts and willful suppression of facts in their product advertisement (e.g., Medimix Sandal Soap). They should give clear and complete details about the product and its usage. So that the effectiveness of ethical values in select advertisement will increase.
- Now-a-days advertisements are common for products, as well as services. Television advertisement reaches the youth effectively. The speed of the advertisement should be controlled by opinion-leaders (Enlighten Citizens) Such as the academicians, economic planners, political thinkers, political elites, technocrats, Bureaucrats, social activists, media experts, development professionals and all other people who have enjoyed the fruits of democracy for ever. These enlightened opinion-leaders will help our youth towards the formation of character, culture, attitude and leadership.

Conclusion

Cultural exaggeration in select advertisement of the products is found in theme, slogan, music and all the factors. In all the 10 products viz., Binco Chips, VVD Gold Coconut Oil, Horlicks, Nescafe Sunrise, KFC Chicken, Medimix sandal soap, Docomo, Motoyuva Y810, Colgate Max Fresh and Spinz Deo, cultural exaggeration is more in action followed by theme and music. Cultural exaggeration is very low in the slogans of the advertisements. According to the respondents unethical under pinning are found in the select advertisement of all the 10 product viz., Binco Chips, VVD Gold Coconut Oil, Horlicks, Nescafe Sunrise, KFC Chicken, Medimix sandal soap, Docomo, Motoyuva Y810, Colgate Max Fresh and Spinz Deo. Majority of the respondents ranging from 28.1 per cent to 41.8 per cent felt that advertisement have unethical values. Another section of the respondents ranging from 16.3 per cent to 39.9 per cent felt that the advertisements have highly unethical values. Only a small section of the respondents felt that advertisements are having ethical moorings. The personal life score index is relatively high for the female respondents, the age group of 22 years, rural area respondents and major students of Arts. (PG, M.Phil) respondents compare to male respondents, the age group of 20 years, 21 years, 23 years, 24 years and above 24 years, urban area respondents and major science students (PG and M.Phil) respondents respectively. The female respondents, the age group of 22 years, rural area respondents and Arts major (PG, M.Phil) respondents are felt that the unethical practices in advertisements are high compare to male respondents, the age group of 20 years, 21 years, 23 years, 24 years and above 24 years, urban area respondents and major Science students (PG and M.Phil) respondents respectively.

There is a significant variation among the respondents about the remembering the content of the advertisement. The forgoing analysis proved beyond doubt that, there is no significant variances among the respondents about the remembering the content of the advertisement. The Chi-square test applied to prove the relationships between group of respondents classified on the basis of age and their remembering pattern shows that there is no significant relation between the age of the respondents and their remembering capability of select advertisements. So the first hypothesis states that there is a significant variation among the respondents and their remembering the content of the select advertisements, is disproved. The second hypothesis which states that the effectiveness of advertisement diverges differs widely among the respondents on the basis on their age, religion, income and major subjects perceived for their studies. This hypothesis the foregoing analysis proves that the effectiveness of the advertisement has not differed widely among respondents on the basis of their age, religion, income and major subjects perceived by the students. The effectiveness of advertisements is viewed from five different criteria namely, opinion about the personal life style, unethical practices in advertisements, comment on advertising, cultural exaggeration in select advertisements and ethical values in select advertisements. Inferring from above five criteria the effectiveness of advertisement has a same impact on respondents irrespective of their age, religion, income and major subjects perceived by them. The notable exception is, there are differences in the different income categories of respondents on their view on unethical practices advertisement. The same result is found for unethical practices for the students perusing different major subjects. Barring these exceptions the over all result is the effectiveness of advertisement is not significantly differing among respondents on the basis of age, religion, income and major subjects. The third hypothesis states that there is a perfect uncertainty of views about unethical dimensions of advertisements among opinion leaders and students respondents. The hypothesis is proved correct. The table no. 5.85 shows that in all the fifteen critical unethical practices in advertisements they have similar views. The following is the opinion of both opinion leaders and students respondents about the unethical practices in advertisements. Majority of the respondents felt that the unethical practices are featuring more in product and consumer advertisement for the sizable section of the opinion leaders and the students respondents feel that the unethical practices in advertisements are found in equal measures in product and service. Another section of respondents comprising opinion leaders and student respondents feel that the unethical practices are more pronounced in services. A very small section felt that the unethical practices are not present in product and service. The above analysis clearly shows that both opinion leaders and students have identical opinions about the occurrence of unethical practices. The third hypothesis which states that there is certainty among opinion leaders and student respondents is proved correct.

Among the 75 respondents nine point three per cent felt that there is always no ethical value in advertising, 36.0 per cent felt that there is frequently, 38.7 per cent felt that there is occasionally, eight point zero per cent felt never and the remaining eight point zero per cent can't say anything about this factor. Among the 75 respondents six point seven per cent felt that advertising is always just an exaggeration, puffery and bluffing, 28.0 per cent felt frequently, 46.7 per cent felt that occasionally, 13.3 per cent felt never and the remaining five point three per cent can't say anything about this factor. Among the 75 respondents five point three per cent felt that advertising is always degenerates our culture, 20.0 per cent felt frequently, 30.7 per cent felt that occasionally, 21.3 per cent felt never and the remaining 22.7 per cent can't say anything about this factor. Among the 75 respondents 32.0 per cent felt that advertising is always prepare young minds (children) for the product, 46.7 per cent felt frequently, 13.3 per cent felt that occasionally, five point three per cent felt never and the remaining two point seven per cent can't say anything about this factor. Among the 75 respondents 10.7 per cent felt that advertising is always giving irrelevant statistical data and disproved scientific jargons, 29.3 per cent felt frequently, 40.0 per cent felt that occasionally, eight point three per cent felt never and the remaining 12.0 per cent can't say anything about this factor.

The Advertising Standards Council of India (1985) which is interested in safe-guarding the interest of consumers, whilst ministering or guiding the commercial communications of practitioners in advertising on behalf of advertisers, for advertisements carried by the media, in their endeavours to influence buying decisions of the consuming public. It is suggested that the young youth can file any complaints against such advertisements by providing the background information like a copy of the advertisement name and date of publications (or) the channel name, date and timing of hearing and brief description of TV Commercial or Radio Spot. The universities and colleges must start a consumer club and make the students to join in it. Through this consumer club as a moment to the students and opinion leaders can registered and raise their voice against such wilful advertisements. The Advertising Standard Council of India should have a control over the all advertising agencies such as O & M, McCann-Erickson, Lowe Lintas, Leo Burnett, JWT, Mudra, Grey World Wide, Rediffusion DYR, Contract, FCB Ulka, RK Swamy, Saatchi and Saatchi, Bates enterprise, Euro RSCG and Ambiene Publics. Their media-mix should be edited and censored by the Advertising Standards Council of India, Mumbai. The celebrities of advertisements and opinion leaders should take a lead to be gained by the youth of our country. Most celebrities' endorsement comes from the entertainment world. (Suriya, Vijay) Close Sports World (Tendulkar, Dhoni) appear in the advertisements. These celebrities should check, verify and satisfy themselves whether the advertisement in which they act has moral, ethical, social values. Similarly opinion-leaders inturn should also inculcate the students about puffery, exaggeration, unnecessary and unwanted technical jargons, disproved scientific jargons, cultural degenerations, creating ambiguities in the minds of the consumers, creating fear, criticizing the competitors, use of sex in advertisements, subliminal message and irrelevant statistical data.

The researcher used the recall memory method to find out the effectiveness of selected advertisements among the youth in Tiruchirappalli Corporation limit. The effectiveness of advertisement is checked by recall, remembering the content and the accepting the message. The selected 10 advertisements are very effective and they found a suitable place in the minds of the young youth. With the help of the opinion leaders, the youth can be checked and make them in fall in line to fight against the puffing, exaggeration, false, misleading, unnecessary and unwanted technical jargons, disproved scientific jargon, cultural de-generation, creating ambiguity in the minds of consumers, creating fear, criticizing the competitors, use of sex in advertisement, subliminal message and irrelevant statistical data. The suggestions made by the researcher could be used to channalise the youth to fight against such false and misleading advertisements.

Remember – Don't react, Act
Together we will set it right.

Bibliography

Books

1. Agarwal (2005), Advertising and Salesmenship, Pragati Prakashar, Meerut.
2. Gerad J. Tellis (2004), Effective Advertising, Response Book, A division of Sage Publications India (P) Ltd., New Delhi .
3. Gupta, C.B., (2009), Advertising and Personal Selling, Sultan Chand & Sons, New Delhi.
4. Mathur U C (2002), Advertising Management, New Age International (P) Ltd., New Delhi.
5. Rao. S.L., (1992), Socio-Economic Effects of Advertising in India, National Council of Applied Economic Research, New Delhi.
6. William H. Antrin and Eugene L Dorr (1978), "Advertising", 2nd Edition, Mc-Graw Hill Company, New Delhi, p. 143-150.

Journals

7. Abhilasha Metha (1999), "Using Self-Concept to Assess Advertising Effectiveness" Journal of Advertising Research, 32 (8) 81-88.
8. Adams H.F. (1915), "The adequacy of the laboratory test in advertising", *Psychological Review*, 22(5), 402-422.
9. Alpert, Mark L., Golden, Linda L., Hoyer, Wayne D (1983), "The Impact of Repetition on Advertisement Miscomprehension and Effectiveness", *Advances in Consumer Research*, 10(1) 130-135.
10. Amitav Chakravarti, Chris Janiszewski (2004), "The Influence of Generic Advertising on Brand Preferences", Journal of Consumer Research, 30, 25-38.
11. Anand Kumar (2000), "Interference Effects of Contextual Cues in Advertisements on Memory for Ad Content", *Journal of Consumer Psychology*, 9 (3) 155-166.
12. Andrew L. Mendelson, Paul D. Bolls(2002), "Emotional effects of advertising on young adults of lower socio-economic status" *Journal of Marketing*, 59 (3) 53-62.
13. AnjaZurcher Wray Nancy Nelson Hodges (2008), "Response to activewear apparel *advertisements* by US baby boomers: An examination of cognitive versus chronological age factors", *Journal of Consumer Marketing*, 12 (1) 8-23.
14. Anusorn Singhapakdi, Mohammed Y.A. Rawwas, Janet K. Marta, Mohd Ismail Ahmed (1999), "A cross-cultural study of consumer perceptions about marketing ethics", *Journal of Consumer Marketing*, 16 (3) 257-272.
15. Appiah, Osei(2007), "The Effectiveness of "Typical-User" Testimonial Advertisements on Black and White Browsers' Evaluations of Products on Commercial Websites: Do They Really Work?" *Journal of Advertising Research*, 47 (1), 14-27.

16. Appiah-Adu, Kwaku(1999), "Assessing the Effectiveness of Travel Agency Print Advertisements", *Journal of International Marketing & Marketing Research*, Vol. 24, no.3, p. 145-160.
17. Arch G. Woodside, Chris Dubelaar (2003), "Increasing Quality in Measuring Advertising Effectiveness: A Meta-Analysis of Question Framing in Conversion Studies", Journal of Advertising Research, 45(28) 78-84.
18. Bagozzi, Richard P, Silk, Alvin J (1983), "Recall, Recognition, and the *Measurement* of Memory for Print *Advertisement", Marketing Science,* 2(2) 95. Leigh, James H (1984), "Recall and Recognition Performance for Umbrella Print Advertisements", *Journal of Advertising*, 13 (4)5-30.
19. Baird, Amy L.; Grieve, Frederick G (2006), "Exposure to Male Models in Advertisements Leads to a Decrease in Men's Body Satisfaction", *North American Journal of Psychology*, 8, no.1, p115-121.
20. Beattie, Geoffrey, Shovelton, Heather(2005), "Why the spontaneous images created by the hands during talk can help make TV advertisements more effective", *British Journal of Psychology*, 96 (1)21-37.
21. Beomjoon Choi, Crandall, Christian S (2008), "Permission to be Prejudiced: Legitimacy Credits in the Evaluation of Advertisements with Black and White Models", *Advances in Consumer Research - North American Conference Proceedings*, 35, 724-725.
22. Boles, James, Scot Burton (1992), "An Examination of Free Elicitation and Response Scale Measures of Feelings and Judgments Evoked by Television *Advertisements", Journal of the Academy of Marketing Science* , 20 (3) 225.
23. Boonghee Yoo, Rujirutana Mandhachitara (2003), "Estimating Advertising Effects on Sales in Competitive Setting" *Journal of Advertising Research*, 28 (3) 310-319.
24. Bruce A. Austin (1986), "Cinema Screen Advertising: An Old Technology With New Promise For Consumer Marketing", *Journal of Consumer Marketing*, 3 (1) 45 – 56.
25. Bruce F. Hall(2004), "Measuring The Effectiveness Of The Promotional Program - Presentation Transcripty" *Mcgraw-Hill/Irwin.*
26. Burton, Scot, Lichtenstein, Donald R (1988), "The Effect of Ad Claims and Ad Context on Attitude Toward the Advertisement", *Journal of Advertising*, 17(1) 3-11.
27. Bush, Alan J.; Bush, Victoria Davies (1994), "The Narrative Paradigm as a Perspective for Improving Ethical Evaluations of Advertisements", *Journal of Advertising*, 23 (3) 31-41.
28. Bush, Ronald F.; Hair Jr., Joseph F.; Solomon, Paul J (1979), "Consumers' Level of Prejudice and Response to Black Models in Advertisements" *Journal of Marketing Research*, 16 (3)341-345.
29. Carol Kaufman-Scarborough (2001), "Accessible advertising for visually-disabled persons: the case of color-deficient consumers", *Journal of Consumer Marketing*, 18(4) 303 – 318.
30. Chan, Kara; Prendergast, Gerard P. (2008), "Social comparison, imitation of celebrity models and materialism among Chinese youth." *International Journal of Advertising*, 27(5) 799-826.
31. Chandon, Jean Louis, Chtourou, Mohamed Saber; Fortin, David R (2003), "Effects of Configuration and Exposure Levels on Responses to Web Advertisements", *Journal of Advertising Research*, 43(2) 217-229.
32. Chang-Hoan Cho (2003), "The Effectiveness of Banner Advertisements: Involvement and Click-through", *Journalism & Mass Communication Quarterly*, 80 (3)623-645.

33. Chanthika Pornpitakpan; Tan, Tze Ke Jason(2000), "The Influence of Incongruity on the Effectiveness of Humorous Advertisements The Case of Singaporeans", *Journal of International Consumer Marketing,* 12(3), 27-45.

34. Charles F. Hofacker, Jamie Murphy (1998) "World Wide Web banner advertisement copy testing", *European Journal of Marketing,* 32 (7/8) 703 – 712.

35. Christian, Richard C (1965), "How Much Does an Industrial Logotype Add to the Effectiveness of an *Advertisement?", Journal of Marketing,* 29 (2)57-59.

36. Christian, Richard C, Gordon, Howard L (1967) "Yes, Virginia, Research Helps Better *Advertisements", Journal of Marketing,* 31 (1)64-66.

37. Christine Communal, Barbara Senior (1999), "National culture and management: messages conveyed by British, French and German advertisements for managerial appointments", *Leadership & Organization Development Journal,* Vol 20, no.1, P 26 – 35.

38. Chung-Kue Hsu Daniella McDonald, (2002), "An examination on multiple celebrity endorsers in advertising", *Journal of Product & Brand Management,* 11(1), 19-29. Hs

39. Chun-Tuan Chang (2006), "Is a Picture Worth a Thousand Words? Influence of Graphic Illustration on Framed Advertisements", *Advances in Consumer Research,* 33 (1) 104-112.

40. Clarence E. Eldridge (1958), "Advertising Effectiveness: How Can It Be Measured?", *The Journal of Marketing,* 22 (3) 241-251.

41. Clow, Kenneth E Berry, Christine T, Kranenburg, Kristine E, James, Karen E,(2005), "An Examination of the Visual Element of Service Advertisements", *Marketing Management Journal,* 15 (1), 33-45.

42. Cornelia Pechmann, Susan J. Knight (2002), "An Experimental Investigation of the Joint Effects of Advertising and Peers on Adolescents' Beliefs and Intentions about Cigarette Consumption", *Journal of Consumer Research,* 29, 101-125 .

43. Dahlen, Micael, (2001), "Banner Advertisements through a New Lens", *Journal of Advertising Research,*.41(4), 23-30.

44. David Corkindale (1976), "Setting objectives for advertising", *European Journal of Marketing,* 10(3) 109 – 126.

45. David H. Silvera, Benedikte Austad, (2004) "Factors predicting the effectiveness of celebrity endorsement advertisements", *European Journal of Marketing,* 38 (11/12), 1509 – 1526.

46. David S. Waller (1999), "Attitudes towards offensive advertising: an Australian study", *Journal of Consumer Marketing,* 16 (3) 288 – 295.

47. David S. Waller, Kim-Shyan Fam, B. Zafer Erdogan(2005), "Advertising of controversial products: a cross-cultural study", *Journal of Consumer Marketing,* 22 (1) 6-13.

48. David Szetela(2008), "Measuring a Text Ad's Effectiveness" *Search Engine Watch Webcast* 1, 10-15

49. David W. Lloyd, Kevin J. Clancy (1991), "Television program involvement and advertising response: some unsettling implications for copy research", *Journal of Consumer Marketing,* 8 (4) 61 – 74.

50. Day, Robert L(1990), "Revisiting the Rough/Finished Issue in Advertisement Pre-testing: A Practitioner's Viewpoint", *Marketing Research,* 2 (3) 22-29.

51. Deborah Roedder John(1999), "Consumer Socialization of Children: A Retrospective Look At Twenty Five Years of Research", *Journal of Consumer Research,* 26 68-77.

52. Deborah Y. Cohn (2005), "Current Ethical Dilemmas of Advertising Professionals", *Research in Ethical Issues in Organizations*, 6, 149 – 168.
53. Decrop, Alain(2007), ".The influence of message format on the effectiveness of print advertisements for tourism destinations" *International Journal of Advertising*, 26(4), 505-525.
54. Demetrios Vakaratsas and Zhenfeng MA, (2005), "A look at the long-run effectiveness of multimedia advertising and its implications for budget allocation decisions, *Journal of Advertising Research*, 17 (2), 241-255.
55. DeRosia, Eric D (2008), "The effectiveness of nonverbal symbolic signs and metaphors in advertisements: An experimental inquiry", *Psychology & Marketing*, 25 (3) 298-316.
56. Doyle & Saunders, (1990), "Measuring advertisement effectiveness—a neural network approach" *Neuro-Fuzzy Laboratory* funded by A.I.C.T.E. (All India Council for Technical Education), New Delhi, Government of India.
57. D'Souza, Goes, Rao, Ram C (1995), "Can repeating an *advertisement* more frequently than the competition affect brand preference in", *Journal of Marketing*, 59 (2) 32.
58. Earl, Ronald L., Pride, William M (1980), "The Effects of Advertisement Structure, Message Sidedness, and Performance Test Results on Print Advertisement in formativeness", *Journal of Advertising*, Vol. 9, no.3, p36-46.
59. Edward Rosbergen, Rik Pieters, Michel Wedel (1997), "Visual Attention to Advertising: A Segment Level Analysis", *Journal of Consumer Research*, 24, 78-87.
60. Elizabeth Cowley, Eunika Janus (2004), "Not Necessarily Better, but Certainly Different: A Limit to the Advertising Misinformation Effect on Memory", *Journal of Consumer Research*, 31 55-63.
61. Elizabeth S. Moore, Richard J. Lutz (2000), "Children, Advertising, and Product Experiences: A Multi method Inquiry", *Journal of Consumer Research*, 27, 98-109.
62. Encyclopedia Britannia, Vol.16, 1960, p.17.
63. Finn, Adam (1992), "Recall, Recognition and the *Measurement* of Memory for Print *Advertisements:* A Reassessment", *Marketing Science*, 11, (1) 95
64. Fortin, David R.; Dholakia, Ruby Roy(2005), "Interactivity and vividness effects on social presence and involvement with a web-based advertisement", *Journal of Business Research*, 58 (3) 387-396.
65. Fotini Patsioura, Maro Vlachopoulou, Vicky Manthou, (2009) "A new advertising effectiveness model for corporate advertising web sites: A relationship marketing approach", Benchmarking: *An International Journal*, 16(3), 372 – 386.
66. France Leclerc and John D. C. Little (1997), "Can Advertising Copy Make FSI Coupons More Effective?", *Journal of Marketing Research*, 34 (4)473-484.
67. France, Karén Russo; Park, C. Whan(1997) "The Impact of Program Affective Valence and Level of Cognitive Appraisal on Advertisement Processing and Effectiveness", *Journal of Current Issues & Research in Advertising*, 19 (2) 1-21.
68. Franzen, Raymond (1942), "Inequalities Which Affect Scores of *Advertisements*", *Journal of Marketing*, 6 (4)128-132.
69. Friedman, Hershey H, Termini, Salvatore, Washington, Robert (1976), "The Effectiveness of Advertisements Utilizing Four Types of Endorsers", *Journal of Advertising*, 5 (3) 22-24.
70. Fry, Marie-Louise (2006), "Message processing of fear-based anti-drink driving advertisements" *Message processing of fear-based anti-drink driving advertisements.*

71. Garcia, Eli, Yang, Kenneth C. C (2006), "Consumer Responses to Sexual Appeals in Cross-Cultural *Advertisements", Journal of International Consumer Marketing*, 19 (2) 29-52.

72. Gates, Fliece R (1986), "Further Comments on the Miscomprehension of Televised *Advertisements", Journal of Advertising*, 15(1) 4-9.

73. George S. Low, Charles W. Lamb Jr (2000), "The measurement and dimensionality of brand associations", *Journal of Product & Brand Management*, 9 (6) 350 – 370.

74. Gerard Prendergast, Po-yan Liu, Derek T.Y. Poon (2009), "A Hong Kong study of advertising credibility", *Journal of Consumer Marketing*, 26 (5) 320 – 329.

75. Gitav Enkataramani Johar (1995), "Consumer Involvement and Deception from Implied Advertising Claims", *Journal of Marketing Research*, 32 (3) 267-279.

76. Goldsmith, Ronald E.; Lafferty, Barbara A.; Newell, Stephen J.(2000), "The Impact of Corporate Credibility and Celebrity Credibility on Consumer Reaction to Advertisements and Brands", *Journal of Advertising*, 29 (3)43-54.

77. Grant McCracken (1989), "Who is the Celebrity Endorser? Cultural Foundations of the Endorsement Process", *The Journal of Consumer Research*, 16 (3) 310-321.

78. Grønhaug, Kjell, Kvitastein, Olav, Grønmo, Sigmund (1991), "Factors moderating advertising effectiveness as reflected in 333 tested advertisements", *Journal of Advertising Research*, 31 (5) 42-50.

79. Gunne Grankvist, Hans Lekedal, Maarit Marmendal (2007), "Values and eco- and fair-trade labelled products", *British Food Journal*, 109 (2) 169 – 181.

80. Hanssens, Dominique M., Weitz, Barton A (1980), "The Effectiveness of Industrial Print Advertisements Across Product Categories", *Journal of Marketing Research (JMR)*, 17 (3) 294-306.

81. Hee-Sook Yoon, Doo-Hee Lee(2007), "The Exposure Effect of Unclicked Banner Advertisements", Advances in International Marketing, 18(12) 211- 229.

82. Henry Petroski; Henry Petroski (1986), "Dress For Success: The Dust Jacket As Art, Advertisement And Nuisance", *New York Times Book Review*, 21.

83. Herbert e. Krugman (1966), "the Measurement of Advertising Involvement" *Public Opinion Quarterly*, 30 (4)583-596.

84. Hoggard, Jesse T (2007), "Moving towards a Very Long Engagement: The Effects of Interactivity on Prolonging Engagement with Online Movie Advertisements", Master's Thesis.

85. Howard, Daniel J.; Kerin, Roger A(2004), "The Effects of Personalized Product Recommendations on Advertisement Response Rates: The "Try This. It Works!" Technique", *Journal of Consumer Psychology (Lawrence Erlbaum Associates)*, 14 (3) 271-279.

86. Hudson, S, Hung, C. L, Padley, L(2002), "Cross-national standardisation of advertisements: a study of the effectiveness of TV advertisements targeted at Chinese Canadians in Canada", *International Journal of Advertising*, 21 (3)345-366.

87. Hyunjoo Oh, (2005) "Measuring affective reactions to print apparel advertisements: a scale development", *Journal of Fashion Marketing and Management*, 9 (3), 283 – 305.

88. Ioni Lewis, Barry Watson, Richard Tay(2007), "Examining the effectiveness of physical threats in road safety advertising: The role of the third-person effect, gender, and age", *Transportation Research Part F: Traffic Psychology and Behaviour* 10(1), 48-60.

89. Jagdish Agrawal and Wagner A. Kamakura (1995), "The Economic Worth of Celebrity Endorsers: An Event Study Analysis", *The Journal of Marketing*, 59 (3) 56-62.

90. Jakob Nielsen (2007), "ethical aspects of Internet advertising", *Library & Information Update*, 6 (11) 10-10.

91. Janssens, Wim; De Pelsmacker, Patrick (2005), "Advertising for New and Existing Brands: The Impact of Media Context and Type of Advertisement", *Journal of Marketing Communications*, 11 (2) 113-128.

92. Jason C. G. Halford, Jane Gillespie, Victoria Brown, Eleanor E. Pontin, Terence M. Dovey (2004), "Effect of television advertisements for foods on food consumption in children", *Appetite*, 42 (2) 221-225.

93. Jay (Hyunjae) Yu; Cude (2009), "Hello, Mrs. Sarah Jones! We recommend this product!' Consumers' perceptions about personalized advertising: comparisons across advertisements delivered via three different types of media", *Brenda. International Journal of Consumer Studies*, 33, 4, 503-514.

94. Jennifer edson escalas barbarab. stern (2003), ". Sympathy and Empathy: Emotional Responses to Advertising Dramas" *Journal of Consumer Research*, 294, 566-578.

95. Jennifer Edson Escalas, Mary Frances Luce (2004), "Understanding the Effects of Process Focused versus Outcome Focused Thought in Response to Advertising", *Journal of Consumer Research*, 31, 78-86.

96. Jim Novo(2007)., "Marketing Mix Modeling - Measuring the effectiveness of "Brand" Advertisement" *Marketing Modeling* -Permalink.

97. Joel J. Davis (1993), "Strategies for environmental advertising", *Journal of Consumer Marketing*, 10(2) 19 – 36.

98. Johnson, G. D.(2009), "The social dimension of multi-racial advertising: Its impact on consumers' attitude", *South African Journal of Business Management*, 40 (2) 45-52.

99. Jones, Lara(2002), "Are advertisements featuring local business owners effective or detrimental", *Enterprise/Salt Lake City*, 31 (31) 1.

100. Jourdan, Philippe (1999), "Creation and Validation of an Advertising Scale Based on the Individual Perception of the Emotional or Informational Intent of the *Advertisement*", *Advances in Consumer Research*, 26 (1) 504-512.

101. Julie Verity (2005), "Interpreting the successful transformation of Shell's advertising activity 1997-2002", *Management Decision*, 43 (1) 72 – 85.

102. Kara Chan, Lyann Li, Sandra Diehl, Ralf Terlutter, (2007) "Consumers' response to offensive advertising: a cross cultural study", *International Marketing Review*, 245 606 – 628.

103. Katherine Gallagher, Jeffrey Parsons and K.Dale Foster, (2001), "A tale of two studies: Replicating "Advertising Effectiveness and content evaluation in print and on the web" *Journal of Advertising Research*, July-August, 71-81.

104. Kathleen Mortimer, (2008), "Identifying the components of effective service advertisements", *Journal of Services Marketing*, 22(2), 104-113.

105. Kathryn A. Braun (1999), "Post experience Advertising Effects on Consumer Memory", *Journal of Consumer Research*, 25, pp57-68.

106. Kanti Prasad V. (1976), "Communications-Effectiveness of Comparative Advertising: A Laboratory Analysis", *Journal of Marketing Research*, 13(2) 128-137.

107. Kilbourne, William E, Painton, Scott, Ridley, Danny (1985), "The Effect of Sexual Embedding On Responses to Magazine *Advertisements", Journal of Advertising*, 14 (2) 48-56.

108. Kim Shyan Fam, David S. Waller, B. Zafer Erdogan (2004), "The influence of religion on attitudes towards the advertising of controversial products", *European Journal of Marketing*, 38,(5/6) 537 – 555.

109. Kim-Shyan Fam, Reinhard Grohs, (2007) "Cultural values and effective executional techniques in advertising: A cross-country and product category study of urban young adults in Asia", *International Marketing Review*, 24(5), 519 – 538.
110. Kuehl, Philip G, Dyer, Robert F (1977), "Application of the "Normative Belief" Technique for Measuring the Effectiveness of Deceptive and Corrective Advertisements", *Advances in Consumer Research*, 4.(1) 204-212.
111. Kumar, Anand(2000)," Interference Effects of Contextual Cues in Advertisements on Memory for Ad Content", *Journal of Consumer Psychology (Lawrence Erlbaum Associates)*, 9(3)155-166.
112. Kyoko Fukukawa, Christine Ennew, Steve Diacon (2006), "An Eye for an Eye: Investigating the Impact of Consumer Perception of Corporate Unfairness on Aberrant Consumer Behavior", *Research in Ethical Issues in Organizations*, 7 187-221.
113. Laczniak, Russell N, Teas, R. Kenneth (2002), "Context Effects in the *Measurement* of Attitude Toward the *Advertisement* ", Journal of Current Issues & Research in Advertising, 24 (1) 11, 14.
114. Lana Hall and Ingrid Foik(1983), "Generic versus Brand Advertised Manufactured Milk Products: The Case of Yogurt" *North Central Journal of Agricultural Economics*, 5 (1) 19-24.
115. Lau, Richard R.; Sigelman, Lee(1999), 'The effects of negative political advertisements: A meta-analytical assessment", *American Political Science Review*, 93 (4) 851.
116. Lees, Gavin; Healey, Ben(2005), "A Test of the Effectiveness of a Mouse Pointer Image in Increasing Click through for a Web Banner Advertisement". *Marketing Bulletin*, 16, 1-6.
117. Lewis, I, Watson, B, et al (2008) "An examination of message-relevant affect in road safety messages: Should road safety *advertisements* aim to make us feel good or bad", *Transportation Research*, 11 (6) 403-417.
118. Lohtia,Ritu,Donthu,Naveen,Yaveroglu, Idil(2007), "Evaluating the efficiency of Internet banner *advertisements" Journal of Business Research*, Vol. 60 no 4, p365-370.
119. Loken, Barbara, Howard-Pitney, Beth (1988), 'Effectiveness of Cigarette Advertisements on Women: An Experimental Study", *Journal of Applied Psychology*, 73 (3) 378-382.
120. Luther,Catherine A (2009), "Importance Placed on Physical Attractiveness and Advertisement-Inspired Social Comparison Behavior Among Japanese Female and Male Teenagers.", *Journal of Communication*, 59 (2) 279-295.
121. Lynn R. Kahle and Pamela M. Homer (1985), "Physical Attractiveness of the Celebrity Endorser: A Social Adaptation Perspective", *The Journal of Consumer Research*, Vol.11, (4) 954-961.
122. Mark Loughney, martin Eichholz, Michelle Hagger (2008), "Exploring the Effectiveness of Advertising in the ABC.com Full Episode Player" Journal of Advertising research, 25 (5) 322-328.
123. Mark Robertson (2008), "Video Banner Ads vs. Traditional Banner Ads - Measuring Effectiveness" *International Journal of Advertising*, 9 (2) 15-22.
124. Mark Uncles(2000), "The Alpha, Beta, Gamma Approach to Measuring Change and its use for Interpreting the Effectiveness of Service Quality Programs",.*A transcript of record.*
125. Mark R. Forehand,Andrew Perkins(2005), "Implicit Assimilation and Explicit Contrast: A Set/Reset Model of Response to Celebrity Voice Overs", *Journal of Consumer Research*, 32 45-56.

126. Mark Ritson, Richard Elliott (1999), "The Social Uses of Advertising: An Ethnographic Study of Adolescent Advertising Audiences" *Journal of Consumer Research*, 26 79-86.

127. Marla Royne Stafford, Thomas F. Stafford (2002), "A Contingency Approach: The Effects of Spokesperson Type and Service Type on Service Advertising Perceptions", *Journal of Advertising*, 31 (2) 17-35.

128. Mathew Joseph, Deborah F. Spake, Zachary Finney (2008), "Consumer attitudes toward pharmaceutical direct-to-consumer advertising: An empirical study and the role of income" *International Journal of Pharmaceutical and Healthcare Marketing*, 2, (2)117 – 133.

129. Mazursky, David, Schul, Yaacov (1988), "The Effects of Advertisement Encoding on the Failure to Discount Information: Implications for the Sleeper Effect", *Journal of Consumer Research* , 15(1) 24-36.

130. McMenemy, David (2006), "What Would You Do?: Reflecting on the Importance of Ethical Values in Librarianship", *Journal of the Career Development Group*, 9 (4) 71-73.

131. Melewar T.C., Claes Vemmervik (2004) "International advertising strategy: A review, reassessment and recommendation", *Management Decision*, 42 (7) 863-881.

132. Mercia Selva Malar S., (2008), "The "ethics" of being profit focused", *Social Responsibility Journal*, 4 (1/2) 136 – 142.

133. Michael A. Kamins (1990), "An Investigation into the "Match-up" Hypothesis in Celebrity Advertising: When Beauty May Be Only Skin Deep", *Journal of Advertising*, 19 (1)4-13.

134. Michael A. Kamins, Meribeth J. Brand, Stuart A. Hoeke, John C. Moe (1989), "Two-Sided versus One-Sided Celebrity Endorsements: The Impact on Advertising Effectiveness and Credibility", *Journal of Advertising*, 18 (2)4-10.

135. Michael Fay (2006), "Cyclical patterns in the content of advertisements: Replication, confirmation, extension and revision", *European Journal of Marketing*, 40 (1/2) 198 – 217.

136. Michael J Baker(1998), "*The Westburn Dictionary of Marketing*" Westburn Publishers Ltd 2002.

137. Michael Volkov, Debra Harker, Michael Harker (2002), "Complaint behaviour: a study of the differences between complainants about advertising in Australia and the population at large" *Journal of Consumer Marketing*, 19 (4) 319-332.

138. Micu, Camelia C, Coulter, Robin A, Price, Linda L (2009), "How Product Trial Alters The Effects of Model Attractiveness", *Journal of Advertising*, 38 (2) 69-81.

139. Miller, Darryl W, Hadjimarcou, John, Miciak, Alan (2000), "A scale for measuring *advertisement*-evoked mental imagery", *Journal of Marketing Communications*, 6,(1), 1-20.

140. Minamizawa,(2009), "Advertisement Effect Measurement Device, Advertisement Effect Measurement Method Used In The Advertisement Effect Measurement Device And Advertisement Effect Measurement Control", *ITO, Naoko.*

141. Mortimer, Kathleen(2008), "*Journal of Services Marketing*, 22, (2/3) 104-113.

142. Muehling, Darrel D, Bozman, Carl S (1990), "An Examination of Factors Influencing Effectiveness of 15-Second Advertisements", *International Journal of Advertising*, (4) 331-344.

143. Nicholas Reading, Steven Bellman, Duane Varan, Hume Winzar (2006), "Effectiveness of Telescopic Advertisements Delivered via Personal Video Recorders" *Journal of Advertising Research*,.41(6) 217-225. 126a.

144. Norris, Claire E.; Colman, Andrew M(1992), "Context Effects on Recall and Recognition of Magazine Advertisements", *Journal of Advertising*, Vol. (21) (3) 37-46.

145. Okechuku, Chike, Gongrong Wang (1988), "The effectiveness of Chinese print advertisements in North America", *Journal of Advertising Research*, 28(5) 25-34.

146. Orenstein, Frank E (1967), "Attempts at Measuring the Effectiveness of Advertising/ Do People Really Read Advertisements?/ How to Choose Between Major Categories of Media", *Journal of Marketing Research (JMR)*, 4 (4) 409-410.

147. Pablo Briñol, Richard E. Petty, Zakary L. Tormala (12004), "Self Validation of Cognitive Responses to Advertisements", *Journal of Consumer Research*, 30, 45 -55.

148. Pamela M. Homer and Lynn R. Kahle (1990), "Source Expertise, Time of Source Identification, and Involvement in Persuasion: An Elaborative Processing Perspective", *Journal of Advertising*, 19(1), 30-39.

149. Patzer, Gordon L (1980), "A Comparison of Advertisement Effects: Sexy Female Communicator Vs Non-Sexy Female Communicator", *Advances in Consumer Research*, 7 (1)359-364.

150. Paul M. Fischer, Dean M. Krugman, James E. Fletcher, Richard J. Fox, Tina H. Rojas (1993), "An Evaluation of Health Warnings in Cigarette Advertisements Using Standard Market Research Methods: What Does It Mean to Warn?", *Tobacco Control*, 2 (4) 279-285.

151. Pechmann, Cornelia; Reibling, Ellen T(2006), "Antismoking Advertisements for Youths: An Independent Evaluation of Health, Counter-Industry, and Industry Approaches", *American Journal of Public Health*, 96(5) 906-913.

152. Peck, Joann; Loken, Barbara (2004), "When Will Larger-Sized Female Models in Advertisements Be Viewed Positively? The Moderating Effects of Instructional Frame, Gender, and Need for Cognition", *Psychology & Marketing*, 21 (6) 425-442.

153. Pei-Luen Patrick Rau, Duye Chen (2006), "Effects of watermark and music on mobile message advertisements", *International Journal of Human-Computer Studies*, 64 (9) 905-914.

154. Pirisi, Angela (1997), "Eye-catching *advertisements" Psychology Today*, 30 (1) 14.

155. Pradeep Korgaonkar, Ronnie Silverblatt, Bay O'Leary (2001), "Web advertising and Hispanics", *Journal of Consumer Marketing*, 18 (2) 134 – 152.

156. Quester, Pascale G (1998), "Antecedents of Anti-Smoking Advertisements' Effectiveness: A Bi-Cultural Study", *Journal of International Consumer Marketing*, 10(4) 29.

157. Rae, Nathan; Brennan, Mike(1998), "The relative effectiveness of sound and animation in Web banner advertisements", *Marketing Bulletin*, 9 76.

158. Rama Yelkur, Chuck Tomkovick, Patty Traczyk (2004), "Super Bowl Advertising Effectiveness: Hollywood Finds the Games Golden" *Journal of Advertising Research*, 56(8) 143-156. 126b.

159. Richard E. Petty, John T. Cacioppo, David Schumann (1983), "Cntral and Peripheral Routes to Advertising Effectiveness: The Moderating Role of Involvement", *The Journal of Consumer Research*, 10 (2) 135-146.

160. Rick T. Wilson, Brain D. Till (2007), "Direct-to-consumer Pharmaceutical Advertising: Building and Testing a Model for Advertising Effectiveness", Journal of Advertising Research, 38 (10) 270-280.

161. Robert J. Fisher, David Ackerman (1998), "The Effects of Recognition and Group Need on Volunteerism: A Social Norm Perspective", *Journal of Consumer Research*, 25, 13-21.

162. Robert J. Fisher,David Ackerman (1998), "The Effects of Recognition and Group Need on Volunteerism: A Social Norm Perspective", *Journal of Consumer Research*, 25, 38-46.

163. Robert J. Fisher, Laurette Dubé (2005), "Gender Differences in Responses to Emotional Advertising: A Social Desirability Perspective", *Journal of Consumer Research*, 31,107-114.

164. Rohini Ahluwalia, Robert E. Burnkrant (2004), "Answering Questions about Questions: A Persuasion Knowledge Perspective for Understanding the Effects of Rhetorical Questions", *Journal of Consumer Research*, (31) 49-56.

165. S John Gabriel (2006), "The Impact of Television Advertisements on Youth: A Study", *The ICFAI journal of Marketing Management*, V, (3) 71-79.

166. Samu, Sridhar; Bhatnagar, Namita(2008), "The efficacy of anti-smoking advertisements: the role of source, message, and individual characteristics", *International Journal of Nonprofit & Voluntary Sector Marketing*, 13 (3) 237-250.

167. Schleifer, Stephen, Dunn, S. Watson (1968), "Relative Effectiveness of Advertisements of Foreign and Domestic Origin", *Journal of Marketing Research (JMR)*, 5(3) 296-299.

168. Schweidel, David A., Bradlow, Eric T., Williams, Patti (2006), "A Feature-Based Approach to Assessing Advertisement Similarity", *Journal of Marketing Research (JMR)*, 43 (2) 237-243.

169. Shanker Krishnan H. and Dipankar Chakravarti (2003), "A Process Analysis of the Effects of Humorous Advertising Executions on Brand Claims Memory", *Journal of Consumer Psychology*, 13 (3) 230-245.

170. Shen, Fuyuan (2002), "Banner *Advertisement* Pricing, *Measurement*, and Pretesting Practices: Perspectives from Interactive Agencies", *Journal of Advertising*, 31(3) 59-67.

171. Shin Yi Chou, Inas Rashad, Michael Grossman (2008), "Fast Food Restaurant Advertising on Television and Its Influence on Childhood Obesity", *The Journal of Law and Economics*, vol. 51, 114-119.

172. Shou-Shiung Chou(2006), "Effects of Trope Advertisement on Chinese Consumers", *Journal of American Academy of Business, Cambridge*, 9 (1) 229-232.

173. Silvera, David H.; Austad, Benedikte(2004), "Factors predicting the effectiveness of celebrity endorsement advertisements", *European Journal of Marketing*, 38 (11/12), 1509-1526.

174. Smith, Karen h.; Stutts, Mary Ann(2006), "The Influence of Individual Factors on the Effectiveness of Message Content in Antismoking Advertisements Aimed at Adolescents", *Journal of Consumer Affairs*, 2006, 40 (2), 261-293.

175. Spike Cramphorn (2004), "Measuring Effectiveness Of Business-to-business Advertising" *Journal of advertising research*, 2, (3), 2-5.

176. Starch, Daniel (1923), "Testing the Effectiveness of Advertisements", *Harvard Business Review*, 1(4)464-474.

177. Stephen Ansolabehere and Shanto Iyengar (1994), "Riding the Wave and Claiming Ownership Over Issues: The Joint Effects of Advertising and News Coverage in Campaigns", *The Public Opinion Quarterly*, 58(3) 335-357.

178. Stephen R. McDaniel, Gary R. Heald (2000), "Young Consumers' Responses to Event Sponsorship Advertisements of Unhealthy Products: Implications of Schema-triggered Affect Theory", *Sport Management Review*, 3 (2) 163-184.

179. Stephens, Nancy (1982), 'The Effectiveness of Time-Compressed Television Advertisements With Older Adults", *Journal of Advertising*, 11(4) 48-76.

180. Stewart, Patrick A.; Schubert, James N (2006), "Taking the "Low Road" with Subliminal Advertisements: A Study Testing the Effect of Precognitive Prime "RATS" in a 2000 Presidential Advertisement", *Harvard International Journal of Press/ Politics*, 1 (4) 103-114.

181. Stocks, J. M. B (1965), "Validating Television Advertisement Tests", *Commentary: The Journal of the Market Research Society*, 7 (3) p159-165.

182. Subhash C. Jain and Edwin C. Hackleman(1978), "How Effective Is Comparison Advertising for Stimulating Brand Recall?", *Journal of Advertising*, 7 (3)20-25.

183. Surendra N. Singh and Gilbert A. Churchill (1986), "Using the Theory of Signal Detection to Improve Ad Recognition Testing", *Journal of Marketing Research*, 23(4) 327-336.

184. Svante Andersson, Anna Hedelin, Anna Nilsson, Charlotte Welander (2004), "Violent advertising in fashion marketing", Journal of Fashion Marketing and Management, 8 (1)96 – 112.

185. Terje I. Vaaland, Morten Heide, Kjell Grønhaug (2008), "Corporate social responsibility: investigating theory and research in the marketing context", *European Journal of Marketing*, 42 (9/10) 927 – 953.

186. Thomas, Jerry W (1997), "Looking for results? Track your *advertisements", Air Conditioning Heating & Refrigeration News*, 200 (4), 76.

187. Tina M. Lowrey (1998), "The Effects of Syntactic Complexity on Advertising Persuasiveness", *Journal of Consumer Psychology*, 7 (2) 187-206.

188. Tom, Gail, Clark, Rebecca, Elmer, Laura, Grech, Edward, Masetti Jr., Joseph, Sandhar, Harmona,(1992), "The Use of Created Versus Celebrity Spokespersons in Advertisements", *Journal of Consumer Marketing*, 9 (4)45.

189. Turley, L. W.; Shannon, J. Richard, (2004), "The impact and effectiveness of advertisements in a sports arena", *Journal of Services Marketing*, 14 (4/5) 323.

190. United States Patent 5991734, (2009) "Method of measuring the creative value in communications"- *ViscosityJournal.com*-24th-Sep-2009 at 11.05a.m.

191. Utpal M. Dholakia,Vicki G. Morwitz(2002), "The Scope and Persistence of Mere Measurement Effects: Evidence from a Field Study of Customer Satisfaction Measurement", *Journal Of Consumer Research*, 29 57-68.

192. Vanden Abeele P., P. Luysterman, (1981) "The Evaluation of Pre-tests by Advertising People: Results of a Survey in Belgium", *European Journal of Marketing*, 15(1) 48-57.

193. William H.Antrin(1978), "Advertising Effectiveness" *International Journal of Advertising*,19 (3), 299-315.

194. William H.Bolen(1984), "Advertising Effectiveness"-*www. science direct.com*-24th sep 2009, at 11.15a.m.

195. William T. Moran (1951), "Measuring exposure to advertisements", *Journal of Applied Psychology*, 35(1) 72-77.

196. Wim Janssens, Patric De Pelsmaker, et al (2007), "The moderating role of the persolity trait discomfort with ambiguity", *Journal of Marketing Communication*, 9(3)110-125.

197. WoonBong Na, Roger Marshall, Arch G. Woodside (2009), "Decision system analysis of advertising agency decisions", *Qualitative Market Research: An International Journal*, 12 (2) 153 – 170.

198. Yong Zhang, James P. Neelankavil, (1997) "The influence of culture on advertising effectiveness in China and the USA: A cross-cultural study", European Journal of Marketing, 31(2)134-149.

199. Yoon, Sung-Joon; Choi, Yong-Gil(2005), 'Determinants of successful sports advertisements: The effects of advertisement type, product type and sports model", *Journal of Brand Management*, 12 (3) 191-205.

200. Zhang, Jie, Wedel, Michel, Pieters, Rik (2009), "Sales Effects of Attention to Feature *Advertisements:* A Bayesian Mediation Analysis", *Journal of Marketing Research (JMR)*, 46 (5)669-681.

201. Zhao, Xinshu, Bleske, Glen L (1995), "*Measurement* effects in comparing voter learning from television news and campaign *advertisements*", *Journalism & Mass Communication Quarterly*, 72 (1) 72-83.

News Paper

202. The Hindu, 10th June, 2010.

Web Sources

203. www.trichy.co.in accessed on 2nd November 2009.

204. www.tn.co.in accessed on 2nd November 2009.

205. www.periyarevrcollege.org accessed on 15th November 2009.

206. www.sjctni.edu accessed on 15th November 2009.

207. www.holycrossedu.org accessed on 8th January 2010.

208. www.cauverycollege.ac.in accessed on 8th January 2010.

209. www.andavancollege.ac.in accessed on 10th January 2010.

Index